Praise for *Foucault and Feminist Philosophy of Disability*

"Sets the scene for philosophy of disability and opens new paths for critical disability studies. . . . Tremain carefully corrects misreadings and misappropriations of Foucault among disability theorists and feminists alike, and shows how these thinkers inadvertently reinscribe the status quo when it comes to theorizing disability. In working through the many ways disability is constructed, the book radicalizes philosophical consideration of topics ranging from epistemic injustice to stem cell research."
  —Melinda Hall, Stetson University

"A much-needed contribution to the general intellectual discussion of disability, to Foucault studies, and to feminist theory. Tremain plows into some central tenets of disability theories and some of the most taken-for-granted feminist criticisms of Foucault. She also indicts professional philosophy in North America for its structural exclusion of disabled scholars. The evidence she presents and the arguments she makes are strong and sound."
  —Ladelle McWhorter, Stephanie Bennett-Smith Chair in Women,
    Gender, and Sexuality Studies, University of Richmond

Foucault and Feminist Philosophy of Disability

Corporealities: Discourses of Disability

Series editors: David T. Mitchell and Sharon L. Snyder

Recent Titles

A complete list of titles in the series can be found at www.press.umich.edu

Foucault and Feminist Philosophy of Disability

SHELLEY L. TREMAIN

University of Michigan Press
Ann Arbor

Published in the United States of America by the
University of Michigan Press
Printed and bound by CPI Group (UK) Ltd, Croydon, CR0 4YY

2020   2019   2018   2017   4   3   2   1

A CIP catalog record for this book is available from the British Library.

Library of Congress Cataloging-in-Publication Data

Names: Tremain, Shelley, author.
Title: Foucault and feminist philosophy of disability / Shelley L. Tremain.
Description: Ann Arbor : University of Michigan Press, 2017. | Series:
   Corporealities: discourses of disability | Includes bibliographical references
   and index.
Identifiers: LCCN 2017023341| ISBN 9780472073733 (hbk : alk.
   paper) | ISBN 9780472053735 (pbk : alk. paper) | ISBN 9780472123476
   (e-book)
Subjects: LCSH: Foucault, Michel, 1926–1984. | Sociology of
   disability. | Feminist theory. | Disability studies.
Classification: LCC HV1568 .T77   2017 | DDC 362.401—dc23
LC record available at https://lccn.loc.gov/2017023341

Cover description for accessibility: The words and image are framed within a thin rectangular border within the edges of the cover. The title appears on three lines at the top, two words on each line. The author's name appears across the bottom. A sculpture by Judith Scott is in the center; its shape and composition resemble a mammal's heart. The sculpture consists of various colors of yarn and string wound around objects such as a plastic coffee cup lid, pieces of cellophane, and spirals of tubing, the latter of which resemble the ventricles of a heart.

Credit: Judith Scott, 2004. Photograph courtesy of Sylvian Deleu.

Dedicated
to my mother,
Elizabeth Jean Fisher Tremain,
and
to the memory of my father,
Robert Frederick Tremain

People know what they do; they frequently know why they do what they do; but what they don't know is what what they do does.

—Michel Foucault

Preface and Acknowledgments

A History of the Present

———— ৽৵ ————

Where We Are Now

During my first year in a temporary teaching position, I scheduled a meeting with an accomplished female faculty member of the philosophy department in which I was employed to ask for some advice about how to enhance my chances of securing a tenure-track position. When I had initially approached her with the request to meet, she seemed enthusiastic about doing so; hence, I had high expectations about the many valuable tips that she would offer me based on her years of experience in the field. Our meeting was brief, during which time the most salient and memorable piece of advice that she gave me was that I should shift the focus of my philosophical work away from disability because, if I didn't, I would never get a job in philosophy. The subtext of her advice was clear and distinct: you may think you are a philosopher, but what you write (about) is not philosophy. The exasperated expression on her face when I suggested that considerations about the nature of disability constitute metaphysical reflections underscored the subtext of her advice. The general lesson that my esteemed colleague was concerned to convey to me and that countless other philosophers—before and after, dead and alive—have implicitly and explicitly aimed to convey is this: there exists a predetermined and determinate set of philosophical questions and approaches to them, outside the scope of which fall the phenomena of disability. In the view of my colleague (and of many other philosophers, living and dead), the phenomena of disability are not proper objects of philosophical inquiry.

Notwithstanding my esteemed colleague's sentiments, some discussions about disability have, since about the mid-twentieth century, been increasingly prevalent in the subfields of moral and political philosophy, bioethics, and cognitive science. In these discussions, disability has almost invariably been conceived as a natural human disadvantage, an inherent human flaw, and politically neutral human characteristic. Claims advanced about disability that assert otherwise, that is, claims that variously assert that disability is a social and political phenomenon, have been regarded as misguided, ideological, interested, or naïve. Even now, critical philosophical approaches to disability remain marginalized in most subfields of philosophy and completely ignored in the other subfields of the discipline.

This bias, that is, the bias in the profession that only certain approaches to disability and its conceptual objects are appropriate subject matter for philosophical inquiry has both constrained my career in professional philosophy and determined the direction that it would take. I was the first philosopher (and certainly the first disabled philosopher) to attempt to establish a career in philosophy with the production of critical philosophical work on disability: I wrote my doctoral dissertation on disability and social justice and gave the name "Philosophy of Disability" to a subfield that had not previously existed. In the years since the disappointing meeting with my former colleague, furthermore, I have steadily turned my intellectual pursuits and professional activism to the articulation of arguments and development of projects designed to resist and counter the message that my colleague had conveyed, doing so while almost always underemployed under exploitative working conditions or unemployed, a set of circumstances that is all too common among disabled philosophers and disabled academics in general.

The assumption that any philosophical inquiry about disability is fundamentally biomedical in nature has also seriously constrained how my work and the work of other philosophers of disability are understood and represented in philosophy. Indeed, the way in which critical philosophical work on disability is currently classified and categorized in the field has significant ramifications for how widely the work will receive consideration; how, which, and even whether philosophers will engage with it; and whether the work will deliver professional benefits in the form of employment, publication, and so on for the given philosopher who produces it. I and other philosophers of disability have persistently

tried to undermine these constraints and show that medicalized understandings of disability misconstrue it and are reductionist. Nevertheless,
the current representation and positioning in the discipline of philosophy of disability in general and feminist philosophy of disability more
specifically remains an intransigent obstacle.

Consider, for example, the position that feminist philosophy of disability is afforded in PhilPapers: Online Research in Philosophy (n.d.),
the large and influential database of research and writing in philosophy
that is organized according to areas of specialization, subfields, and topics that are themselves hierarchically arranged in a descending order of
importance in accordance with prevailing ideas in the Euro-American,
Western philosophical tradition and discipline about which areas, subfields, and topics: (1) have the most/less philosophical import; (2) have
the most/less explanatory power; and (3) should be endowed with the
most/less authoritative status. The so-called core or fundamental areas
of the discipline—Metaphysics and Epistemology; Value Theory; Science, Logic, and Mathematics; History of Western Philosophy; and Philosophical Traditions—are designated as the supreme categories on the
system and, in turn, other areas of inquiry are designated as subcategories of these supreme categories, or subcategories of the subcategories of
the supreme categories, or ("leaf") subcategories of the subcategories of
the subcategories of the supreme categories, where a category's distance
from the supreme categories marks the diminished import, explanatory
power, and authoritative status within philosophy of the areas of inquiry
that it encompasses. However, classification of items, states of affairs, and
other phenomena is no mere value-neutral reportage or representation
of objective differences, relations, and similarities that await discovery
and recognition; on the contrary, classification (and classification systems) is *performative* insofar as it contributes to the constitution of the
very value-laden resemblances, distinctions, associations, and relationships that it puts into place.

The *constitutive* categories that the PhilPapers database uses to classify research and writing position feminist philosophical work on disability under the rubric of a "leaf" subcategory—namely, "Feminism:
Disability"—that is subordinate to the subcategory of "Topics in Feminist Philosophy," a subcategory of the superior category of "Philosophy
of Gender, Race, and Sexuality," which in turn is a subcategory of the
supreme category of "Value Theory." In the schema of the PhilPapers
database, that is, feminist philosophy of disability is conceived as on par
with "topics" in feminist philosophy such as "Autonomy," "Love," "Iden-

tity Politics," and "Reproduction" rather than on par with, an element of, and in relationship with other formative political and discursive categories of identity and subjection—in this context, gender, race, and sexuality—in a more comprehensive and politically astute category of "Philosophy of Gender, Race, Sexuality, and Disability," to which the subcategory of "Topics in Feminist Philosophy" would be subordinate. Although the superior category of "Philosophy of Gender, Race, and Sexuality" includes subcategories of "Philosophy of Gender," "Philosophy of Race," and "Philosophy of Sexuality," it does not encompass an offspring category of "Philosophy of Disability." The relegated status of work in feminist philosophy of disability in the PhilPapers database reflects a political decision that operates as an institutional and structural mechanism to preclude and even prevent the incorporation of disability into an intersectional or other integrated analysis, thereby reinforcing depoliticized conceptions of disability and contributing to the marginalization and diminution of work on disability within the subfield of feminist philosophy and the discipline more generally.

I initially wrote about the marginalized positioning of (feminist) philosophy of disability in the PhilPapers database in an article that I published in 2013 (see Tremain 2013b). After the article appeared and received attention in some philosophical circles, the PhilPapers database was expanded to include additional sub-subcategories for work on disability. Although the addition of these categories on PhilPapers enables philosophers of disability to situate their work in more places within the database, the infrastructural problems with the database nevertheless remain.

Implications of a causal connection that this book addresses between the conception of disability that prevails in philosophy and the underrepresentation of disabled philosophers are even more strikingly evident if one considers how philosophy of disability is positioned in another database that the PhilPapers Foundation has created and cohosts with the American Philosophical Association (APA): PhilJobs: Jobs for Philosophers (n.d.), now the most popular job board for listings in professional philosophy. To create PhilJobs, the co-directors of PhilPapers transported a rudimentary framework of the latter's classificatory system to the new database, where the superordinate categories of the latter database came to designate areas of specialization (AOS) and areas of competence (AOC) on the former.[1]

Given the AOS and AOC categories in the PhilJobs database, search committees are implicitly discouraged and even directly prevented from posting advertisements that place disability on par with gender, race, and sexuality or that reflect the fact that philosophy of disability (like philosophy of gender and philosophy of race) crosses the subdisciplines of epistemology, metaphysics, philosophy of language, and so on. Whereas there are AOS and AOC categories for "Philosophy of Gender" and "Philosophy of Race," under the banner of which employers can post jobs within the category of "Value Theory," there are no AOS or AOC categories for "Philosophy of Disability" within the category of "Value Theory" under which employers can post jobs. Instead, the guiding assumption of PhilJobs seems to be that job postings for philosophical work on disability are most appropriately situated on the job site under the rubric of "Biomedical Ethics" or "Applied Ethics," an ableist sequestration that (among its other deleterious effects): (1) perpetuates the medicalization and depoliticization of disability within philosophy; (2) constrains how philosophers of disability can represent their research to prospective employers; (3) limits the extent to which hiring committees can recruit practitioners of philosophy of disability; (4) contributes to the diminution and marginalization of critical philosophical analyses of disability; and (5) contributes to the underrepresentation of disabled philosophers and other philosophers of disability in the profession (see PhilJobs n.d.). Job postings influence what philosophers regard as emerging and current research and as important areas of the field to develop in their own departments. Hiring departments, insofar as they do not see other departments recruit and hire specialists in the subfield of philosophy of disability (a large percentage of whom are disabled), are neither motivated, nor compelled, to recruit and hire specialists in philosophy of disability themselves. In short, the current classificatory scheme of PhilJobs (and PhilPapers) and the classification of philosophical work on disability in the database in particular are implicated in the underrepresentation of disabled philosophers in philosophy.

Some of the work in this book was previously published in other forms, in other venues. I am grateful to the editors of these publications for their permission to draw upon work published as: "Knowing Disability, Differently," from *The Routledge Handbook on Epistemic Injustice*, edited by I. J. Kidd, J. Medina, and G. Pohlhaus Jr. (New York: Routledge, 2017), 175–83; "This Is What a Historicist and Relativist Feminist Philosophy of Disability Looks Like" in *Foucault Studies* 19 (2015): 7–42; "Introducing Feminist Philosophy of Disability," in *Disability Studies Quarterly* 33, no. 4 (2013); "Educating Jouy," in *Hypatia: A Journal of Feminist Philosophy* 28, no. 4 (2013): 801–17; "Biopower, Styles of Reasoning, and What's Still Missing from the Stem Cell Debates," in *Hypatia: A Journal of Feminist Philosophy* 25, no. 3 (2010): 77–609; "Reproductive Freedom, Self-Regulation, and the Government of Impairment in Utero," in *Hypatia: A Journal of Feminist Philosophy* 21, no. 1 (2006): 35–53; and "On the Government of Disability," in *Social Theory and Practice* 27, no. 4 (2001): 617–36.

My remarks about the PhilPapers and PhilJobs databases originally appeared in the guest editor's introduction (see Tremain 2013b) to a special issue of *Disability Studies Quarterly* (*DSQ*) whose theme was "Improving Feminist Philosophy by Taking Account of Disability" and whose contributions showed, among other things, how critical work on disability has been left out of feminist philosophy. The introduction to the special issue was intended to create a context within which the readership of *DSQ*, composed primarily of nonphilosophers, could situate the contributions to the issue. Thus, the introduction is a relatively comprehensive survey of various aspects of the profession, including percentages of disabled faculty employed in philosophy departments in North America; the lack of representation of disabled feminist philosophers in anthologies, on editorial boards of feminist philosophy journals, and in conference lineups; the inaccessibility of feminist philosophy conferences; and the (in)accessibility of the operations of the APA.

Many feminist philosophers did in fact read my introduction to the issue, which in turn precipitated changes in the field almost immediately after the issue's appearance online, including these: an increasing number of calls for papers in feminist philosophy conferences and journal issues solicited work in philosophy of disability; fewer calls for papers for feminist philosophy conferences included ableist language; conference and workshops organizers began to address the accessibility of their events; feminist philosophers of disability were recruited for editorial boards; and some feminist philosophers began to consider the question of how to reconceptualize disability. These changes in institutional and professional practice notwithstanding, many nondisabled feminist philosophers continue to implicitly construe gender as prior to, more fundamental than, and indeed separable from disability and other apparatuses of subjecting power, even though they explicitly claim to endorse and uphold the political, theoretical, and discursive value of intersectionality. In other words, many feminist philosophers continue to presume that insofar as "women" share so many experiences in virtue of their (conventional) gender—and are, therefore, similarly situated in the most significant ways with respect to privilege and oppression—an analytic focus on gender in isolation from, say, disability, race, ethnicity, class, sexuality, age, and nationality constitutes a legitimate project. For these feminist philosophers, women are first and foremost oppressed *as women* and are oppressed *as different groups of women*—that is, as disabled lesbians of color, as disabled bisexual white women, as nondisabled heterosexual women of color, and so on—only secondarily and less significantly.[2] The analytical purity of this conception of the category of gender is achieved, however, only by obscuring other apparatuses of power with which gender is complicit and coexists, usually through the implicit institution of a nondisabled white norm. Thus, much work remains to be done to incorporate an accountable and sophisticated understanding of disability into feminist philosophy and indeed the discipline of philosophy more broadly, as well as to improve the situation for disabled (feminist) philosophers in the profession. It is my hope that the arguments of *Foucault and Feminist Philosophy of Disability* will be instrumental to this activity.

How I Got Here

Many people have influenced the shape of my thinking and praxis with respect to disability and the current situation of disabled philosophers. I am very grateful to Barry Allen, my friend and former teacher who, years ago, urged me to read Foucault and taught me how to write philosophy. I want to extend thanks to Les Green, my PhD supervisor, who once told me that although lovers may come and go, philosophy will always be there for me. I also want to thank Ian Hacking, whose fascinating graduate seminar on the topic of styles of reasoning enabled me to think more schematically about disability as a historical artifact.

The support, camaraderie, and appreciation for my work on disability that these friends and colleagues provided has sustained me through difficult times: Melinda Hall, Zara Bain, Jane Dryden, Komarine Romdehn-Romluc, Maeve O'Donovan, Andrea Nicki, Joe Stramondo, Ray Aldred, Audrey Yap, Thomas Nadelhoffer, Kevin Timpe, Anne McGuire, Sally Haslanger, Tommy Curry, Lauren Guilmette, Catherine Clune-Taylor, Elvis Imafidon, Joshua Knobe, Devonya Havis, Jennifer Scuro, Cecilea Mun, Axel Arturo Barceló, Whitney Mutch, Olúfẹ́mi Táíwò, Samantha Brennan, Lori Gruen, Carol Gould, Joshua Keton, Edouard Machery, Gaile Pohlhaus Jr., José Medina, Tanya Titchkosky, Ada Jaarsma, Kathryn Pauly Morgan, Anna Mudde, Aimi Hamraie, Eric Winsberg, Chandra Kumar, Suze Berkhout, Stephen Kuusistro, Bill Peace, John Drabinski, John Altmann, Eric

Schwitzgebel, Lori Gabrielson, Mike Matheson, Darleen Burnett, Joshua St. Pierre, Michael Gillan-Peckitt, Evan Simpson, and Tipsy Tullivan.

I want to convey my deep gratitude to all the disabled philosophers whom I have had the great honor to interview in the Dialogues on Disability series at the *Discrimination and Disadvantage* blog. I also want to convey my sincere thanks to Kevin Rennells, Production Editor at the University of Michigan Press who, in addition to patiently accepting my repeated requests to make revisions after I submitted the final manuscript, guided me through the production process of the book. Thanks also to David Mitchell and Sharon Snyder, the editors of the Corporealities: Discourses of Disability series at the University of Michigan Press, for their enthusiasm about the book.

I am very grateful for the comradeship, friendship, and encouragement of Kelly Fritsch and Jay Dolmage, who nominated me for the 2016 Tanis Doe Award that the Canadian Disability Studies Association-Association Canadienne des Études sur L'Incapacité conferred upon me, giving public recognition to my philosophical work on disability. I am also very grateful to the University of Michigan for selecting this book as the winner of the Tobin Siebers Prize for Disability Studies in the Humanities for 2016. LeAnn Fields, Aquisitions Editor at the University of Michigan Press, has believed in me, advised me in the best ways, and displayed tremendous generosity in her interactions with me.

Bryce Huebner and Tracy Isaacs have nurtured me in more ways than either of them know. For many years, Christine Overall has offered me guidance, mentorship, and feminist support in her distinctively humble and gracious way. Ladelle McWhorter, whose fabulous body of work on Foucault tangibly influences my own, has stuck with me through thick and thin. I am extremely grateful for Ladelle's enduring friendship. Jesse Prinz has brought so much light into my life. In so very many ways, Jesse made writing this book possible. Oreo was a steadfast companion who provided unconditional love and trust. Writing this book has enabled me to live with the sorrow of losing him. My sister Heather Kerr and brother-in-law Craig Kerr, my sister Tracy Talosi and brother-in-law Zak Talosi, my sister Christine Wilson and brother-in-law Steve Wilson, and my nieces and nephews have also loved and supported me unconditionally. My mother, Elizabeth Tremain, and my father, Robert Tremain, motivated me to recognize injustice, taught me by example why I should not accept it, and fought for me when I could not fight for myself. This book is dedicated to my parents.

Contents

Contents

CHAPTER 1

Groundwork for a Feminist Philosophy of Disability

―――――ᴥ―――――

A Naturalized Narrative

Throughout the last decades of the twentieth century, discussions about disability became increasingly prevalent in mainstream philosophy, especially with the resurgence of work on social justice since the publication of John Rawls's *A Theory of Justice* in 1971 and the emergence and expansion of the subfields of cognitive science and bioethics. Since the mid-twentieth century, that is, mainstream philosophers have engaged in philosophical discussions about disability formulated around questions such as these: What (if anything) does society owe to disabled people? How should society compensate disabled people for their natural disadvantages and brute bad luck? On what grounds is it justifiable to euthanize disabled people? Is it morally permissible to conduct experimentation on cognitively disabled research subjects? What can we learn about the (normal) mind from the fact that "people with autism" lack a theory of mind? What can we learn about the operations of the (normal) brain, its emotions, perceptions, and so on, from study of people who have experienced brain injuries?

Notwithstanding the apparent variety of questions that mainstream philosophers have asked (and continue to ask) about disability, the cluster of motivational assumptions that underpins almost all these inquiries

takes for granted the metaphysical status and epistemological character of the category of disability, casting disability as a self-evident and
thus philosophically uninteresting designation that science and medicine can accurately represent. On the terms of this cluster of assumptions, disability is a prediscursive, transcultural, and transhistorical
disadvantage, an objective human defect, that is, a non-accidental, biological human property, attribute, or characteristic that ought to be
prevented, corrected, eliminated, or cured.[1] That these assumptions
are contestable, that it might be the case that disability is a historically
and culturally specific and contingent social phenomenon, a complex
apparatus of power rather than a natural attribute or property that certain people possess, is not considered, let alone seriously entertained.
Indeed, most feminist philosophers uncritically accept the aforementioned assumptions about what disability is, though they may not derive
the same normative conclusions from this ontology[2] as mainstream philosophers do. Even most philosophers of disability do not rigorously
question the metaphysical and epistemological status of disability, but
rather advance ethical and political positions that largely assume the
self-evidence of that status.

Although critical analysis of disability has made significant inroads
elsewhere in the humanities and social sciences, such inquiry remains
severely marginalized within philosophy, a state of affairs that should
be attributed to a complex and complicated set of interrelated factors,
including the historical composition and demographics of professional
philosophy itself; the narrowing concentration of the prevailing subject
matter and techniques of philosophy; the increasingly close association
between philosophy and the sciences; and the otherwise limited theoretical, discursive, and political focus of much philosophy. The seemingly intransigent bias in philosophy according to which the inequalities
that accrue to disabled people are self-evidently natural and inevitable
has yielded the belief that these disadvantages are most appropriately
addressed in the domains of medicine, the life sciences, and related
fields rather than in philosophy departments. Thus, the assumption that
critical analysis of the status of disability is not appropriate subject matter
for philosophical inquiry has shaped philosophy departments, influencing hiring practices and decisions as well as course curricula, conference
lineups, the composition of professional networks and editorial boards,
the contents of edited collections, and so on (see Tremain 2013b; also
see Tremain 2014, 2010). In short, the assumption that disability is a
philosophically uninteresting human characteristic and the underrepre-

sentation of disabled philosophers within the profession are inseparably embedded in the institutional infrastructure of the discipline, mutually constitutive and mutually reinforcing.

A distinctive mixture of selection bias[3] and confirmation bias[4] restricts the professional opportunities available to disabled philosophers generally and disabled philosophers of disability particularly, especially when combined with the prestige bias, sexism, racism, cisheterosexism, classism, and ageism that condition hiring in philosophy and academia in general at present. In the context of philosophy, I want to argue, the assumption that disabled people are biologically or naturally disadvantaged—that is, physiologically inferior or naturally flawed—has the following effects, among others: it (1) contributes to the hostile environment that disabled philosophers confront within philosophy and (2) enables the exclusion of disabled philosophers from the profession that thereby (3) bolsters other subjecting apparatuses (such as race, gender, sexuality, nationality, age, and class) with which the apparatus of disability is co-constitutive and, in addition, (4) sustains and reproduces the homogeneous and monolithic character of both the discipline of philosophy and the persona of the professional philosopher, thereby (5) contributing to the conditions of possibility for the epistemology of domination (a notion explained later in this chapter) and epistemic injustice that beset philosophy while (6) reinforcing and perpetuating the deeply entrenched ableism of the Euro-American, Western philosophical tradition that is part and parcel of, and facilitates, the widespread discrimination that disabled people confront elsewhere in the university and beyond it (see also Dolmage 2017).

One of my central aims in this book is to identify and defy practices that contribute to the prevailing cluster of assumptions that produce these pernicious effects. The book responds to this question (among others): What concrete institutional, professional, and disciplinary effects does the conception of disability that predominates in philosophy produce? To accomplish this aim, I interrogate the very self-evidence, inevitability, and transparency of disability and its discursive objects that, with few exceptions, philosophers currently take for granted. I also identify accepted institutional practices and entrenched professional habits that contribute to these effects and enable their reproduction. Indeed, the book calls for a "conceptual revolution" (to borrow Rae Langton's term), a critical ontology of what philosophers think disability is, of what they think about how disability is produced, and of what their current thinking about disability does.

Insofar as philosophers have conceived the social inequalities that accrue to disabled people as the inevitable consequences of a self-evident physiological, or natural, human characteristic (property, difference, or attribute), they have presupposed certain assumptions about the relation between biology and society—that is, between nature and nurture—that I aim to undermine. Dorothy E. Roberts (2016) has distinguished heuristically between two approaches to the question of the relation between biology and society: "the old biosocial science" and "the new biosocial science."[5] As Roberts explains it, the old biosocial science posits that biological differences produce social inequality, whereas the new biosocial science posits that social inequality produces biological differences. The biological determinism of the old biosocial science, she notes, is achieved in several ways: first, the old biosocial science approach separates nature from nurture in order to locate the origins of social inequalities in inherent traits rather than imposed societal structures; second, the old biosocial science postulates that social inequalities are reproduced in the bodies, especially the wombs, of socially disadvantaged people rather than reinvented through unjust ideologies and institutions; third, the old bioscience identifies problems that stem from social inequality as derived from the threats that oppressed people's biology itself poses to society rather than from structural barriers and state violence imposed upon oppressed people; and fourth, the old bioscience endeavors to intervene and fix perceived biological deficits in the bodies of oppressed people rather than end the structural violence that dehumanizes them and maintains an unjust social order.

By contrast, the new biosocial science, Roberts explains, posits that every single biological element, every single biological process in the human body, every human cell, and everything that happens to a human cell is affected by society. All of life, Roberts remarks, is at once biological and social. There is, in short, no natural body. Genes do not determine anything. Moreover, our brains are plastic, with the ability to be modified by social experience. Both epigenetics and social neuroscience, Roberts points out, show that biology is not a separate entity that interacts with the environment; rather, biology is constituted by these interactions (2016; see also Roberts 1998, 2012; Prinz 2012; Gilman and Thomas 2016). With Roberts, various authors have pointed out, furthermore, that critical analyses of biosocial science must consider how claims about the social construction of biological phenomena are produced, in what contexts they are mobilized, and for what political purposes. Victoria Pitts-Taylor (2010, 635) argues, for example, that if we are to take the plasticity of the brain seriously, we must think critically about the historicity of this ontology and the political and economic forces that have produced the historical and epistemological conditions of possibility for its uptake. As Andy Clark (1998) states, the plastic brain is a situated brain, culturally, biologically, and socially.

I want to denaturalize and debiologize the ways that philosophers understand disability. In my view, Michel Foucault's insights provide the most sophisticated and most philosophically and politically astute tools with which to proceed with this intellectual, political, and practical enterprise. Many of Foucault's insights upon which I draw for this purpose were introduced and refined in his own discussions of abnormality, madness, deviance, and other discursive objects that intellectuals and nonintellectuals alike commonly associate with disability. In many respects, my argument extends these discussions and is most aptly characterized as a feminist philosophical inquiry into what Foucault referred to as the "problematization" of phenomena in the present. Foucault's studies of abnormality, madness, and deviance (among other things) were not intended to provide normative responses to these phenomena, but rather were designed to show how these phenomena became thinkable, that is, emerged as problems to which solutions came to be sought. Equally, I do not offer an explicitly normative feminist proposal or response to the phenomena of disability, nor do I provide a (normative) feminist critique of a given normative response to the phenomena of disability. Such a given proposal, response, or critique would allege to show that there is a certain definitive solution to the "problem" of disability. The feminist philosophical inquiry into the problematization of disability that I develop is designed in large part to indicate how a certain historically and culturally specific regime of power has produced certain acts, practices, subjectivities, bodies, relations, and so on *as a problem* for the present, as well as to indicate the role that philosophy has played and continues to play in the elaboration of this problem. I follow Foucault's suggestion that inquiry into the problematization of a given state of affairs attempts to uncover how the different solutions to a problem have been constructed, as well as how these different solutions resulted from the problematization of that given state of affairs in the first place (Foucault 2003e, 20–24).

Thus, another aim of my inquiry is to show how a certain regime of power has produced impairment as both the prediscursive—that is, natural and universal—antecedent of culturally variant forms of disability and a problem for this regime of power to which the regime offers solu-

tions. In other words, one of my aims is to indicate how a certain apparatus of power has brought impairment—the naturally disadvantageous
foundation of disability—into being as that kind of thing. Throughout
this inquiry, I implicitly and explicitly address questions such as these:
How have impairment and disability been constituted within philosophy,
including within its professional and institutional practices and its theoretical discourses? How has philosophy construed disability—and its naturalized antecedent, impairment—as a certain kind of problem for the
present and, in doing so, propped up the apparatus of disability? What
is the relation between this conceptualization of disability as a problem
that ought to be rectified, what is taught about disability in philosophy,
and the underrepresentation of disabled philosophers in the profession?

Using Phineas Gage

Consider the story of Phineas Gage, now institutionalized in introductory textbooks in cognitive science, philosophy of psychology, and cognate subfields. In 1848, Gage, a railroad supervisor, was impaled by a
tamping iron that entered his left cheek and exited the back of his skull.
Malcolm Macmillan (2002), in *An Odd Kind of Fame: Stories of Phineas
Gage*, notes that two-thirds of introductory psychology textbooks mention Gage. Over the course of more than a century and a half, in fact,
an almost mythical narrative has been elaborated within psychology and
medical textbooks about the aftermath of Gage's injury, a mythology to
which philosophers and cognitive scientists have subscribed and have
promoted. As Allan Ropper (a neurologist at Harvard Medical School
and Brigham and Women's Hospital) puts it, Gage's "famous case"
helped to "establish brain science as a field." "If you talk about hard core
neurology and the relationship between structural damage to the brain
and particular changes in behavior," Ropper says, "this is ground zero."
Ropper explains that Gage's brain injury offered scientists and medical practitioners "an ideal case" because it involved one region of the
brain, was very evident, and the resulting changes in personality "were
stunning" (Ropper qtd. in Hamilton 2017). These sorts of claims about
the impact of Gage's injury have led philosophers of mind and cognitive scientists (among others) to use the story of Gage (and stories of
other real or hypothetical people who have sustained brain injuries) as a
springboard to advance arguments, develop experiments, and formulate
positions on, inter alia, personal identity, the true self, the moral self,

and so on (Strohminger 2014; Knobe 2016; Tobia 2016). I submit, however, that the uses to which philosophers of mind and cognitive scientists routinely put the story of Gage deserve more careful consideration.

Steve Twomey (2010) notes that "John Martyn Harlow, the doctor who treated Gage for a few months afterward, reported that Gage's friends found him 'no longer Gage.'" To Harlow, Twomey remarks, "the balance between Gage's 'intellectual faculties and animal propensities' seemed to have [disappeared]." Gage was "unable to stick to plans, uttered 'the grossest profanity' and showed 'little deference for his fellows.'" Macmillan points out that subsequent accounts of Gage's changed character have gone far beyond Harlow's observations, transforming Gage into an ill-tempered, shiftless drunk (2002). As Twomey asserts, and as my own research on Gage indicates, these accounts about Gage's demeanor post-accident vilify him, seem exaggerated, and in fact seem largely fabricated. Consider that Harlow, to whom most references in the literature appeal, treated and observed Gage for only a few months, a relatively short span of time given Gage's injury and the changes in his life that it would have entailed. Furthermore, Harlow's description of the post-injury-Gage does not seem to warrant the dispositional and personality changes—cruel, mean, and so on—that have been attributed to Gage in the scientific and philosophical literature over the years. In short, the ways that (if not the very fact that) cognitive scientists and philosophers use the story of Gage are highly contestable. They cannot be sure that the cited reports from Gage's friends (if in fact made) were not in some way conditioned by their own misunderstandings of his behavior, their revulsion and prejudices about his changed physical appearance, or simply their own impatience as he learned new ways to comport himself in the world. Some accounts of Gage's life post-injury contradict the oft-cited reports, indicating that Gage had a pleasant enough demeanor post-injury, but was socially outcast and unable to find employment. Macmillan, who allows that Gage did undergo a change in personality post-injury, remarks nonetheless that the personality change that Gage experienced "did not last much longer than [two or three years]" (2002). As Macmillan points out, Gage eventually secured employment as a long-distance stagecoach driver in Chile, an occupation that would have required considerable skill, focus, and amicable behavior.

That Gage's situation has been exaggerated and embellished within the contexts of the literature of (inter alia) neuroscience, cognitive science, philosophy of mind, and medicine reminds us that science, philosophy, and medicine are embedded social practices rather than disinterested domains that exist apart from and immune to ableist biases and other elements of the apparatus of disability. Indeed, I contend that we should ask these questions (among others) about this line of inquiry in cognitive science, philosophy of mind, and related fields: How has this (embellished) narrative about Gage contributed to the problematization of disability in philosophy? In what ways has this mythical narrative about Gage enabled the naturalization and materialization of impairment within certain subfields of the discipline and thus further enabled the consolidation of the relation between philosophy and the apparatus of disability? In what ways does this mythology about certain disabled people ultimately shape, condition, and determine research programs and teaching in cognitive science, neuroscience, and philosophy of mind? How has this vilification of Gage within academic contexts relied upon and reproduced pervasive social prejudices and assumptions of the sort that I examine in chapter 4, that is, relied upon and reproduced biased social prejudices and assumptions according to which certain disabled people are aggressive, violent, and even dangerous? How, and to what extent, do the repeated articulations of this myth about Gage confirm what philosophers already believed about (some) disabled people? Finally, to what extent does the repeated articulation of this fanciful narrative about Gage (and there are surely others, including the discourses in ethics and cognitive psychology on "psychopaths") foster the hostile environment that disabled philosophers confront in philosophy and sustain their underrepresentation in it?[6]

Two Spheres of Analysis

In the chapters that follow, I indicate how Foucault's technique of genealogy, his analyses of biopower, his innovative conception of the subject, and his prescient claims about liberalism and neoliberalism (among others) can be used to investigate the ways that the tradition, discipline, and profession of philosophy have contributed to both the problematization and apparatus of disability, as well as to the naturalization of the allegedly objective antecedent of disability—namely, impairment. To examine the *problématique* of disability in this way, especially as it is produced within philosophy, I advance claims that derive from and extend two distinct, but interrelated, spheres in which I have conducted research. I refer to these spheres as a reconstructive-conceptual sphere and a metaphilosophical sphere.

In the first sphere—the reconstructive-conceptual sphere—I have used Foucault's insights to develop a conception of disability that does not rely upon a natural, transhistorical, and transcultural metaphysical and epistemological foundation (impairment). This conception of disability, the argument of which I introduced in an article entitled "On the Government of Disability" (Tremain 2001), is elaborated in chapter 3. In the article, I use Foucault's technique of genealogy and claims about the performative character of a distinctly modern form of power to consider how impairment has been brought into being as the naturalized foundation of disability. This new antifoundationalist conception of disability provides philosophers of disability and disability theorists with a theoretically sophisticated alternative to the conceptions of disability that have prevailed in the literature of disability studies internationally. In chapter 3, I offer a detailed outline of these latter conceptions of disability and distinguish them from the alternative approach to disability that I have developed. Nevertheless, I shall now introduce these conceptions in order to situate the stance on disability from which my arguments in subsequent chapters proceed.

In much of the interdisciplinary literature of disability studies, disparate conceptions of disability are carelessly conflated and terminology is often used ambiguously and equivocally. In some cases, the conflations involve the simultaneous use of conceptions of disability that rely upon different assumptions about what disability is, the recommendation of contradictory social responses to disability, and conflicting representations of disability, not least of all through the language that each of the conceptions promotes. In some cases, the conflation arises when both of two senses of the term *social model of disability* (or, *social model*) are used in the space of one claim or argument, although these two senses operate at different levels of generality. In technical terms, the conflation of these two senses of *social model* involves confluence of what philosophers of language refer to as "type" and "token." In the international discussions of disability studies, that is, the term *social model* is used in two ways: (1) broadly and loosely, to refer to just about any counterhegemonic (i.e., nonmedical model) understanding of disability, that is, to a type of approach to disability; and (2) narrowly, to refer to a specific understanding of disability that originated in the United Kingdom in the 1970s (henceforth referred to as the British social model, or BSM), that is, to a token of the aforementioned type of approach to disability (see Tremain 2016).

On the latter, narrow, sense (or conception), the term *disability* refers to a form of social oppression that is imposed upon "people with impairments," where these impairments are claimed to be neutral human characteristics (a claim that my alternative antifoundationalist conception of disability was designed to undermine). This latter conception of disability, which has motivated the BSM, is grounded in the assumptions of historical materialism and thus holds that the improvement of "disabled people's" circumstances requires systemic social, political, and economic transformation. In the first sense—that is, the broad and loose sense of the term *social model*—the term *disability* may be used (1) as proponents of the BSM use it, or (2) to refer to the ostensible functional limitations of a given individual who has an allegedly natural disadvantage—namely, an impairment, or (3) in some other, hybrid, way—for instance, some philosophers of disability and disability theorists use the term *disability* to refer to both a biological characteristic or difference and a functional limitation. The medial conception of disability, on which disability is a functional limitation, relies upon an individualized conception of disability whereby minor adjustments to a given environment, such as a workplace, are made that enable a given "person with a disability" to be "accommodated" into an environment that, itself, remains intact overall. Insofar as individual functions and capacities are the focus of this conception, the conception fits well with the tenets of liberal individualism and, as I show in chapter 3, does not avoid the eugenic impulse of the "medical model"[7] of disability that it is claimed to counter.

The conflation of the two senses of the term *social model* and the conflation of different conceptions of the social model are ubiquitous in philosophy of disability and disability studies more generally. For example, when authors use the terms *disabled people* and *people with disabilities* interchangeably to refer to the same social group, they have either conflated the first (historical materialist) and second (individualist) conceptions of the broad sense of the social model or they have conflated the broad and the restrictive senses of the term *social model*. To be sure, some philosophers and theorists of disability self-consciously combine the two senses of the social model, using the language of both the historical materialist and individualist conceptions of disability in a hybrid way to circumvent the excesses that they perceive with the former conception and the shortcomings that they perceive with the latter conception. Although this move might seem as if it is a worthwhile way to reconcile the two conceptions, the two conceptions are in fact incompatible; hence, conflation of them, and of the two senses of the term *social model*, can render an argument or claim confusing or incoherent. In my work, I use the term *British social model* (or *BSM*) to refer to the second, restricted sense of the notion of a social model and the terms *sociopolitical* (or *social-political*) *conception* and *sociopolitical interpretation* to refer to a broad, counterhegemonic understanding of disability.

Though a more detailed explication and critique of both the BSM and the individualist conception constitutes part of my discussion in chapter 3, suffice it to say in this context that the BSM is formulated around a structuralist distinction between impairment and disability analogous to the familiar feminist distinction between sex and gender (discussed in subsequent chapters) and is claimed, like the latter feminist distinction, to have universal applicability. In the 2001 article in which I introduce my alternative understanding of disability, therefore, I draw on Foucault's idea about the constitutive character of power and Judith Butler's work on the performativity of gender to formulate an argument about the performativity of impairment and disability. I have subsequently used the new conception of disability in several contexts to advance novel arguments about (for instance) the performativity of impairment and disability in the contexts of prenatal testing and genetic counseling discourse, human embryonic stem cell (hESC) research, and cognitive impairment (see Tremain 2006a, 2006b, 2008, 2010, 2013a). My arguments in the articles on these topics are, in certain respects, designed to show, first, how philosophers, especially feminist and nonfeminist bioethicists, have constituted impairment by and through their implicit assumptions and explicit claims about disability; second, the uncritical acceptance and systematization in philosophical argumentation of prevalent ideas and biases about disability; third, the neglect of certain important epistemological and ontological questions about disability in philosophy; and fourth, the general disregard for critical approaches to disability that conditions most of these other discursive and theoretical practices. In short, I have aimed to show how critical analysis of disability has been left out of both mainstream and feminist philosophy in important and formative ways as well as used in both domains in oppressive and other harmful ways.

These conceptual issues and their ethical, political, institutional, cultural, and discursive implications and effects are inextricably linked in numerous ways to the underrepresentation of disabled philosophers within the profession of philosophy and the marginalization of philosophy of disability within the discipline. Thus, in the second sphere of my research—that is, the metaphilosophical sphere—I have been concerned to investigate mechanisms, practices, and policies that sustain the marginalization of philosophy of disability within the discipline and the virtual exclusion of disabled philosophers from the profession (Tremain 2010, 2013b, 2014). Empirical data and theoretical analyses relevant to various institutional, organizational, and discursive influences in the discipline and profession have driven my research and analysis in this sphere, including data and analyses about professional associations for philosophers, influential sites of social media for philosophers, philosophy conferences, job boards for philosophers, edited philosophy collections and journals, and philosophical research databases. Some of this metaphilosophical analysis was presented in the preface to this book. Later in this introductory chapter, I revisit my earlier work, offering additional, updated data and analyses in order to provide a context within which my subsequent discussions can be considered.

Historicizing and Relativizing the Problem of Disability

Over the course of this book, I weave together arguments drawn from the two spheres of my research to articulate an analytically robust and empirically grounded feminist philosophy of disability. *Feminist philosophy of disability* is the term that I have coined to instigate the emergence of a field of inquiry that simultaneously employs, contributes to, and widens the scope of feminist philosophy, philosophy of disability, and the interdisciplinary field of (feminist) disability studies, with all of which theoretical domains feminist philosophy of disability shares many theoretical assumptions, social values, and political goals, but from all of which domains feminist philosophy of disability is distinct: it remains beholden to none of these other domains. Given the non-foundationalist conception of impairment and disability that I have elaborated and continue to hold, it should come as no surprise that the feminist philosophy of disability that I advance is both relativist and historicist. I define *relativism* as the philosophical doctrine according to which different societies and cultures create different beliefs and values under different historical conditions. I define *historicism* as the philosophical doctrine according to which beliefs and values emerge as a consequence of historical events and circumstances (see Prinz 2007, 215, 234–35).

An interlocutor might point out that the aforementioned definition of relativism refers to a form of it—namely, descriptive relativism—that is uncontroversial among philosophers: most philosophers grant that different cultures have different beliefs and practices. Such an interlocutor might in turn argue that I need an additional argument if I wish to advance a stronger relativism whereby different cultures have different beliefs and practices that have equal claims epistemologically and ethically. Let me point out, therefore, that although philosophers generally agree that descriptive relativism is true with respect to science, religion, and values—i.e., every culture has its own beliefs about these things—most of them implicitly presuppose a kind of universalism about certain categories taken to be fundamental, especially categories that they believe are based in biology, categories such as life and death, health and disability, and pleasure and pain.[8] Thus, not even descriptive relativism is an obvious thesis. Nevertheless, the relativism of my position does not require the sort of epistemological or ethical appeal upon which the interlocutor insists. For the relativism of the feminist philosophy of disability that I aim to articulate is established and substantiated by and through its historicism; that is, the historicism of my feminist philosophy of disability should be conceived as both theoretically prior and antecedent in practice to its relativism, which is, therefore, a derivative of the historicism. Insofar as I argue for the historicist and artifactual character of disability, I establish its relativist character. Claims about the historical transformation of concepts and practices need not necessarily imply their improvement and progress. By both definition and design, the relativist and historicist feminist philosophy of disability that I elaborate offers a new approach to the questions and concerns about disability that philosophers (including feminist philosophers) of disability and disability theorists raise, an approach that is dynamic and historically and contextually sensitive to an extent that other (feminist) philosophies of disability are not.

My choices of relativism and Foucault's historicism as vehicles through which to articulate a feminist philosophy of disability will be unpopular, if not dismissed, in many circles within philosophy, including within feminist philosophy. Indeed, Foucault himself explicitly denied that his work was relativist (see Foucault 1982, 212). Although he offered no explanation for this denial, the fact that in the same context Foucault also denied that his work relies upon skepticism[9] suggests that he may have assumed that a relativist approach required that he refuse even historicist claims to truth, a refusal that, as I indicate in my discussion of his work on subjectivity in general and sexual subjectivity in particular, he did not make. Nevertheless, many philosophers trained in Anglo-American philosophy continue to refer to Foucault's work as relativist as means to discount its philosophical significance and complexity. As David Wong (2006), who has written extensively about relativism, points out, most philosophical discussions of relativism in Anglo-American philosophy are designed to make relativism an easy target for derision and condemnation, seldom revealing what motivates people who are attracted to it as a philosophical approach. Such discussions, Wong notes, usually come early in standard introductory textbooks in order "to get relativism out of the way so that the 'serious' philosophy can start" (xi). The strategy, he explains, is almost always negative or purports to show some incoherence in relativist argumentation. Rarely do philosophers who are critical of relativism attempt to formulate a version of it that is "nuanced and plausibly motivated" (xi).

Despite Foucault's own denial that his claims were relativist, I nevertheless associate both his refusal to universalize and his historical approach with a form of relativism to develop a historicist and relativist feminist philosophy of disability that is nuanced and plausible, politically informed and provoked. In my view, the historicism at the heart of Foucault's claims establishes them as relativist or, at least, makes them amenable to a relativist approach.

Uncritical appeal to the charge of relativism as a form of dismissal is, of course, not confined to philosophical circles, but rather is expressed throughout the academy. Many feminist theorists and disability theorists variously disregard Foucault's work because of (inter alia) his reluctance to make universal and ahistorical pronouncements about values such as justice, equality, and truth; his reluctance to advance normative prescriptions for political and ethical action; and his articulation of claims about the constitutive character of discursive power and their implications for our understanding of subjectivity, identity, and embodiment. In chapter 3, I introduce and respond to objections that revolve around some of these concerns.

That Foucault used historical approaches to the phenomena that he investigated rather than purportedly ahistorical conceptual analysis, deductive reasoning, and logical argumentation, is another reason why many, if not most, mainstream "analytic" philosophers dismiss or at least disregard his work. Jesse Prinz (himself a relativist), who draws on the work of Friedrich Nietzsche to recommend a genealogical method for philosophical inquiry, is a notable exception to this rule in mainstream analytic philosophy. Prinz asserts that the important lessons to derive from Nietzsche's genealogical approach to morality are that each of the values that we currently cherish has a history, that these histories may not be favorable, and furthermore, that these histories may not suggest our progression toward ideas that are truer or more beneficial. Our disregard for the historicity of our values, Prinz writes, gives us a "false sense of security" in them: "We take our moral outlook to be unimpeachable" (2007, 217). In other contexts, Prinz has drawn upon Nietzsche's genealogical method and the sentimentalism of David Hume to develop a historicist and relativist approach to morality that takes account of historical contingency and cultural variation in ways that, and to an extent that, normative ethical theories do not. Prinz's aim is to show that the genealogical method can be effectively used to inquire into the genesis of human values. A genealogical investigation of human values, Prinz explains, confirms that moral convictions are products of social history and accident rather than derived from intuition, revelation, or deductive reasoning from normative principles. Philosophers who investigate where moral beliefs and values originate are usually said to commit the "genetic fallacy," according to which the origins of morality are irrelevant; however, Prinz (217, 235) argues that genealogy—as a method to investigate origins—can enable us to discern when a given value originated in circumstances that are ignoble and therefore is especially suitable for reassessment. Genealogy, he states, "is an under-utilized tool for moral critique" (243).

Ian Hacking (2002), whose work is indebted to Foucault, has also addressed resistance to historical and historicist approaches in philosophy. Hacking too points out that philosophers who attend to the context of discovery, rather than the context of justification, are said to commit the genetic fallacy, according to which it is erroneous "to expect that the content of an idea, or the credibility of a proposition, can in any way be illuminated by our routes to it." Thus Hacking, who pithily remarks that the charge of genetic fallacy is "insubstantial name-calling" (63), explains his counter-positivist use of genealogy in this way:

> Plenty of philosophical problems surround concepts such as "normal" (said of human behavior, characteristics, or customs) or "chance." Or, to pursue the Foucauldian chain: "Mad," "criminal," "diseased," "perverse." I believe that specific details of the origin and transformation of these concepts is important to understanding them and for understanding what makes them "problematic." I do not see . . . my investigations of chance or abuse as solving the problem of free will or of the respective rights of state, parents, children. I certainly do not have the ludicrous self-indulgent conception that the problems go away when I am through. But I can show why these matters are prob-

lematic, whereas before we knew only that they were problematic. Sometimes one can hope to make a concept more problematic than before, for example, "information and control." And of course to use history in this way for the understanding of philosophical problems is not to resign one's right to use it in other ways. (71–72)

Feminist Philosophies of Disability

Feminist epistemologists and feminist philosophers of science have for quite some time argued that philosophical inquiry must take account of information about the social contexts from which both philosophical questions emerge and responses to them are generated, including the subjectivity and social positioning of any given questioner and respondent. Sandra Harding (among others) has argued that information about the subjectivity and social situation of knowers can provide valuable insights into the assumptions and biases on which a given position relies (for instance, see Harding 1986, 1991, 2015). Harding and other feminist philosophers maintain that any given proposition, argument, or other discursive practice is a product of the enculturation along gendered, racial, classist, and national lines of the subject (or group of subjects) who articulates it and the sociocultural milieu from which it emerges. Harding and other feminist philosophers claim, in short, that there is no such thing as a view from nowhere. To argue this way, Harding and a growing number of feminist (and other) philosophers assume some version of "standpoint epistemology." Feminist standpoint epistemologies variously postulate that people in subordinated social positions have, in virtue of their subordinated social status, understandings of social relations that are superior to—that is, more complete and objective than—the understandings of these relations that members of privileged social groups have (see Harding 1986, 2015; Hartsock 1983; Dotson 2011, 2012). Alison Wylie points out that standpoint theory is an explicitly political social epistemology whose "central and motivating insight is an inversion thesis" (2003, 26). As Wylie explains it,

> [T]hose who are subject to structures of domination that systematically marginalize and oppress them may, in fact, be epistemically privileged in some crucial respects. They may know different things, or know things better than those who are comparatively privileged (socially, politically) by virtue of what they experience and how they

understand their experience. Feminist standpoint theorists argue that gender is one dimension of social differentiation that may make a difference epistemically. Their aim is to both understand how the systematic partiality of authoritative knowledge arises—specifically, its androcentrism and sexism—and to account for the constructive contributions made by those working from marginal standpoints (especially feminist standpoints) in countering this partiality. (2003, 26)

Feminist philosophers in professional, institutional, and social positions of relative privilege must do more than they have thus far done to put these epistemological and methodological claims to work in practice, especially with respect to disability (and disabled philosophers); nevertheless, feminist philosophical insights about situated knowledges contribute to the background of the relativist and historicist philosophy of disability that I aim to advance, especially given the commitment of feminist standpoint theorists who—however much they otherwise disagree—concur that standpoint theories must not "presuppose an *essentialist* definition of the social categories or collectivities in terms of which epistemically relevant standpoints are characterized" (Wylie 2003, 26; emphasis in Wylie). Indeed, the relativist and historicist feminist philosophy of disability that I sketch in the pages that follow provides implicit and explicit responses to questions that have been central to (Euro-American) feminist philosophy and the Eurocentric Western philosophical tradition more generally, including: Are concepts universal, objective, and transhistorical? Are social categories real? Is social change determined by a society's material conditions? What is the nature of oppression? Do we have agency?

Given the historicism and relativism of the feminist philosophy of disability that I articulate in what follows, I assume broad metaethical and metaphilosophical positions with respect to moral and political questions and concerns. For if, as I hope, readers accept my arguments that the epistemological and ontological status attributed to disability and its putative foundation (impairment) are historically and culturally relative and specific, then they should also accept—or at least seriously entertain—the argument that morality with respect to disability too can be shaped by culture and history. That is, anyone who accepts my arguments that people's nonmoral (metaphysical and epistemological) beliefs about disability are shaped by cultural practices and historical events should probably concede that moral beliefs and values (i.e., about disability) that derive from, or presuppose, the "nonmoral" beliefs are also shaped by cultural practices and historical events.

This observation about the plasticity of both nonmoral and moral beliefs about disability challenges both the ways in which moral and political philosophers, cognitive scientists, and bioethicists (among others) currently understand the relation between morality and disability and the self-evidence that they confidently confer upon their claims with respect to a number of highly charged issues concerning disability that have emerged with its problematization by and through the apparatus of disability, including the claim that a defining feature of autistic people is that they lack the capacity for empathy; claims about euthanasia and physician-assisted suicide; claims about psychopathology; social determinist justifications for infrastructural and institutional inaccessibility; and arguments for prenatal testing and selective abortion. Notice that my idea of a historicist and relativist feminist philosophy of disability affects a methodological reversal of the way that philosophers approach disability. Typically, when and if philosophers of mainstream ethics, political philosophy, or bioethics inquire into disability, they take as their point of departure a normative moral and political theory that is somehow subsequently "applied" to disability, which itself is assumed to comprise a philosophically uninteresting, natural, and inert entity. By contrast, the historicist and relativist feminist philosophy of disability that I articulate in what follows takes as the starting point of inquiry the assumption that disability is an apparatus of force relations, a product of human invention and intervention all the way down.

A historicist and relativist feminist philosophy of disability improves upon the accounts of disability generated in the theoretical domains of feminist philosophy, philosophy of disability, and both feminist and nonfeminist disability studies in virtue of its insistence on attention to historical contingency and cultural specificity and variation, its political potency, and its analytical rigor. Thus, a historicist and relativist approach holds out subversive potential for feminist philosophy, for philosophy of disability, and indeed for feminist philosophy of disability, subversive potential precluded by the failure of analytic philosophers to appreciate the value of historical and systematically nonnormative approaches to philosophical questions and concerns. In chapter 3, I suggest that if philosophers of disability and disability theorists were to take up Foucault's historicist, genealogical approach to theoretical questions and political concerns about (for instance) identity, subjectivity, materiality, and power, they would avoid the reproduction of transhistorical and transcultural claims that currently condition much of the work done in philosophy of disability and disability studies. In chapter 4, furthermore, I use a well-known feminist critique of Foucault to show that if feminist philosophers were to employ Foucault's historicism in their philosophical analyses of questions and concerns, they would likely bypass the inclination to obscure disability and ableism in order to advance evocative universalizing claims.

Feminist philosophers take a critical approach to many of the methods and values of traditional areas of philosophy, questioning the assumptions and biases on which these areas of philosophy rely and identifying how these assumptions and biases reinforce forms of social subordination, especially with respect to gender. Feminist philosophers of disability (e.g., Silvers 1995; Wendell 1996; Kittay 1999; Carlson 2009; Barnes 2016) variously concentrate on the assumptions and biases about disability on which philosophical claims rely, as well as on how disabled people have been either vilified within the tradition of Euro-American, Western philosophy or exiled from it. The approaches to disability that they advance resist and run counter to the dominant conceptualization of disability that is persistently elaborated within bioethics, cognitive science, and mainstream political philosophy and ethics especially, according to which disability is a deficit, personal misfortune, or pathology that necessarily reduces the quality and worth of disabled people's lives and inevitably leads to the social and economic disadvantages that disabled people confront. Insofar as practitioners of the Euro-American philosophical tradition have, with few exceptions, cast disability as a natural, negative, and inert state of affairs in this way, they have largely removed the category of disability from the realm of philosophical inquiry and kept at bay philosophical debate and questioning about its epistemological, ethical, and political status. Feminist philosophers of disability, by contrast, both use and take a critical stance toward the history of philosophy and the contemporary practice of mainstream philosophy to variously elaborate new ways in which to think about disability and about the current social, political, cultural, and economic position of disabled people. They do so by employing the very methods, concepts, analytical rigor, and argumentative tools of the Euro-American, Western philosophical tradition and the discipline of philosophy in which they were trained, in addition to critically evaluating these practices and tools through the concepts, political commitments, critical insights, and personal investments that shape feminist, anti-ableist, antiracist, class-conscious, and antihetero-sexist theory and practice.

The feminist philosophy of disability that I want to elaborate shares many features with other feminist philosophies of disability. Some of these shared features distinguish varieties of feminist philosophy of disability from work done elsewhere in the broad, interdisciplinary field of feminist disability studies. Nevertheless, the feminist philosophy of disability that I hold relies upon an understanding of disability that distinguishes it from other feminist philosophies of disability, in addition to distinguishing it from other theories in feminist disability studies.

Other feminist philosophies and theories of disability uncritically retain some of the unsavory elements of dominant theoretical approaches to disability insofar as they variously conceive disability as (1) the functional manifestation of an intrinsic characteristic, a biological difference, or a property (attribute)—for example, an impairment—that certain people embody or possess and that gives rise to particular forms of social discrimination against them; or (2) the form of discrimination and oppression imposed upon people who have an intrinsic characteristic, attribute, or property construed as a human difference; or (3) some hybrid of (1) and (2), in which the relation between disability (as a functional limitation or form of social oppression) and, say, impairment (as an intrinsic characteristic, a property, or a difference that some people embody or possess) may not be clearly defined or may fluctuate from one context to another context, though, terminologically speaking, emphasis is placed upon the former (that is, disability). Feminist philosophies and theories that assume (1) construe disability as a natural feature of human existence, an aspect of human diversity that has historically been devalued and must be redeemed, revalued, and even celebrated. Feminist philosophies and theories of disability that assume (2) construe disability as a social, economic, and political problem directed at an already-existing group of people. Whereas feminist philosophies and theories of disability that assume (3) tend to be ambiguous about the actual character of disability and are, in some cases, inadvertently self-contradictory.

To be sure, these apparently distinct conceptions of disability diverge from each other in some important ways; nevertheless, these seemingly disparate conceptions each depend upon roughly the same assumptions about the epistemological and ontological status of impairment and disability, as well as upon the same assumptions about social power, including the assumption according to which power is fundamentally repressive and external to preexisting objects upon which it acts. I disagree with all these assumptions. In the next chapter, I argue, following Foucault, that social power is productive of the objects on which it acts and is diffused throughout society and culture rather than first and foremost repressive and centralized, as these other (feminist) conceptions of disability assume. In other words, my disagreement with these other conceptions of disability stems from the assumptions about causation that they make and the epistemological and ontological status that they implicitly confer upon the categories of impairment and disability. Whereas other feminist philosophers and theorists of disability variously conceive of disability as the functional outcome of a natural human characteristic, a human variation or difference, an identity, or a form of oppression in relation to which impairment is assumed to be the anterior, or prediscursive, foundation, I regard disability as what Foucault referred to as an "apparatus" (*dispositif*) of relatively recent force relations. Impairment, I contend, is an element of this apparatus produced as its naturalized and naturalizing foundation; that is, impairment is both an effect of and a mechanism of the apparatus of disability.

The Apparatus of Disability

In "The Confession of the Flesh," Foucault (1980a, 194) defined an apparatus (*dispositif*) as a thoroughly heterogeneous and interconnected ensemble of discourses, institutions, architectural forms, regulatory decisions, laws, scientific statements, administrative measures, and philosophical, moral, and philanthropic propositions that responds to an "urgent need" in a certain historical moment. In other words, an apparatus is a historically specific and dispersed system of power that produces and configures practices toward certain strategic and political ends. My use of Foucault's idea of apparatus enables me to move philosophical discussion about disability away from restrictive conceptualizations of it as (for instance) a personal characteristic or attribute, a property of given individuals, an identity, a difference, or a form of social oppression. In addition, my assumption that disability is an apparatus, in Foucault's sense, moves philosophical discussion of disability toward a more comprehensive conceptualization of it than the other conceptions of disability provide, a conceptualization of disability that is (among other things) historicist and relativist and, hence, culturally sensitive in ways that other conceptions of it are not. As an apparatus, disability is a historically specific aggregate that comprises, constitutes, and is constituted by and through a complex and complicated set of discourses, technologies, identities, and practices that emerge from medical and scientific research, government policies and administrative decisions, academic initiatives, activism, art and literature, mainstream popular culture, and so on. Although some of the diverse elements of the apparatus of disability seem to have different and even conflicting aims, design strategies, and techniques of application, the elements of the apparatus are nevertheless co-constitutive and mutually reinforcing.[10]

To understand disability as an apparatus is to conceive of it as a far-reaching and systemic matrix of power that contributes to, is inseparable from, and reinforces other apparatuses of historical force relations. On this understanding, disability is not a metaphysical substrate, a natural, biological category, or a characteristic that only certain individuals embody or possess, but rather is a historically contingent network of force relations in which everyone is implicated and entangled and in relation to which everyone occupies a position. That is, to be disabled or nondisabled is to occupy a certain subject position within the productive constraints of the apparatus of disability. In the terms of this understanding of disability, there are no "people with disabilities" and "able-bodied people"; rather, there are "disabled people" and "nondisabled people." Just as people are variously racialized through strategies and mechanisms of the apparatus of race, but no one "has" a race or even a certain race and, furthermore, just as people are variously sexed through strategies and mechanisms of the apparatus of sex, but no one "has" a sex or even a particular sex, so too people are variously disabled or not disabled through the operations of the apparatus of disability, but no one "has" a disability or even a given disability. In short, disability (like race and sex) is not a nonaccidental attribute, characteristic, or property of individuals, not a natural biological kind (see Tremain 2001, 2015; Haslanger 2000, 2006, 2012; Spencer 2017).

In the terms of the feminist philosophy of disability that I wish to advance, to refer to someone as "a person with a disability" is in fact to commit a category mistake. That females and people of color (which are by no means mutually exclusive social groups) have been perceived in the recent histories of Western and Northern nations as the bearers of sex and race, respectively, does not mean that males are not also sexed in accordance with the apparatus of sex, nor that white people are not racialized in the terms of the apparatus of race.[11] Equally, the fact that one is not subjected as a disabled person does not indicate that one occupies a space apart from the apparatus of disability. The apparatus of disability is expansive and expanding, differentially subjecting people to relatively recent forms of power on the basis of constructed perceptions and interpretations of (inter alia) bodily structure, appearance, style and pace of motility, mode of communication, emotional expression, mode of food intake, and cognitive character, all of which phenomena are produced and understood within a culturally and historically contingent frame and shaped by place of birth, place of residence, gender, education, religion, years lived, and so on. My analysis of the apparatus of disability treats these phenomena as the outcomes of contextually specific and performative relations of power rather than as transcultural and transhistorical objective and determined facts about humans.

I assume, furthermore, that key classificatory schemes and distinctions made in disability theory—such as the distinctions between visible disabilities and invisible disabilities; mental disabilities versus psychological disabilities; physical disability versus cognitive disability; physical impairments as opposed to sensory impairments; severe disabilities versus moderate or mild disabilities; high functioning and low functioning—are themselves strategies of these relations of power; that is, these distinctions and designations are performative artifacts of the apparatus of disability that naturalize this state of affairs, reinstituting disability as a personal attribute or individual characteristic.[12] That disabled people reify these (and other) historically contingent products of the apparatus of disability and incorporate them into their sets of beliefs, theories, values, and practices in a host of ways, interpreting them as the substratum or ground of putatively natural or even socially constructed identities, should be recognized as a strategic mechanism of the "polymorphism" of (neo)liberalism (as Foucault referred to it), that is, the continuous capacity of a liberal regime of force relations to respond to critique by (among other things) molding the subjectivities of individuals in particular ways. I return to consider this claim when I address the issue of the identity of the disabled subject in chapters 2 and 3. I shall argue that when disability is situated within the domain of force relations, that is, when disability is construed as an apparatus of power, its collaboration with other apparatuses of force relations— such as settler colonialism and white supremacy—can be more readily identified and more thoroughly investigated than has been done thus far. Indeed, as I indicate in the next chapter, Foucault's (2003g) idea of a "racism against the abnormal" anticipates the conception of disability as an apparatus.

The conception of disability as an apparatus is premised on an understanding of the relation between power and causation that runs counter to current and emerging work in philosophy of disability and disability studies. For the conception of disability does not rely upon some variation of the assumption that impairment and disability could be taken up as politically neutral and value-neutral objects of inquiry were it not for disabling practices and policies of exclusion that the ideological requirements of power place upon them. This assumption is fundamental to the BSM (and most other extant sociopolitical approaches to disability), which, as I have indicated, construes impairment as a politically neutral human characteristic on which disability (construed as social oppression) is imposed. With the conception of disability as an apparatus, by contrast, no domain of impairment or disability exists apart from relations of power. Impairment and disability can never be freed from power, nor, furthermore, can there be a phenomenology that articulates these supposedly prediscursive domains. Power relations are not external to impairment and disability and their nexus in the apparatus of disability, but rather are integral to this relationship, constituting the knowledge and objects that these historical artifacts affect, as well as the artifacts themselves. As Foucault explained,

> Relations of power are not in a position of exteriority with respect to other types of relationships (economic processes, knowledge relationships, sexual relations), but are immanent in the latter; they are the immediate effects of the divisions, inequalities, and disequilibriums which occur in the latter, and conversely they are the internal conditions of these differentiations; relations of power are not in superstructural positions, with a role of prohibition or accompaniment; they have a directly productive role, wherever they come into play. (1978, 94)

Since there is no exteriority between techniques of knowledge and strategies of power, and insofar as knowledge-power relations are constitutive of the objects that they affect, one of my aims is to identify and examine discussions within philosophy around which historically specific responses to disability, produced in accordance with the requirements of the apparatus of disability, have coalesced; that is, I aim to identify and examine "especially dense transfer point[s] for relations of power" (Foucault 1978, 98) within philosophy that the apparatus of disability has produced, thereby contributing to its expansion and to the constitution of its naturalized elements, of which impairment is only one. Within the discipline of philosophy, the subfields of bioethics and cognitive science are most easily recognizable as domains within which the constitutive effects of the apparatus of disability are produced; however, such sites of power can be identified across and throughout the discipline. Notice that Foucault's insight that knowledge-power relations are constitutive of the very objects that they are claimed to merely represent and affect dissolves the binary distinctions between (for instance) description and prescription, fact and value, and form and content. Among other things, the insight indicates that any given description is indeed a prescription for the formulation of the object (person, practice, or thing) to which it is claimed to innocently refer. Knowledge-power relations have not only brought impairment into being, but have brought it into being as a certain kind of thing, that is, as negative, as a natural disadvantage, as a problem to be corrected or rectified. Impairment has emerged as an area of investigation only because productive relations of power established it as a possible object of inquiry and a particular kind of object of a particular kind of inquiry in the first place, inquiry that has been possible and remains possible only because techniques of knowledge and discursive practices have been able to invest it as such. I am concerned to show how various discourses within feminist philosophy and the broader discipline and profession of philosophy have coalesced around "local centers" that demarcate differential power relations between subjects, as well as how these discursive demarcations contribute to the production of impairment and other elements of the apparatus of disability through the very inquiry into them in which philosophers engage.

Situating the Problem of Disability

Insofar as I aim to denaturalize impairment and disability, the question of how to position this analysis within philosophy is an integral concern of the investigation. In the remainder of this chapter, therefore, I introduce empirical data and theoretical arguments that establish a context within which readers can situate my subsequent discussions. To begin to create such a context, I shall first briefly address remarks that I make at the outset of the chapter about the relation between bioethics and disability. As I note there, the subfield of bioethics is one of the only areas of mainstream philosophy in which disability—that is, a certain conception of disability—is treated as appropriate subject matter for investigation; thus, the institutional and disciplinary pressure to configure critical philosophical work on disability in bioethical terms can be substantial. Indeed, the decision to (re)define and categorize one's critical philosophical work on disability as disability bioethics (or feminist bioethics, or simply bioethics) can be professionally prudent and even financially lucrative, enhancing one's opportunities for (say) publication, employment, or substantial government, university endowment, and corporate research grants, as well as other benefits that derive from recognition and advancement in a preestablished subfield. Yet, the social, institutional, and critical price of these rewards is high.[13] In another context, Roberts, speaking about the conditions under which current research on race is conducted within academia, makes a similar argument, pointing out that there is an economic incentive for researchers to "biologize race," that is, to conduct research on race that has a biological element. Such incentives, Roberts argues, threaten to undermine critical work on race because, as she explains it, "the biological" is often added to the research without sufficient scrutiny (2016; also see Roberts 2012).

Philosophers of disability should resist the compulsion to re-depoliticize philosophy of disability (and race), that is, to re-biologize philosophy of disability (and race) by configuring it as a form of bioethics, not least because of the role that the field of bioethics has played and continues to play in the apparatus of disability (and the apparatus of race) and the problematization of impairment and disability that has emerged by and through that apparatus in the context of professional philosophy. In chapter 5, I draw on Foucault to argue that a (neo)liberal governmentality of eugenics—in support of which the apparatus of disability has coalesced—undergirds the field of bioethics and has motivated its emergence and expansion. The assumptions on which the subfield of bioethics relies, I argue, run counter to efforts to improve the social position of disabled people and the professional situation of disabled philosophers in particular. To be sure, I recognize that some feminist bioethicists might object to my assertions in this regard by arguing that these sorts of criticisms of bioethics misrepresent the field; that is, they might argue that bioethics is a diverse field, covering a wide range of topics and a variety of approaches, and that their feminist work on these wide-ranging topics is politically oriented and informed, thereby rendering my cautionary proviso moot. Although I do aim to offer responses to such objections, I set them aside for now and address them in some detail in chapter 5.

I want, nonetheless, to point out that there are in fact additional reasons why philosophers and theorists of disability should refuse to describe their work on disability as "disability bioethics" (or some other form of bioethics). These additional reasons ought to be especially compelling for feminist philosophers. To draw an analogy with feminism, consider that given the historical medicalization of women's lives, most (if not all) feminist philosophers would likely object if the subject matter of feminist philosophy was prone to be comprehensively redescribed as "feminist bioethics." Feminist philosophers, to secure recognition and respect for feminist insights across the subdisciplines of philosophy, have long struggled against elements of systemic sexism in the profession that trivialize the serious character of these insights and discount them as genuinely philosophical subject matter. Not everything about feminist philosophy, nor even everything that feminists say about the body, gets redescribed as "feminist bioethics"; likewise, not everything about philosophy of disability is suitably repackaged as "disability bioethics." The implicit suggestion that any and all work that pertains to disability is in some sense biomedical or bioethical in nature—even when this work primarily addresses evidently metaphysical and epistemological concerns and questions—is reductive and sequesters (feminist and nonfeminist) philosophy of disability in the oft-derided realm of "applied ethics," as well as depoliticizes and remedicalizes disability in ways that facilitate its continued omission from complex intersectional and integrated feminist philosophical analyses.

The institutional, disciplinary, and professional compulsion to redescribe philosophy of disability as some variation of bioethics contrives to limit the philosophical scope and transgressive prospects of this emerging subdiscipline by both tying critical work on disability to a medicalizing discourse that is the crux of the institutionalized, discursive, and structural ableism of the discipline and profession of philosophy and reinforcing the widely held assumption that philosophical analyses of disability are "not really"—that is, not "hard," not "core," not "rigorous"—philosophy. Philosophers of disability confront enormous challenges to the philosophical merit and rigor of their work, as well as to its importance, challenges that are in no way abated by reductionist misconceptions of it. The refusal of the profession to recognize that specializations in metaphysics, epistemology, philosophy of language, and so on can be accomplished through philosophy of disability—that is, that the focus of the work of a given philosopher of disability could be (for instance) metaphysics or epistemology or philosophy of language—ensures that philosophers of disability who specialize in such areas of the discipline are not taken seriously as applicants for jobs in these (and other) areas, nor as potential presenters at conferences in these areas, nor as contributors to edited collections in these areas, and so on.

In another context, Tommie Shelby has pointed out various ways that African American philosophy is diminished and delegitimized within the discipline of philosophy, some of which resemble ways that philosophy of disability too is discounted and delegitimized in the discipline. In *We Who Are Dark: The Philosophical Foundations of Black Solidarity*, Shelby writes, "Within the broader discipline of philosophy as practised in the United States, African American philosophy is still largely marginalized. Many philosophers regard it as not real philosophy at all. And when it is considered philosophical, it is given the label *applied philosophy*, a term often used derisively to denote work that is considered 'soft' or only marginally philosophical" (2007, 13). In fact, this distinction between "real" philosophy and "applied" philosophy maps roughly onto the metaphilosophical distinction between ideal theory and nonideal theory that Rawls (1971) advanced. On the terms of Rawls's distinction, ideal theory is concerned with universals derived from unmitigated reflection and conceptual analysis, whereas nonideal theory is concerned with particularities derived from empirical observation and experience. For Rawls, the former sort of theory ought to be regarded as an ethical, political, and philosophical improvement upon the latter kind of theory: the reliance on observation and experience renders nonideal theory susceptible to arbitrary factors such as bias in ways that ideal theory is not. As Charles Mills (2005) and others have pointed out, however, and as I agree, Rawls's famous distinction between ideal and nonideal theory is reductive and undermines, if not ignores, the knowledges that members of marginalized groups produce.

Exceptional Marginality and Ableist Exceptionism

Among the humanities and social sciences, philosophy is the most conservative and homogeneous discipline, rivaling only the STEM (science, technology, engineering, and mathematic) fields in this regard. Women philosophers make up an estimated 25 percent of full-time philosophy faculty in the United States (Schwitzgebel and Dicey Jennings 2016); about 30–35 percent in Canada; an estimated 25 percent in Australia; and similar numbers elsewhere. Black philosophers constitute approximately 2 percent of full-time philosophy faculty in North America. Philosophers of color constitute an estimated 10 percent or less (see Tremain 2013b, 2014). A recent membership survey conducted by the American Philosophical Association suggests that disabled philosophers constitute roughly 2 percent of its faculty members (American Philosophical Association 2016), although disabled people make up roughly 22 percent of the general North American population (Centers for Disease Control and Prevention 2015). A comparable survey conducted by the Canadian Philosophical Association (CPA) in 2013 suggests that disabled philosophers constitute less than 1 percent of faculty members employed in philosophy departments in Canada. In other words, the profession of philosophy is made up almost entirely of nondisabled white people (see Tremain 2013b, 2014).

The low percentage of disabled philosophers employed as full-time faculty in philosophy departments can be attributed in part to the widespread employment discrimination and bias against disabled faculty across the university and the exclusion of disabled people from the workforce at large. An article in the *Chronicle of Higher Education* reports that a Freedom of Information Act request at the University of California at Berkeley indicates that only twenty-four of the university's 1,552 fulltime faculty members—roughly 1.5 percent—are disabled (Grigely 2017). In a recent collaborative study, furthermore, researchers at Rutgers University and Syracuse University found, for example, that employers expressed an interest in candidates who identified as disabled 26 percent less frequently than they did in candidates who did not identify as disabled. These researchers had devised a study—designed to track bias and discrimination against disabled candidates—in which résumés and cover letters for identically qualified fictitious job candidates were sent out for jobs in accounting. The only salient distinction between the fictitious candidates was that some of them indicated in their cover letters that they were disabled and others did not. Similar studies have been conducted to identify bias and discrimination against people due to gender and race. The Rutgers-Syracuse study showed that employers were 34 percent less likely to express an interest in experienced disabled job candidates and 15 percent less likely to express an interest in disabled job candidates at the beginning of their career (Scheiber 2015).

Data compiled by the Institute on Disability at the University of New

Hampshire indicates that, in the general population, only 34 percent of working-age disabled people are employed, compared to 74 percent of working-age nondisabled people (Institute on Disability 2016). Data compiled by the U.S. Department of Labor's Office of Disability Employment Policy roughly confirms these figures, indicating that only 32.0 percent of working-age disabled people were employed on average in the 2010–12 period, compared to over 72.7 percent of nondisabled people (Office of Disability Employment Policy, n.d.). Furthermore, as the Office of Disability Employment Policy points out, most employed disabled people work in low-paying jobs. Due to the high rate of unemployment among disabled people and the segregation of disabled people in low-paying jobs, many of them live in poverty. The Annual Disability Statistics Compendium reports that, in 2014, 28.2 percent of disabled people living in the community in the United States lived in poverty, compared to 13 percent of nondisabled people (Institute on Disability 2016). When the increased housing, transportation, and other living expenses with which many disabled people contend are taken into account, the disparity between the two groups widens significantly.

The grievous unemployment and poverty that accrue to disabled people are due at least in part to the fact that most institutions of higher education remain largely inaccessible to disabled people, not having incorporated the principles of universal design into their infrastructure, physical design, and day-to-day operations. An individualized, medicalized, and privatized conception of disability and inclusion of disabled people underlies the accessibility policies of most universities and colleges, a conception (deemed to be most cost effective for these institutions) wherein disabled students, faculty, and staff are tacitly expected and coercively compelled to assimilate into inaccessible educational and work environments. Within the terms of this conception of inclusion and its concrete instantiations, the requirements of a certain group of people are taken for granted and naturalized as "normal," regular, and typical, the preferential allocation of resources for which is rendered invisible precisely insofar as these requirements are considered "standard" and basic. The materialization of this conception involves the implicit perception and bias according to which the requirements of certain other people are "special needs," idiosyncratic, and extraordinary, the allocation of resources to which is supererogatory and supplementary, regarded as "accommodation," and taken into account only if and when these people make "special," "confidential" requests to university and college administrations for the provisions and services that they require (and to which they are entitled). The administrative recognition of such requests for accommodation almost always depends upon some sort of medical validation and certification. Hence, insofar as universities and colleges operate with this accommodationist approach, people in the latter group—namely, disabled people—must usually medicalize their circumstances and enter a bureaucratic morass in order to get the social goods that they require, that is, must make *more* effort (and usually *considerably more* effort) to get the services and resources that they require than nondisabled people make to get comparable services and resources (for instance, see Stramondo 2015; Tremain 2013b).

Philosophers should note that this "accommodationist" understanding of the inclusion of disabled people is reminiscent of the way that the claims to entitlement of disabled people were "set aside" in Rawls's influential approach to social justice, to be considered after the parties in the original position determined the basic structure of a just society for "normal and cooperating" people (Rawls 1971). The Americans with Disabilities Act (ADA) of 1990, to which universities and colleges in the United States appeal in order to administer and justify such accommodationist approaches to inclusion of disabled people, was initially hailed as a landmark piece of civil rights legislation; however, an increasing number of disability scholars and activists recognize (and a series of successful court challenges has demonstrated) that the concept of "reasonable accommodation," which is at the center of the ADA, is a limiting concept, that is, a regulative instrument that actually naturalizes disability, limiting and restraining the extent to which disabled people can make demands upon employers, businesses, organizations, and service providers for the goods and resources to which they are entitled.

In another context (2013b), I identify and outline many of the institutional structures, disciplinary mechanisms, and discursive practices that restrict the employment and other professional opportunities available to disabled philosophers. In this context, I am concerned to show that a distinctive combination of discursive practices, institutionalized disciplinary mechanisms and structures, and institutionalized biases and prejudices substantially restricts the opportunities available to disabled philosophers generally and to disabled philosophers of disability especially. The assumption that disability is a philosophically uninteresting human characteristic and thus not the appropriate subject matter of philosophy is one (but only one) component of this mixture.

The continued institutionalization of ableist language in philosophical discourse is an exceptional reminder of the marginalization and exclusion of critical philosophical analyses of disability from mainstream philosophy. Even now, disability remains ever-present in philosophy in the form of these rhetorical devices. Indeed, some philosophers hold on to these rhetorical practices so resolutely that they seem to imply that not another sentence could be written in the historical discourse of philosophy if they were to refrain from their use of phrases such as *blind to the implications* and terms such as *morally blind*. Due to the seeming inescapability of the association between sight and knowledge in the Eurocentric philosophical tradition, ocular ableist metaphors such as these phrases and terms are the most prevalent examples of this deleterious practice in philosophical writing. Nevertheless, auralist metaphors, that is, metaphors that disparage deaf people, are also commonly used, along with metaphors that disparagingly allude to nonverbal people, people who do not walk, people who hear voices, and so on. To be sure, some philosophers reluctantly concede that the aforementioned phrases are ableist; however, they attempt to draw the line there with respect to ableist metaphors in philosophical discourse. These philosophers argue that we should distinguish the unseemly uses of ocular metaphors from what they regard as benign metaphorical appeals to blindness; that is, they hold out for phrases such as *blind review* and *justice is blind*, citing the allegedly positive valence of these metaphors. For some of these philosophers, the integrity of the latter metaphors serves to dismantle the critique of ableist metaphors and ableist language altogether.

Should we accept this distinction between ableist and "benign" metaphors? That is, are the former metaphors "negative" and the latter "positive"? Consider the metaphor *justice is blind*. Now, this phrase seems sacrosanct in American society; thus, one might assume that it is harmless. Justice is good, virtuous, ethical, and so on. That is what the metaphor figuratively tells us, is it not? To some philosophers, the answer is yes. They concur with this straightforward understanding of the metaphor; that is, they argue that insofar as the metaphor *justice is blind* associates blindness with what is good, virtuous, and ethical, it is a mistake to claim that the metaphor is ableist. A similar argument is made with respect to the term *blind review*.

Notice, however, that philosophers who argue in this way misunderstand how these metaphors work. For the metaphor *justice is blind* is intended to describe the process by which justice is achieved; it is not meant to refer to the (positive) value of that ideal. If the phrase *justice is blind* were a statement about the merit of justice, then it would be a contradiction to claim that justice is "blind" (i.e., good) and that is a bad thing. Yet the latter claim is not at all a contradiction. Legal theorists such as feminists Martha Minow (1991) and Martha Fineman (2005), among others, have written eloquently about the shortcomings of notions of justice that purport to transcend the influence on decision making of allegedly natural human differences and circumstances. Transcendence of these human differences is, however, precisely what the metaphor of *justice is blind* purports to achieve: it describes a system of justice in which personal characteristics, attributes, and contingent circumstances are deemed arbitrary and, therefore, withheld from available knowledge. In short, the metaphor *justice is blind* draws an association between lack of knowledge and blindness. It is the association between lack of knowledge and blindness that makes this apparently redeeming rhetorical device a pernicious artifact of ableism. A similar argument applies to the term *blind review* (Tremain 2011; see also May and Ferri 2005; Dolmage 2005; M. Bailey 2011; Schalk 2013).

My critiques of ableist metaphors and other ableist language in philosophical discourse have met with considerable opposition from nondisabled philosophers and even some disabled philosophers. Usually, their dismissals of, and disagreements with, these critiques assume that language and discourse are politically neutral purveyors of value-neutral information and facts, an assumption about linguistic and discursive practices that continues to dominate philosophy and other areas of the academy. As Foucault (1972) convincingly argued, however, language and discourse do not innocently reflect, or "mirror," a transparent, pregiven reality, but rather construct social reality *as* pregiven. Feminists, critical race theorists, and Marxist theorists (among others) have shown, furthermore, that linguistic and discursive practices are primary mediums through which asymmetrical forms of social power are generated, sustained, and reproduced. Nevertheless, although feminist philosophers and philosophers of language (among others) argue that linguistic and discursive practices contribute to the constitution of inequalities due to sexism and racism, many of them engage in a form of ableist exceptionism insofar as they are reluctant or even refuse to acknowledge that these practices are formative of, sustain, and perpetuate the inequalities that accrue to disabled people. *Ableist exceptionism* is the term that I have coined to refer to the phenomenon whereby disability, because it is assumed to be a prediscursive, natural, and politically neutral human characteristic (difference, attribute, or property), is uniquely excluded from the production and application of certain values, beliefs, principles, and actions that circulate in political consciousness.[14] My claim is thus that philosophers (and other theorists, activists, and so on) commit ableist exceptionism when they assume that the metaphorical and other use to which they put disability in language and discourse is politically neutral and innocent, although they politicize virtually all other speech acts, identifying them as value laden and interested. It would be very strange indeed if linguistic and discursive practices were constitutive of other social inequalities, yet somehow remained outside of, apart from, and indifferent to, the domain of disability and ableist oppression. In fact, ableism (and the forms of power with which it is co-constitutive) saturates language and discourse—both everyday and philosophical—and is reconstituted through them.

In recent years, philosophers, especially some feminist philosophers, have increasingly attended to the influence of implicit biases on the composition of the profession and discipline of philosophy, producing a substantial body of literature that, they argue, shows that these biases can have demonstrable effects upon hiring practices, student evaluation, journal refereeing, promotion, and so on (for instance, see Brownstein and Saul 2016). Implicit biases are generally defined in this literature as nonconscious, reflexive attitudes that detrimentally affect the ways in which people perceive, evaluate, and interact with members of stigmatized social groups (see Gendler 2011). Contributions to this literature usually take as their starting point or rely upon data derived from the Implicit Association Test (I.A.T.), a research tool that psychologists Mahzarin Banaji and Anthony Greenwald (n.d.) introduced in 1998, claiming that the test facilitates the identification of nonconscious discriminatory attitudes. Closely associated with the philosophical literature on implicit bias is a growing body of work in philosophy that draws attention to the phenomenon of stereotype threat, an idea said to account for the fact that people's (usually nonconscious) awareness of their membership in a stigmatized social group can negatively impact their performance in certain situations, such as job interviews.

Discussions within philosophical circles about how psychological phenomena condition the perceptions and assessments (including self-perceptions and self-assessments) of members of marked groups have played a significant role in endeavors to overcome the homogeneity of professional philosophy, leading to a variety of successful outcomes. Notwithstanding these outcomes, however, the notions of implicit bias and stereotype threat, as well as prior discussions about implicit bias and stereotype threat in philosophy, warrant more critical consideration.

First, claims about implicit bias and the I.A.T. itself—that is, the validity and reliability of the I.A.T.—have been sharply criticized by some philosophers of science, while claims about stereotype threat have been at the heart of a replication crisis in social psychology (for instance, see Machery 2016; Bartlett 2017; Spencer 2017). Second, virtually all the heretofore discussions about implicit bias and stereotype threat in the profession have concentrated exclusively on how these phenomena affect subjects marked by gender, or by race, or by gender and race, with these categories conceived as mutually exclusive of each other and of other categories of subjection. Thus, even if concerns with respect to the methodological and theoretical nature of philosophical work on implicit bias were assuaged, the ways in which philosophers have put the I.A.T. and the notion of implicit bias into practice would be very disconcerting.

None of the studies of implicit bias in hiring, promotion, and publication to which philosophers routinely refer reports on empirical inquiry and analyses—as in the Rutgers-Syracuse cover-letter study—of the biases and prejudices that disabled philosophers confront. Some philosophers who refer to the studies on gender and race biases speculate that the findings of these studies likely apply in the same ways to the situations and circumstances of disabled philosophers (as well as working-class philosophers, lesbian and gay philosophers, and other marginalized philosophers). However, this speculation implies that sexism and racism are paradigmatic forms of marginalization and exclusion that other forms of marginalization and exclusion from the discipline and profession replicate. This assumption—that is, the assumption that ableism and the exclusion of disabled philosophers from the profession are produced through the same techniques and mechanisms as the exclusion of non-disabled philosophers (however gendered and racialized)—obscures the distinct forms of discrimination that disabled philosophers confront and is, in effect, another means by which the relative homogeneity of the discipline and profession is enabled to persist. Indeed, the routine exclusion of substantive consideration of disability from the research on bias in philosophy is a form of ableist exceptionism, that is, a political decision with detrimental consequences for disabled philosophers (however gendered and racialized).

Although it is incumbent upon feminist philosophers (and others) who produce work on implicit bias in philosophy to enlarge the purview of their studies in ways that encompass the biases that disabled philosophers confront, the preoccupation with psychological factors in discussions about the homogeneity of philosophy and the exclusion of considerations of ableism from these discussions has entailed that the structural, institutional, and discursive mechanisms and apparatuses

that contribute to the production in philosophy of a hostile environment for disabled philosophers remain largely obfuscated. To be sure, a
growing number of feminist philosophers (and others) argue that institutional and structural mechanisms of power must be given primacy in
accounts of social power, including accounts of how power circulates
within philosophy. Other philosophers argue, furthermore, that structural and individual factors cannot be analytically separated and ranked
according to the priority that they should be given in such accounts (see
Madva 2016). In other words, the preoccupation with implicit biases and
psychological explanations of power imbalances in the profession and
elsewhere seems to be on the decline. Nevertheless, this recent shift in
emphasis of philosophical work on the operations of power both within
the profession and beyond seems thus far as limited in scope as the earlier explanations with respect to implicit biases, that is, limited to analyses
of macropolitical factors that produce sexism and racism alone.[15]

Put directly, the exclusion of disabled philosophers (however gendered and racialized) from the profession is in addition variously produced by and through distinct mechanisms and techniques that continue to be ignored in these discussions about the demographics of
the profession, factors such as the segregating conceptual and built
environments—including inaccessible conferences, classrooms, lectures,
course materials, and workshops—in which the very practice of philosophy takes place, as well as research agendas, arguments, instruments,
databases, and influences that revolve around an array of notions that
operate to subjugate disabled people, including "normality," "quality of
life," "well-being," "natural disadvantage," "death with dignity," "compensation," "defect," "cure," "pathology," and "risk." Indeed, insofar as
claims according to which disabled people are (for example) "abnormal," "defective," "worse off," "permanently dependent," and "losers in
the natural lottery" continue to be both articulated and taken seriously
as possible candidates for theoretical endorsement within various subfields of philosophy, it is no wonder that disabled people are not regarded as viable colleagues in the profession, nor considered worthy of the
role of "professional philosopher," as the low representation of disabled
philosophers in the profession vividly demonstrates (see Tremain 2014).
In short, much of the very subject matter of philosophy is incompatible with efforts to increase the representation of disabled people in the
profession. A feminist philosophy of disability that draws on Foucault
to investigate the problematization of disability—especially as it is produced in philosophy—must take account of this state of affairs.

Knowing Disability

Feminist philosophers have convincingly argued that there are correlations between the demographics of the profession and the content of philosophical inquiry, correlations conditioning (among other things) which questions are prioritized, how they get asked, what kinds of answers are sought, and what methods of investigation are employed. The efforts of feminist philosophers have had lasting and far-reaching effects, raising the consciousness of professional philosophers about gender inequality and sexism within the profession, discipline, and tradition of philosophy. These efforts and the fruits of them include the publication of several anthologies and edited collections of feminist philosophy; the establishment of professional associations for women philosophers and feminist philosophers; the founding and development of several journals of feminist philosophy; special issues of mainstream philosophy journals on feminist philosophy or topics of interest to feminist philosophers especially; the establishment of a blog for feminist philosophers; the election of quite a number of women and feminist philosophers to leadership positions within national philosophy associations internationally; and the growing presence of feminist philosophy at national philosophy association meetings worldwide. Nevertheless, it is quite clear that the benefits that have directly and indirectly accrued to feminist philosophers and women philosophers due to these improvements have not been distributed equally among them, as I documented in a 2013 article (Tremain 2013b).

Despite the links that feminist philosophers have traced between the egregious demographics of professional philosophy and the exclusionary character of philosophical inquiry, critical analyses of disability continue to be systematically left out of most feminist philosophical analyses (as the feminist work on implicit bias and stereotype threat exemplifies), which remain substantively limited to the trilogies of gender, race, and sexuality and gender, race, and class or the duet of gender and race. Many feminist philosophers have received a large portion of, or even all of, their philosophical training in areas and subfields such as mainstream ethics and political philosophy, bioethics, and cognitive science, where individualized and medicalized conceptions of disability are especially prevalent and explicit; thus, these philosophers have almost certainly not been informed (and likely have not informed themselves) about sociopolitical conceptions of disability. Indeed, few feminist (and other) philosophers understand disability as an apparatus of force relations that is inextricable from and mutually constitutive with gender, race, sexuality, ethnicity, class, age, and nationality (among other apparatuses of power). In feminist philosophy (as elsewhere in philosophy), disability is generally not conceived as a product of force relations in which everyone is implicated, but rather is still widely regarded as an intrinsic, unfortunate, and politically neutral characteristic (pathological property) that some individuals possess and embody, offering little that a politically informed feminist philosophy should analyze and interrogate.

An especially disconcerting example of this uncritical stance on (the apparatus of) disability can be found in Miranda Fricker's *Epistemic Injustice: Power and the Ethics of Knowing* (2007), a book that has become quite influential in feminist epistemology and in social epistemology more generally, notably because of its elaboration of the concept of epistemic injustice. Although I think that Fricker's work on epistemic injustice has significant potential for the articulation of feminist philosophy of disability, I approach it with reservations. I believe that Fricker's well-known discussion of hermeneutical injustice reproduces biases about the taken-for-granted apolitical and philosophically uninteresting character of disability. Fricker, I contend, understands disability as external to relations to power, that is, she assumes that force relations are external to the production of knowledge about disability, an assumption that feminist philosophy of disability that draws on Foucault eschews.[16]

Fricker (2007, 146–48) argues that the capacity of relatively powerless social groups to adequately and appropriately understand the world is jeopardized if dominant groups disproportionately influence the interpretive resources available at any given time Asymmetrical relations of social power, she explains, can skew shared hermeneutical resources in ways that both enable members of powerful social groups to understand their social experiences and prevent members of relatively disempowered social groups from understanding their own experiences. Fricker remarks that the mid-twentieth-century feminist consciousness-raising groups, in which women publicly articulated experiences that had previously been systematically obscured and routinely privatized, were, for example, a direct response to the fact that such epistemological resources had hitherto been rendered unavailable to them. To illustrate these claims, Fricker quotes an excerpt from Susan Brownmiller's memoir in which Brownmiller (1990) writes about one woman's revelatory introduction to feminist consciousness raising in a group that embarked on a discussion about postpartum depression. Brownmiller describes how, over the course of the forty-five-minute discussion, the woman realized that the depression she had experienced—and for which both she and her husband had blamed her—was not a "personal deficiency" at all, but rather, "a combination of physiological things and a real societal thing, isolation" (1990, 182, in Fricker 2007, 149). As Fricker explains it, the lack of understanding with which the woman had lived until that life-altering discussion constituted a harm inflicted upon her in her capacity as a knower, that is, it constituted a specific sort of epistemic injustice, namely, a hermeneutical injustice.

Fricker cautions that not all hermeneutical disadvantages amount to hermeneutical injustices; hence, she draws upon the distinction between justice and luck that conditions mid-twentieth-century analytic political philosophy and ethics in order to identify the features that distinguish hermeneutical disadvantages that inflict epistemic injustice from herme-neutical disadvantages that do not involve injustice, a difference that she asserts can easily be recognized (2007, 149, 152). She puts it thus:

If, for instance, someone has a medical condition affecting their social behaviour at a historical moment at which that condition is still misunderstood and largely undiagnosed, then they may suffer from a hermeneutical disadvantage that is, while collective, especially damag-ing to them in particular. They are unable to render their experiences intelligible by reference to the idea that they have a disorder, and so they are personally in the dark, and may also suffer seriously negative consequences from others' non-comprehension of their condition. But they are not subject to hermeneutical injustice; rather, theirs is a poignant case of circumstantial bad luck. (152)

What is remarkable about Fricker's sketch of a hermeneutical disadvan-tage that derives from circumstantial bad luck rather than from injustice is how aptly it describes the hermeneutical disadvantage that only three pages earlier in her book she had associated with a paradigmatic case of epistemic injustice, that is, the lack of hermeneutical resources that in the not-so-distant past had been unavailable to women who experienced postpartum depression. Fricker argues that the salient difference with respect to epistemic injustice between the situation of women with post-partum depression and the situation of the hypothetical subject in the cited example is that in the former case, but not the latter, "background social conditions" prevailed "that were conducive to the relevant herme-neutical lacuna" (152). She explains that revelations about postpartum depression emerged in feminist consciousness-raising groups during a historical moment in which women were still markedly powerless in relation to men. This powerlessness, Fricker asserts, entailed that women had unequal hermeneutical participation, which "sort of inequality provides the crucial background conditions for hermeneutical injustice" (152). She notes, furthermore, that when this kind of unequal hermeneutical participation exists with respect to some area of social experience, members of the relevant disadvantaged group are likely "hermeneutically marginalized" (153).

My argument, however, is that people with an "undiagnosed condition" whose social behavior is subject to "negative consequences" due to the ways in which others perceive them are also members of a hermeneutically marginalized group; that is, the detrimental consequences that accrue to these people are produced by precisely the sort of social conditions from which Fricker claims that a hermeneutical disadvantage must result to qualify as a form of hermeneutical injustice. Certain forms of unequal social power—that is, mechanisms of the apparatus of disability—produce an array of disciplinary norms about appropriate social behavior and interaction, modes of communication, rationality, emotional self-control, and so on. These historically specific forms of unequal power, this historical a priori—that is, these "background conditions"—shape the public perceptions and authoritative epistemologies from which the negative social, political, interpersonal, and economic consequences to which Fricker refers accrue to some people, naturalizing, medicalizing, and depoliticizing these perceptions and epistemologies in ways that conceal their contingent and artifactual character.

The medical and juridical classifications that emerge from these background conditions produce the kinds of subjects that they are claimed to (merely) identify and name or represent. As I demonstrate in subsequent chapters, Foucault labored to point out the constitutive character of human classification and categorization, arguing that people are not naturally—that is, universally and transhistorically—sorted into social groups and kinds in accordance with ontologically preexisting categories such as sane and mad, healthy and sick, normal and pathological. Rather, social groups and kinds of people come into being because we make them that way by and through the practices that we use to describe them. Nevertheless, the performative and artifactual character of human classifications in general and psychiatric diagnoses in particular does not nullify their disciplinary and punitive effects. People who, for any number of reasons, do not conform to highly regulated standards of (for instance) social behavior and interaction—such as people who are classified as "mentally ill" or perceived to be "insane"—are routinely discredited, ignored, vilified, and stigmatized. Until the relatively recent formation and rise of "the mad pride movement" and related social movements, the hermeneutical resources that many disabled people required to collectively understand the political character of their situation were unavailable to them. In short, these people have been, and indeed continue to be, habitually subjected to hermeneutical injustice. That Fricker, in her discussion of kinds of hermeneutical disadvantage, neither takes account of the arguments that philosophers and theorists of disability and disabled activists have articulated with respect to the political origins of the "negative consequences" that become attached to these disabled people, nor recognizes the unequal hermeneutical participation that produces them, seems itself to be an instance of epistemic injustice (see Le François, Menzies, and Reaume 2013; China Mills 2014).

Fricker's assumptions about disability, according to which disability is a disadvantageous personal characteristic that exists apart from and prior to relations of social power and thus is not really philosophically interesting, reinforce and extend the marginalized and subordinated status of feminist philosophical work on disability. The belief that disability is a naturally occurring, disadvantageous phenomenon that exists apart from and prior to force relations and thus is not suitable to philosophical discussions of social power creates a "looping effect" (Hacking 1995, 351) in feminist philosophy that contributes to, expands, and sustains the naturalization of disability both within the discipline and beyond academia in policy and other spheres of social influence and organization. Due to the pervasiveness within philosophy of the belief that disability is separate from social force relations, that is, because of the uncritical acceptance of this assumption in subfields across the discipline, most philosophers do not feel compelled to examine how their theoretical, professional, institutional, and discursive practices reproduce the apparatus of disability, as a growing number of them feel compelled to do with respect to gender, race, and other significant apparatuses. This reluctance (or refusal) on the part of most philosophers to reflect upon how the apparatus of disability structures their own practices is intertwined with and reproduces the continued exclusion of (previously excluded) disabled philosophers from the profession and the persistent marginalization of philosophy of disability within the discipline.

Some philosophers of disability identify the collective refusal of philosophers to critically interrogate disability as an "epistemology of ignorance." For more than two decades, a variety of philosophers have used the term *epistemology of ignorance* to refer to a form of active refusal to attend to certain understandings of and knowledge about social relations of power and oppression. In *The Racial Contract*, Charles Mills writes that the racial contract between white people prescribes for them an "inverted epistemology, an epistemology of ignorance, a particular pattern of localized and global cognitive dysfunctions (which are psychologically and socially functional), producing the ironic outcome that whites will in general be unable to understand the world they themselves have made" (1997, 18). White supremacy, Mills points out, involves a concerted and sustained agreement among whites to engage in an epistemology of ignorance about the actual relations of power and oppression in society. Philosophers of race and feminist philosophers (among others) have subsequently used Mills's idea of an epistemology of ignorance to develop an emerging area of inquiry that has come to be referred to as "ignorance studies." In the introduction to their edited collection on race and epistemologies of ignorance, for instance, feminist philosophers Shannon Sullivan and Nancy Tuana (2007, 1) remark that although ignorance is commonly thought to be a gap in one's knowledge that can easily be remedied, sometimes what we do not know is a lack of knowledge or an unlearning that is actively produced for the purposes of domination and exploitation. As Sullivan and Tuana explain it, these "unknowledges" may be either consciously produced or unconsciously generated and supported.

My argument is that this discourse on epistemology of ignorance itself enlists a refusal to know, that is, a refusal to acknowledge itself as subjugating. Indeed, there are at least two reasons why it is a mistake for philosophers of disability to adopt the notion of an epistemology of ignorance in order to describe the stubborn indifference of (most) philosophers to the urgent philosophical, political, and social questions that disability raises.

First, the idea of an epistemology of ignorance is ableist. Although philosophers who use the idea of epistemologies of ignorance are adamant that their idea refers to far-reaching structural and institutional determinants of knowledge and not to a mere gap in a given individual's knowledge, they seem unable to describe the idea in any detail without reference to some "lack" or "deficit" of cognitive capacity. That is, proponents of the idea of epistemologies of ignorance claim to advance an externalist understanding of the relation between epistemology and domination; yet, their arguments invariably resort to internalist understandings of cognitive phenomena to make their case. Indeed, philosophical discussions of epistemologies of ignorance are peppered with ableist metaphors and other references to cognitive impairment and disability, metaphors and references that, in some respects, serve to paradoxically depoliticize and naturalize the states of affairs to which they are intended to refer: "obliviousness," "delusion," "collective amnesia," "blindness," "moral blindness," and "cognitive dysfunction," to name only a few. Stacy Clifford Simplican (2015), writing about the uses of Mills's theory for the idea of a capacity contract that addresses cognitive disability, argues that although an epistemology of ignorance captures many components of domination, the language of ignorance is inappropriate for an emancipatory project that revolves around cognitive disability. Mills's notion of an epistemology of ignorance is unsuitable, Simplican remarks, because "the familiar Enlightenment category of ignorant/cognizant maps onto morally wrong/right. For Mills," Simplican writes, "ignorance shrouds the morally inferior, whereas the cognitively superior are also morally superior. Better politics demands smarter people" (88). In short, although the idea of an epistemology of ignorance may seem useful in the short term for philosophy of disability, the idea seems counterproductive to the achievement of long-term aims in the field.

Second, the language of ignorance/knowledge and its association with moral inferiority/superiority has classist implications. It just is the case that people's socioeconomic positions significantly condition (among other things) their levels of literacy, access to education, access to technology, social mobility, access to nutritious food and safe shelter, and involvement in a community or some other kind of social arrangement. If people have limited opportunities to avail themselves of these resources and features of modern life, their prospects for acquiring knowledge are severely restricted. As Evan Thompson points out, drawing on the work of Merlin Donald, the human brain is a cultural brain adapted to symbolic culture and must be embedded in a cultural environment. Cultural materials and processes are so densely intertwined with the development and functioning of the brain, Thompson notes, that they operate as a necessary part of human cognition (Thompson 2016, 17; Thompson 2017, 58; Donald 1991, 2001). An epistemology that does not take account of how cultural materials and processes condition, among other things, what people learn; what they know; what knowledge and information they seek; whether they learn; what, whether, and why they remember; how they know; and the extent to which they can learn and know seems elitist and outdated. Thus, I replace the term *epistemology of ignorance* with the more encompassing term *epistemology of domination* (as I did at the outset of this chapter). The latter term, I maintain, can accomplish the conceptual work that needs to be done to capture important elements of the relation between epistemology and domination that the former term was designed to encapsulate, while bypassing the ableist and classist connotations of the term *epistemology of ignorance* that, for many people, compromise its use and indeed its centrality in a critical epistemology.[17]

Map of the Book

Foucault and Feminist Philosophy of Disability is a critical, material, discursive, and institutional intervention into feminist and mainstream philosophy designed to further dismantle the elements of the apparatus of disability that condition these disciplinary domains and shape the profession in general. My hope is that publication of this book will make a flourishing life and career in philosophy possible for more disabled people. The arguments of the book bring together two spheres of inquiry in which my research has been conducted: first, a reconstructive-conceptual sphere, in which I have articulated an antifoundationalist, historicist, and relativist account of impairment and disability that draws primarily upon Foucault; and second, a metaphilosophical sphere, in which I have drawn on empirical data to indicate some of the mechanisms, practices, and policies that perpetuate both the exclusion of disabled philosophers from the profession and the marginalization of philosophy of disability within the discipline. In this introductory chapter, I have offered broad outlines of these two distinct, yet interrelated, spheres. Taken together, the arguments of these spheres demonstrate that the marginalization of philosophy of disability within feminist and mainstream philosophy, the production of impairment by and through discourses of the discipline, the underrepresentation of disabled philosophers (however gendered and racialized) within the profession of philosophy, and the subordinated status of disabled people in society are mutually constitutive and mutually supporting, entangled and entwined.

The historicist and relativist feminist philosophy of disability that I derive from Foucault's approach and from feminist thinkers and other scholars who use his claims has transgressive potential, the extent of which philosophers of disability, feminist philosophers, and indeed, feminist philosophers of disability, have thus far not appreciated. Since both feminist philosophers and disability theorists have advanced arguments according to which many of Foucault's claims are not appropriate for their respective and mutual goals, the third and fourth chapters offer defenses of Foucault's work that aim to show why many of the arguments that feminists and disability theorists have directed at him (and authors who draw upon his claims) ought not to be accepted.

To motivate this task, in the following chapter I introduce ideas in Foucault's work that enable me to articulate a historicist and relativist feminist philosophy of disability. After I indicate how Foucault can be used to elaborate a historicist and relativist conception of disability, I address criticisms that some disability theorists have made of the use of his work for analyses of disability. In the third chapter, that is, I am concerned to dispel arguments that Foucault's claims are counterproductive to the goals of disability theory and activism. I focus on two charges that disability theorists have directed at Foucault: first, the charge that his conception of the subject cannot provide the foundation for a political movement; and second, the charge that his claims deny the materiality of the body and, thus, are tantamount to a form of linguistic idealism. It is within this context that I elaborate the antifoundationalist understanding of impairment and disability on which a feminist philosophy of disability that takes seriously historical contingency and cultural variation rests.

The fourth chapter examines feminist charges that Foucault's work relies upon masculinist and sexist biases. To show that these charges are unsubstantiated, I consider in particular Foucault's use of the case of Charles Jouy, the nineteenth-century farmhand who engaged in "sexual" activity with a girl, Sophie Adam, and subsequently was apprehended and incarcerated for the rest of his life. Chapter 5 zeros in on the subfield of bioethics and the strategic role that it plays in the *dispositif* (apparatus) of disability. The plausibility of the argument in the chapter, which is designed to show that the field of bioethics rationalizes the eugenics of a (neo)liberal governmentality, relies upon Foucault's insight that modern forms of power are intentional and nonsubjective.

CHAPTER 2

Power and Normalization

—⟡—

Discourse and Convention

In the previous chapter, I assert that disability is an apparatus (*dispositif*) of force relations rather than (1) a naturally, or biologically, disadvantageous human characteristic, property, or attribute that exists prior to discourse and cultural practices, that (2) medicine and science can accurately represent, and that (3) is therefore philosophically uninteresting. I endeavor to sketch the outline of the conception of disability as an apparatus, pointing out that this new conception is historicist and relativist. I argue, furthermore, that this reconceptualization has implications for the grave situation of both disabled philosophers vis-à-vis the profession and philosophy of disability vis-à-vis the discipline and its subject matter. Thus, my arguments in the chapter move between and within two spheres, namely, a reconstructive-conceptual sphere and a metaphilosophical sphere.

In this chapter, I continue to flesh out and fill in the sketch of this historically and culturally specific apparatus of power relations that effectively brings disability (and its naturalized antecedent, impairment) into being as a problem. To do so, I unfold some of Foucault's most important claims and draw upon the claims of authors that his work has influenced. For the most part, therefore, metaphilosophical arguments about the relatively homogeneous composition of the profession and the marginalized status of philosophy of disability within the discipline recede into the background of this chapter. These kinds of metaphilo-sophical arguments reappear in the next chapter.

To understand disability as an apparatus that effectively brings dis-ability into being as a problem and produces impairment as its natu-ralized antecedent, one must understand Foucault's idea of discourse. Discourse, for Foucault, is not synonymous with linguistic practices and communication, as many philosophers and disability theorists mistak-enly think. Discourses comprise what is said, how it is said, the social contexts in which statements are made, why they are made, whose com-munications are given authoritative status, and the historical condi-tions of possibility for topics to emerge. As Karen Barad (2008) points out, discourses are not linguistic or signifying systems, or grammars, or speech acts, but rather are the culturally relative and historically specific material conditions that enable and constrain disciplinary knowledge practices such as speaking, writing, thinking, arguing, and analyzing. On Foucault's account, Barad notes, "these 'conditions' are immanent and historical rather than transcendental or phenomenological. . . . They are actual historically situated social conditions" (137). Discursive practices define what will count as a meaningful statement in any given context, that is, discursive practices are the conditions that produce the subjects and objects of knowledge practices, rather than linguistic practices that "merely" describe them. In *The History of Sexuality*, volume 1, Foucault explained that discourses "are tactical elements or blocks operating in the field of force relations; there can exist different and even contradic-tory discourses within the same strategy; they can, on the contrary, circu-late without changing their form from one strategy to another, opposing strategy" (1978, 101–2).

Given these strategic possibilities of discourse, *Foucault and Feminist Philosophy of Disability* should, in one respect, be regarded as a response to this question: How has the combination of (1) philosophical discours-es that reinforce and expand the apparatus of disability and (2) discur-sive practices within professional philosophy that consistently obscure or erase critical analyses of disability enabled (3) resistance to the appara-tus of disability within the discipline and profession of philosophy them-selves? That is, how has this combination of discourses made possible the formation of a "reverse" or "counter" discourse on disability—namely, philosophy of disability—from whence this very book arises? As Foucault wrote, "Discourse can be both an instrument and an effect of power, but also a hindrance, a stumbling block, a point of resistance and a starting point for an opposing strategy. Discourse transmits and produces power;

it reinforces it, but also undermines and exposes it, renders it fragile and makes it possible to thwart it" (101). Where there is power, there are resistances; yet these resistances, too, contribute to the elaboration of the very objects to which they are directed as resistance. Thus, the historical conditions of possibility for resistance to the apparatus of disability are also historical conditions of possibility for its expansion and consolidation.

To advance the argument that medical, administrative, theoretical, and activist discourses (among others) on disability are the culturally relative and historically specific conditions of possibility for and effects of the knowledge-practices that the apparatus of disability produces, I assume a version of nominalism, as did Foucault in his genealogical work on the history of sexuality and the birth of the modern prison.

Barry Allen writes that Foucault's nominalist position represents "a formidable stand against physicalism, or the metaphysics of inherent structure. There is no such thing as nature, not if nature is supposed to be a source of determination or identity independent of historically contingent discourse" (2015, 99). The argument against inherent structure, or physicalism, is that the world does not come divided into categories that humans must discover; rather, humans themselves organize and classify, constructing "facts" and subsequently verifying statements about them. There are no natural kinds, nor is there a natural order. Allen points out that Foucault extended this critique of inherent, physical, or naturally given structure further than William Ockham, Peter Abelard, and other medieval nominalists from whom the philosophy of nominalism derives, insofar as Foucault claimed that identity or structure, like its representation, is an artifact of discourse, of a certain regime of true and false; it is a discursive practice (99). In his treatise on the archaeology of knowledge, Foucault put it thus: "What, in short, we wish to do is to dispense with 'things' . . . to substitute for the enigmatic treasure of 'things' anterior to discourse the regular formation of objects that emerge only in discourse . . . relating them to the body of rules that enables them to form as objects of a discourse and thus constitutes the conditions of their historical appearance" (1972, 47–48). Classical nominalists say that structure is not inherent, but rather comes from language, that is, from names and conventions of representation. To this linguistic structure, Allen (2015, 99) notes, Foucault contributed the idea of social power relations whose economy is as indispensable to knowledge and truth as the names that relations of power cause to combine and circulate.

The nominalist conception of impairment and disability that I wish to advance neither presupposes that the discursive objects of the apparatus of disability are universals nor substantivizes these objects, tendencies to which other conceptualizations of impairment and disability are prone. On my nominalist approach to the objects of the apparatus of disability, the identification of similarities and differences between these objects is a convention of discourse rather than recognition of natural essences, kinds, or identities. Many (if not most) philosophers think that nominalism is a misguided stance. These thinkers hold that objects such as photons, stars, and horses with which the natural sciences concern themselves existed as photons, stars, and horses long before any human being encountered them and presumed to categorize or classify them. Although compelling arguments have been made according to which not even the objects of the natural sciences (say, photons, stars, and Shetland ponies) have identities until someone names them, I want to set aside questions with respect to the ontology of these objects. In this book, the only ontological commitments that concern me pertain to dimensions of human history and practice. As I indicate in the previous chapter, however, I believe that my argument can nevertheless be used to foster and enlarge critical discussions not explicitly articulated herein, including discussions about the relations between human animals and nonhuman animals and humans and the environment.[1]

Biopower and Its Objects

The Industrial Revolution that occurred in Western Europe from about the mid-seventeenth century to the mid-eighteenth century led to dramatic increases in the number of people who migrated to Western European urban centers or were forcibly imported to them through enslavement, with corresponding increases in the material wealth that these people could potentially produce. This influx into and condensation of the Western European metropolis placed unprecedented demands upon monarchs and new republics, affording them new controls. For the first time in the history of Western Europe, governments became more than the collectors of tithes and taxes owed to the sovereign. Now governments became charged with the frugal management of their "populations," a notion that coalesced during this period of societal expansion and amalgamation. "Population," Foucault wrote, "is undoubtedly an idea and a reality that is absolutely modern in relation to the functioning of political power, but also in relation to knowledge and political theory, prior to the eighteenth century" (2007, 11). As Foucault (1978, 25) noted in the first volume of *The History of Sexuality*, the emergence of the population as an economic and political problem was one of the greatest innovations of the techniques of power in the eighteenth century: population as wealth, population as labor capacity, the balance between the growth of a population and the resources it commanded, and so on. The new problems that the phenomena characteristic of a group of living beings, when circumscribed as a population, posed to governmental practice—problems such as sanitation, race relations, overcrowding, poverty and hunger, infant mortality—entailed the emergence of new strategies and techniques of networks of force relations. Foucault used the term *biopower* to refer to the convergence of these immanent strategies and techniques for population management from the eighteenth century onward.[2] One technique used to manage populations involved the introduction of and increasing reliance on mechanisms of security. Notably, it was in this historical context that the idea of "Western culture" first emerged into discourse (Appiah 2016).

From 1971 until his death in 1984, Foucault held the Chair in the History of Systems of Thought at the Collège de France, where, during lectures and seminars held weekly between January and June, he reported on original research in which he was engaged. The published translations of his lecture courses provide English-language readers of Foucault with a rich resource and unprecedented guide to his thinking on a range of topics. For example, Foucault (2003g) began the 1975–76 course (subsequently published in English as *Society Must Be Defended*) with what Paul Rabinow has described as "a despondent, almost despairing apology for what he characterized as his thinking's directionless drift" (1997, xv). As Rabinow explains it, Foucault had intended in these lectures to bring his work of recent years to completion that year, but was at a loss on how to do so. In that first lecture of the course, Foucault lamented,

> I realize that there were more and more drawbacks, for both you and me. Lines of research that were very closely interrelated but that never added to a coherent body of work, that had no continuity. Fragments of research, none of which was completed, and none of which was followed through; bits and pieces of research, and at the same time it was getting repetitive, always falling into the same rut, the same themes, the same concepts. . . . We are making no progress, and it's all leading nowhere. It's all repetitive, and doesn't add up. Basically,

we keep saying the same thing, and there again, perhaps we're not saying anything at all. It's all getting into something of an inextricable tangle, and it's getting us nowhere, as they say. (2003g, 3–4)

Rabinow, in his introduction to the first volume of a three-volume edition of Foucault's writings, suggests that Foucault's confession in that lecture seems harsh, given that he published *Discipline and Punish* in 1975 and *The History of Sexuality*, volume 1, in 1976. In fact, by the end of the 1975–76 lecture course, Foucault had introduced a conception of power that he claimed has been overlooked in political philosophy. This form of power, which crystallizes in the final chapter of the first volume of *The History of Sexuality*, is what he called "biopower." Attention to this form of power, this biopower, has shaped my thinking about disability and, thus, motivates my argument in what follows.

From Aristotle to John Locke and Jean-Jacques Rousseau and on to John Rawls, Euro-American, Western political philosophy has concerned itself with questions about legitimation and sovereignty. What are the foundations of legitimate rule? What is the nature of sovereignty? What is the most just form of government? On what grounds can rights be based? Foucault did not reject outright the significance of these questions for political thinking; however, he did refuse the idea of primal, or natural, universal rights that is presupposed by the "juridico-discursive" conceptions of political power from which these questions arise. In the terms of juridical conceptions, the individual possesses power (as one would possess a commodity) in the form of inherent, inalienable rights, the transfer or surrender of which (through a juridical act or a contract) constitutes a sovereign.

In his lecture of January 7, 1976, Foucault argued to the contrary that power is not something that is exchanged, given, or taken back, but rather is exercised and exists only in action. In addition, Foucault disputed the assumption of juridical conceptions according to which power is fundamentally repressive. Though consensus and violence are the instruments or results of power, he remarked, they do not amount to its essential nature (2003g, 13). As he put it, "The exercise of power can produce as much acceptance as may be wished for: it can pile up the dead and shelter itself behind whatever threats it can imagine. In itself the exercise of power is not violence; nor is it a consent, which, implicitly, is renewable" (1982, 220). For Foucault, the question that political philosophy should ask about power is this: How, that is, by what means, is it exercised? (217). Indeed, one of the most original features of Foucault's analysis is the idea that power is most effectively exercised through productive constraints. Furthermore, he argued that the continued preoccupation with juridical conceptions of power in modern political philosophy has obscured the productive capacity and subtle machinations of a form of power that began to coalesce at the end of the eighteenth century, namely, biopower. In the January 11 lecture of his 1977–78 course at the Collège de France (subsequently published in English as *Security, Territory, Population: Lectures at the Collège de France, 1977–1978*), Foucault described biopower as "the set of mechanisms through which the basic biological features of the human species became the object of a political strategy, of a general strategy of power, or, in other words, how, starting from the eighteenth century, modern [W]estern societies took on board the fundamental biological fact that human beings are a species" (2007, 1). The apparatus of disability has been integral, indeed vital, to the strategies of this relatively recent form of power.

A form of power that targets the biological features of the human being must take account of its reproductive potential, that is, its sex, including sexual practices, partners, potency, and proclivities. Sex has in fact been central to the economic and political problem of population that emerged with biopower and to which biopolitical strategies have responded; that is, with the emergence of biopower came the problematization of sex. Beginning in the eighteenth century, it became increasingly necessary to analyze phenomena such as age at marriage, race of partners, legitimacy of births, precocity and frequency of sexual relations, and impact of contraceptive devices. In this historical moment, a society affirmed, for the first time, and in a persistent manner, that its future existence and fortune were tied to how each individual made use of their sex, in addition to the ties between the future and fortune of the society and the number of its citizens, its rules of marriage, and so on. The sexual conduct of populations became an object of analysis and a target of intervention. Indeed, Foucault pointed out that since the end of the eighteenth century, there has been an explosion in the West of all manner of discourse about and analysis of sex rather than repression of talk about it, as is usually claimed. "Through the political economy of population," Foucault wrote, "there was formed a whole grid of observations regarding sex." It became imperative, he explained, for the state to know what was happening with its citizens' sex, how they put it to use, and that they could control the use to which it was put. "Between the state and the individual," Foucault pointed out, "sex became an issue, and a public issue no less; a whole web of discourses, special knowledges, analyses, and injunctions settled upon it" (1978, 26).

From the eighteenth century forward, biopower, by taking as its object "life itself," has worked toward increasingly efficient and economical management of the problems that variables of sex (and other phenomena) pose for the political economy of populations and individuals. Biopower, Foucault wrote, is "what brought life and its mechanisms into the realm of explicit calculations and made knowledge-power an agent of transformation of human life" (1978, 143). Life—its enhancement, amplification, quality, duration, continuance, and renewal—has become an urgent economic and political concern that government policy and practice addresses to wrest management and control of it. Biopower's management of life has entailed the inauguration of a novel set of strategic measurements, including the ratio of births to deaths, the rate of fertility in the population, and the rate of reproduction, as well as a body of statistical knowledge and administrative cataloging of states of health and perceived threats to it.

Foucault explained that as these phenomena began to be taken account of, a new type of medicine quickly developed whose main function was public hygiene and whose institutions centralized its power, standardized its knowledge, and coordinated the care distributed under its auspices. There were campaigns to educate and medicalize this new composite called a "population," which introduced the notion of a "health risk" and from which, in turn, population-based interventions such as immunization and urban sewage systems were inserted into human social existence. Charitable institutions and economically rational mechanisms—such as insurance, individual and collective savings, and safety measures—were established to deal with accidents, illnesses, and various anomalies. Thus, methods of surveillance and classification of the problem of disability—that is, its problematization—were instrumental in the coalescence of this form of power centered on life, this biopower. Insofar as the phenomena with which biopower is concerned become salient only on a mass level, constants that pertain to the collective were also established. Censuses and other mechanisms that intervene at the level of the collective or group were created to provide forecasts, statistical estimates, and overall measures. These regulatory concerns brought into being other mechanisms in the form of guidelines and recommendations that prescribe norms, adjust differentials to an equilibrium, maintain an average, and compensate for variations within the "general population," a group of living beings whose constitution *as* a population was due to this form of power and the surveillance of sex that it required. Furthermore, security mechanisms emerged that partition and segregate random elements of populations—blind people, lepers, witches, perverts, and so on—from the collective at large as means to maximize the conditions conducive to life (Foucault 2003g, 238–63).

The consolidation of the modern concept of "normal" legitimized and occurred in tandem with the new statistical knowledge and other techniques of population management that stemmed from biopower. As François Ewald (1991, 138) explains, the norm enabled biopower, "which aims to produce, develop, and order social strength," to steadily do the work that juridical modes of governance, characterized by forcible seizure, abduction, or repression, had done in the past. The norm accomplished this expansion by enabling discipline to develop from a simple set of constraints into a mechanism and by transforming the negative restraints of the juridical into the more positive controls of normalization (141). From the eighteenth century on, the function of technologies of normalization has been to isolate so-called anomalies in the population, which can be normalized through the therapeutic and corrective strategies of other, associated technologies. Technologies of normalization are not merely innocuous or even benevolent responses to these anomalies in the social body. On the contrary, technologies of normalization are instrumental to the systematic creation, identification, classification, and control of such anomalies; that is, they systematically contribute to the constitution of the perception of anomalies (such as impairment) and operate as mechanisms through which some subjects can be divided from others. Foucault introduced the term *dividing practices* to refer to modes of manipulation that combine a scientific discourse with practices of segregation and social exclusion to categorize, classify, distribute, and manipulate subjects who are initially drawn from a rather undifferentiated mass of people.[3] Through these practices, subjects become objectivized as (for instance) mad or sane, sick or healthy, criminal or law abiding. Through these practices of division, classification, and ordering, furthermore, subjects become tied to an identity and come to understand themselves scientifically (Foucault 1982, 208).

In the final chapter of *The History of Sexuality*, volume 1, provocatively titled "The Right of Death and Power over Life," Foucault explained the historical shift away from the juridical exercise of power to regulatory control and the coercion of normalization:

[A] consequence of this development of bio-power was the growing importance assumed by the action of the norm, at the expense of the juridical system of the law. Law cannot help but be armed, and its arm, *par excellence*, is death; to those who transgress it, it replies, at least as a last resort, with the absolute menace. The law always refers to the sword. But a power whose task is to take charge of life needs continuous regulatory and corrective mechanisms. It is no longer a matter of bringing death into play in the field of sovereignty, but of distributing the living in the domain of value and utility. Such a power has to qualify, measure, appraise, and hierarchize, rather than display itself in its murderous splendor; it does not have to draw the line that separate the enemies of the sovereign from his obedient subjects; it effects distributions around the norm. I do not mean to say that the law fades into the background or that the institutions of justice tend to disappear, but rather that the law operates more and more as a norm, and that the juridical institution is increasingly incorporated into a continuum of apparatuses (medical, administrative, and so on) whose functions are for the most part regulatory. A normalizing society is the historical outcome of a technology of power centered on life. (1978, 144; emphasis in Foucault)

Foucault regarded normalization as a central—if not the central—mechanism of biopower's management of life, the life of both the individual and the species. Biopower can thus be defined as a historically specific combination of normalization and population management conducted through vast networks of production and social control. Beginning in the eighteenth century, Foucault noted, the power of the normal has combined with other powers such as the law and tradition, imposing new limits upon them. The normal, he explained, was established as a principle of coercion through the introduction of standardized education; the organization of national medical professions and hospital systems that could circulate general norms of health; and the standardization of industrial processes and products and manufacturing techniques. Normalization thus became one of the great instruments of power at the close of the classical age, that is, the power that the norm harnessed has been shaped through the disciplines that began to emerge at this historical moment (Foucault 1977a, 184). For from the end of the eighteenth century, the indicators of social status, privilege, and group affiliation have been increasingly supplemented, if not replaced, by a range of degrees of normality that simultaneously indicate membership in a homogeneous social body (a "population") and serve to distinguish subjects from each other, to classify them, and to rank them in a host of hierarchies.

In *Discipline and Punish: The Birth of the Prison*, Foucault (1977a) noted that normalization initially emerged in eighteenth-century military schools, orphanages, and boarding schools as an effective form of punishment, "a perpetual penalty," a persistent disciplining. In Foucault's terms, discipline is neither an institution nor an apparatus, but rather a type of power and a modality for its exercise, generated by a whole set of instruments, techniques, procedures, levels of application, and targets. Discipline is an "anatomy of power," a technology of power that may be assumed by (1) particular institutions—such as schools or hospitals—in order to achieve a certain end; or (2) authorities that use it as a means to reinforce and reorganize their established means of power; or (3) apparatuses that use it as their mode of functioning; or (4) state apparatuses whose primary function is to assure that discipline reigns over society in general, such as the police (215–16). As a technology that has facilitated the expansion of biopower, disciplinary normalization aims to make the body more efficient and calculated in its acts, movements, gestures, and expression; to produce a body that is "docile," that is, a body that can be subjected, used, transformed, and improved. Modern discipline can be summed up thus: it enables subjects to act in order to constrain them.

Disciplinary "punishment"—that is, normalization—has brought into play five distinct normalizing operations. First, individual actions are referred to a totality that is simultaneously a field of comparison, a space of differentiation, and a rule to be followed. Second, individuals are in turn differentiated from each other in relation to this rule that functions as a minimal threshold, as an average, or as an optimal outcome toward which individuals must move. Third, the natures, grades and levels, and abilities of individuals are hierarchized and quantified. Fourth, these quantifying and hierarchizing measures introduce the constraint of a conformity that must be achieved. Fifth, the limit of difference, the far side of "the abnormal" that will define difference per se in relation to all other specific differences, is codified and enforced by penalty (correction, segregation, and so on). The five elemental modes of normalization are thus comparison, differentiation, hierarchy, homogeneity, and exclusion. The punitive impulse that regulates normalization compares, differentiates, hierarchizes, and excludes individuals in order to homogenize a population that, by virtue of its homogeneity, can be more effectively utilized and modified. In short, the disciplinary power of the norm relies upon coercion rather than open repression or violence. Hence, Foucault pointed out, the centrality of normalization to a form of power (biopower) that aims to exert a more positive influence on life, undertaking to administer it, to multiply it, and to impose on it a system of regulations and precise inspection (1977a, 182–84; see also Knobe 2017).

In his January 25, 1978, lecture at the Collège de France, Foucault described disciplinary power in this way:

> Discipline, of course, analyses and breaks down; it breaks down individuals, place, time, movements, actions, and operations. It breaks them down into components such that they can be seen, on the one hand, and modified, on the other. It is this famous interdisciplinary analytical-practical grid that tries to establish the minimal elements of perception and the elements sufficient for modification. Second, discipline classifies the components thus identified according to definite objectives. What are the best actions for achieving a particular result: What is the best movement for loading one's rifle, what is the best position to take? What workers are best suited for a particular task? What children are capable of obtaining a particular result? Third, discipline establishes optimal sequences or co-ordinations: How can actions be linked together? How can soldiers be deployed for a maneuver? How can schoolchildren be distributed hierarchically within classifications? Fourth, discipline fixes the processes of progressive training (*dressage*) and permanent control, and finally, on the basis of this, it establishes the division between those considered unsuitable or incapable and the others. That is to say, on this basis it divides the normal from the abnormal. (2007, 56–57)

Foucault, in his writing on punishment and his subsequent writing on the history of sexuality, described how knowledges produced about the "normal" case become vehicles for the exercise of disciplinary force relations that target certain people. The etymology of the term *normal* offers clues to the relation between this form of power and the notion of normalcy. Hacking (1990) notes that the first meaning of *normal* that current English dictionaries provide is something like "usual, regular, common, typical." This usage, according to the *Oxford English Dictionary*, became current after 1840, with the first citation of "normal, or typical" appearing in 1828. Hacking remarks that the modern sense of the word *normal* was not, however, furnished by education or cloistered study but rather by the study of life (1990, 161–62). In an illuminating discussion, Hacking explains that the word *normal* became indispensable because it provided a way to be objective about human beings, especially given the inseparability of the notion of normal from its opposite, namely, the pathological. The word *normal,* he writes, "uses a power as old as Aristotle to bridge the fact/value distinction, whispering in your ear that what is normal is also all right" (160). The word *normal* bears the stamp of the nineteenth century just as the concept of human nature is the hallmark of the Enlightenment, says Hacking. Whereas in the past we sought to discover what human nature is, we now concern ourselves with investigations that will tell us what is normal (161). He points out that although the normal stands "indifferently for what is typical, the unenthusiastic objective average, it also stands for what has been, good health, and what shall be, our chosen destiny." "That," he contends, "is why the benign and sterile-sounding word 'normal' has become one of the most powerful ideological tools of the twentieth century" (169). It is especially noteworthy for my argument that, as Hacking explains, the modern usage of the word *normal* evolved in a medical context (165).

Normalization and Implantation

In the late 1700s, there was a significant reconfiguration of the concept of the pathological and its relation to the normal. Disease came to be regarded as an attribute of individual organs rather than as a characteristic of the entire body. Pathology, likewise, was reconfigured, becoming the study of unhealthy organs rather than the study of sick or diseased bodies. Unhealthy organs could be investigated, in part, by the chemistry of fluids, such as urine or mucus, that actual living beings secreted. The concept of the normal came into being as the inverse of this concept of pathology: a given state of affairs or process of the body was normal if it was not associated with a pathological organ. In other words, the normal was secondary to, derivative of, and defined by the pathological. F. J. V. Broussais's principle—that life is a matter of excitation of tissue and disease is "irritation" of the tissue of a given organ—inverted this relation of entailment between the pathological and the normal (Hacking 1990, 82). The pathological became defined as deviation from the normal and all variation became characterized as variation from the normal state. Pathology was no longer conceived as different in kind from the normal, but rather as continuous with it (164). This new understanding of the normal and the pathological that emerged in the late 1700s is one, but only one, component of what I refer to as "the diagnostic style of reasoning," a style of reasoning that has enabled the consolidation and expansion of biopower. Given the importance of statistical knowledge to the operations of biopower, it is not surprising that Broussais—to whom Auguste Comte, for one, attributes our modern understanding of the normal—was connected to the first use of statistical data to evaluate medical treatment (Hacking 1990, 81).

In his Collège de France lecture of January 25, 1978, Foucault (2007) addressed the correlation between the population and a certain technique of power—namely, security—that takes the population as its subject and its object, as well as the mechanisms that operate through this technique of power. To do so, he distinguished between mechanisms of normalization that characterize disciplinary regimes and mechanisms of normalization that characterize regimes of security. Nevertheless, he emphasized that the transition to a regime of security should not be conceived in terms of replacement, whereby sovereign power was replaced by disciplinary power, which in turn was replaced by security. On the contrary, historically, all three forms of power have operated simultaneously. The transition from one form of regime to another has been a matter of emphasis and reorganization with respect to the knowledge and power produced and the mechanisms characteristically deployed rather than the disappearance of an earlier, dominant, form of power and its characteristic mechanisms. As Foucault explained,

> There is not a succession of law, then discipline, then security, but [rather] security is a way of making the old armatures of law and discipline function in addition to the specific mechanisms of security. So, in Western societies, in the domain of law, in the domain of medicine, and in other domains also . . . you can see a somewhat similar evolution and more or less the same type of transformations. What is involved is the emergence of technologies of security within mechanisms that are either specifically mechanisms of social control, as in the case of the penal system, or mechanisms with the function of modifying something in the biological destiny of the species. Can we say then—and this is what is at stake in what I want to analyze—that the general economy of power in our societies is becoming a domain of security? (10)

Whereas discipline functions by circumscribing and isolating a space in which it will operate, the apparatuses of security are centrifugal, constantly expanding and integrating new elements: production, psychology, behavior, how actions are done by producers, buyers, consumers, and the world market, and so on. In other words, whereas discipline encloses a space, security allows the steady development of constantly widening circuits (44–45). Discipline posits a norm; training proceeds with reference to this norm in order to distinguish the normal from the abnormal. By contrast, security plots both the normal and the abnormal, as well as different curves of normativity. The operation of normalization characteristic of apparatuses of security involves the interplay between these different distributions of the normal and the abnormal to incrementally bring the least favorable in line with the more favorable. With respect to force relations whose aim is security, the normal is initially posited and the norm is derived from it. This, Foucault wrote, is normalization in the strict sense (57). For discipline, Foucault pointed out, the norm is fundamental and the normal is derived from it. Thus, he suggested that we refer to forms of coercion characteristic of disciplinary apparatuses as normation, rather than normalization. In chapter 5, I indicate how force relations whose aim of normalization operates incrementally to ensure security rely on the production of notions such as risk, probability, and chance in ways that were not possible before the emergence of this type of force relations.

The category of normal is generally assumed to identify an objective, static, universal, and ahistorical internal disposition or character or state of human beings. As I have indicated, Foucault endeavored to show, however, that the notion of the normal is a historical artifact that emerged through, and facilitates the operations of, a historically specific regime of power—namely, biopower. Following Foucault, Hacking (1990) and other philosophers and theorists have worked to demonstrate how the coercive and contingent character of the normal operates, in specific contexts, circulating in incremental and other ways (for example, McWhorter 1999). These discussions about the historical and cultural contingency of the concept of the normal and its embeddedness in apparatuses of power are vital to my argument; for, once we recognize that the category of the normal is historically and culturally specific, rather than ahistorical and universal, it becomes easier to show that the idea of disability (construed as a disadvantageous human characteristic, property, and so on)—and its antecedent, impairment—too is a historically and culturally specific invention of force relations. If the category of the normal is a historical artifact, then any phenomenon whose identity—including objects and practices that make up the identity—is established and distinguished on the basis of its departure from and relation to that category must also be a historical artifact. In chapter 5, I illustrate how a certain derivation from the category of the normal has gained considerable undeserved influence in the field of mainstream bioethics and has been put in the service of neoliberal eugenics.

Due to its inescapable historical association with pathologization and coercive correction, the idea of normalization has a checkered past in disability theory and research. In the last decades of the twentieth century, some disability theorists and researchers promoted the idea of normalization as emancipatory, both individually and socially, and as a sign of both personal and social progress. Most notably, Wolf Wolfensberger gave birth to a social movement, grounded in the "normalization principle," that denounced the forced institutionalization of "cognitively impaired people." The Normalization Movement (as it was called) aimed to integrate these people into the wider community by enhancing their self-perceptions and potential to advocate for themselves and transforming their appearance to make them more socially accepted (Yates 2015, 66). Michael Oliver explains the principle upon which the Normalization Movement relied in this way: "Normalization theory offers disabled people the opportunity to be given valued social roles in an unequal society which values some roles more than others" (qtd. in Drinkwater 2015, 233). The normalization principle was eventually renamed "social role valorization" to stress the normativity of normalization. Nevertheless, as Chris Drinkwater (2015, 233) has noted, although normalization theory was renamed social role valorization, the power-knowledge regime that is productive of a "normal life" (by any name) remained unexamined. The motivational assumption that underlies these normalizing strategies is that certain people find it difficult to learn how to behave "appropriately," that is, normally. As Drinkwater points out, however, a more tacit assumption that underlies social role valorization is that these people *ought* to learn normal (valued) behaviors as means to acquire normal—that is, "valued"—lifestyles.

Lindsay Williams and Melanie Nind (1999) have drawn attention to the ways that the guiding principle behind the Normalization Movement—namely, that "people with cognitive difficulties" should adhere to dominant cultural values—has regulated these people's sexual liberty, rewarding gender and sexual conformity. With the upsurge of the Normalization Movement in the 1970s, a growing literature on sex education for "people with learning difficulties"[4] was generated. The Normalization Movement, which was composed primarily of people "with cognitive impairments" and their allies, had emerged and coalesced around efforts to deinstitutionalize such people and integrate them into communities. Yet, leaders of the Normalization Movement believed that community living posed certain challenges with respect to sexual activity for people who, due to years of institutionalization, were assumed to be inexperienced sexually. Hence, these representatives of the Normalization Movement argued that this group of people ought to be taught appropriate sexual behavior and roles.

The production of these 1970s sex-education texts constituted an important step in self-advocacy for disabled people "with cognitive impairments," insofar as these texts articulated both how this sector of society has historically been subjugated with respect to sexual self-determination and rights[5] and the role that forced sterilization and gender segregation have played in this subjugation. Nevertheless, as Williams and Nind point out, the sex-education literature of the Normalization Movement reinforced traditional values and norms with respect to gender and sexuality. As they explain it, "Talk of access to ordinary lifestyles and valued status referred after all, not just to housing and work, but to sex and marriage" (William and Nind 1999, 662). This sex-education literature assumed that love, sex, and fulfillment would—and should—be combined. Discussion of same-gender love and sexual practices was completely omitted from these sex-education texts, even well into the 1990s. Indeed, some authors of the Normalization Movement's sex-education texts from this period represented same-gender relationships and sexual practices as "deviant and inappropriate" rather than as relationships and practices that involve valued behaviors and roles. Other authors of this literature were keen to distinguish between "true homosexuals" and "people with cognitive impairments" who, according to these authors, had taken recourse in same-gender sexual activity because they lacked opportunities for (normal) heterosexual sex (663). The sex-education literature of the Normalization Movement has, in other words, been instrumental in the reproduction of the apparatuses of gender and heterosexism, in addition to the ways that the literature has expanded the apparatus of disability. In short, the Normalization Movement is an exemplary product of modern power insofar as it was both enabling and constraining.

Preoccupation with and scrutiny of the sexuality of "deviants" is not a twentieth-century phenomenon. The establishment—at the end of the eighteenth century—of the norm as the central technology to facilitate the expansion of discipline succeeded, in large part, due to the enormous attention paid to the regulation and surveillance of sex for the identification of abnormalities in the proper operation of the "sexual instinct"—that is, identification of perversions. In chapter 4, I provide an example of how this intense interest and investment in the sexuality of perverse and deviant subjects contributed to the constitution of impairment in the context of nineteenth-century rural France and even in the context of twentieth-century feminist philosophy. Writing in the generation before Sigmund Freud, the Viennese psychiatrist Richard von Krafft-Ebing remarked that "with opportunity for the natural satisfaction of the sexual instinct, every expression of it that does not correspond with the purpose of nature—i.e. propagation—must be regarded as perverse" (1965, 86, in Allen 2015, 94). As Foucault read this history, the more that psychiatrists and scientists looked for sexual deviants, the more sexual deviants they were apt to find. Nevertheless, sexual perversions are not human conditions discovered by medicine, but rather are artifacts of expert discourses, implanted in the subjects who are claimed to embody them.

The motivation for the implantation thesis that Foucault advanced with respect to perversions in the first volume of *The History of Sexuality* derives from his innovative conception of power as primarily productive, rather than merely repressive. The implantation thesis can also be used to support the claim that impairments, like perversions, are natural*ized*, rather than natural; invented, rather than discovered; implanted, rather than inherent. Allen (2015) has suggested this sort of argument for the implantation of impairment, pointing out that there can be no notion of impairment without reference to a statistically "normal case," just as there can be no criminal except by reference to the law. As Allen explains it, "A discourse about biomedical norms, scientific though it may be, is no more true to nature, or physically true, than a discourse about criminals" (94). Any norm is an artifact of the discipline that measures it: it has no physical being or reality apart from that practice.

The Diagnostic Style and the Power of History

A certain style of reasoning that emerged through and propelled the vast network of biopower has facilitated the implantation of impairment and the production and distribution of technologies and disciplines that comprise, sustain, and reproduce the apparatus of disability. I call this style "the diagnostic style of reasoning." As is characteristic of a distinct style of reasoning, the diagnostic style has effectively brought into being new types of objects, individuated with the style, which had not previously been noticeable among the things that exist (see Hacking 1992b, 10–11). Hacking claims that the idea of styles of reasoning is required for an understanding of what gets called objectivity, not because styles are objective, but rather because what is obtained by conducting a certain sort of investigation are truths of a certain sort, answering to certain standards. As Hacking explains it, each style of reasoning is the historically and culturally specific canon of objectivity about the phenomena—new types of objects, new types of evidence, new ways of being a candidate for truth and falsehood, new types of laws, and new types of possibilities—which the style has itself brought into being as these types of things. He argues that "there are neither sentences that are candidates for truth, nor independently identified objects to be correct about, prior to the development of a style of reasoning" (10). Sentences of the relevant kinds are candidates for truth or falsehood only when a style of reasoning makes them so. "The truth of a sentence (of a kind introduced by a style of reasoning)," Hacking writes, "is what we find out by reasoning using that style. Styles become standards of objectivity because they get at the truth. But a sentence of that kind is a candidate for truth or falsehood only in the context of the style." Hacking's claim is that styles are in a certain sense "self-authenticating" (13).

Hacking acknowledges that there is an apparent circularity in the self-authentication of styles of reasoning. However, he regards this apparent circularity as a virtue of the idea of a style of reasoning: it goes some distance to explain why styles of reasoning are stable and enduring. Each style of reasoning, he remarks, has its own characteristic techniques of self-stabilization and persists, in its own unique and peculiar way, because it has harnessed these self-stabilizing techniques. He states, furthermore, that if the self-authenticating character of styles of reasoning were understood, we would have gone some way toward grasping the "quasi-stability" of science (14–16). Among the styles that Hacking and other scholars have thus far identified are the laboratory style, the statistical style, and the psychiatric style. To this list can now be added the diagnostic style of reasoning that, as I indicate in the chapters that follow, has brought into being new types of laws, possibilities, candidates for truth and falsehood, and objects, among which impairment is one token of a new type of the latter.[6]

Hacking's account of styles of reasoning is the compelling response to disdain for historical approaches in analytic philosophy that a historicist and relativist feminist philosophy of disability that draws upon Foucault requires. Foucault described the requirements and assumptions of a historicist approach to inquiry in this way, underscoring the importance to such an approach of contingency and of questioning what has been taken for granted as self-evident:

> The recourse to history . . . takes on its import to the extent that history has for its function to show that that which exists didn't always exist, that is to say, that it is always at the confluence of encounters, accidents, through the course of a fragile, precarious history that things are formed that give us the impression of being the most obvious. What reason experiences as its necessity or rather what different forms of rationality present as their necessary condition one can perfectly well do the history of, and recover the networks of contingencies from which it has emerged; which does not mean however that these forms of rationality were irrational; it means that they rest on a base of human practice and of human history and since these things have been made, they can, provided that one knows how they were made, be unmade. (1994, 448–49, in Davidson 2001, 189)

Foucault used genealogy to critically inquire into the history of necessity on a given topic and the historical emergence of the necessary conditions of a certain state of affairs. In his work on the history of the modern prison and the history of sexuality, Foucault took up and adapted the genealogical method that Nietzsche famously introduced in work on the descent of Western morals, variously referring to his own incarnations of genealogy as "histories of the present" and "historical ontologies of ourselves." Foucault's genealogies are concerned with questions about the conditions of possibility for who we are now, that is, questions about *how* our current ways of thinking and acting came into being. They are not concerned with questions about *why* we think and act as we do. This distinctive orientation is crucial, for the latter type of question—that is, "why" questions—usually seeks answers about why we think and act as we do by appealing to a discourse that takes subjectivity as a given, that is, assumes subjectivity from the outset. Phenomenology and psychoanalysis were, for Foucault, exemplars of such "transcendental," ahistorical discourse. By contrast, the genealogist asks (as did Foucault): Of what is given to us as universal, necessary, and obligatory, how much is occupied by the singular, the contingent, the product of arbitrary constraints? A critical ontology of ourselves, Foucault (1997b) explained, must not be considered as a theory, doctrine, or permanent body of knowledge but rather as a "limit-attitude," that is, an ethos, a philosophical life in which the critique of what we are is at the same time the historical analysis of the limits imposed on us. Indeed, the questions with which genealogy concerns itself—that is, "how" questions—aim to identify how historically contingent practices, encounters, events, and accidents have enabled the emergence of current modes of thinking and acting and the limits that they impose (see Foucault 1982, 216–19). As Ladelle McWhorter (2010) explains it, genealogies help us "to make sense of how we are now, in this historical moment, by looking at how we got here and how this, here, now, is historically possible."

Subjectivities—that is, specific types of identity and active and affective possibility—are, in other words, secondary phenomena whose historical emergence and descent genealogy is especially designed to trace. Subjectivities are productions of force relations that can be analyzed. A genealogical analysis of subjectivities is intended to reveal the networks of power relations in which subjects find themselves, to reveal the formations and transformations of these force relations, their strengths, and their vulnerabilities. Hence, genealogies of disabled subjectivity and of the experience of disability as a phenomenon are subversive. Genealogy, Foucault wrote, is "the union of erudite knowledge and local memories which allows us to establish a historical knowledge of struggles and to make use of this knowledge tactically today" (1980b, 83). Genealogies, he pointed out, are not positivistic returns to a form of science that more accurately represents phenomena. Genealogies are, rather, "antisciences." What characterizes genealogies is not that they reject knowledge or appeal to, or even celebrate, some immediate experience that knowledge has yet to capture. "That," Foucault stressed, "is not what they are about." Rather, genealogies, he explained, "are about the insurrection of knowledges . . . An insurrection against the centralizing power effects that are bound up with the institutionalization and workings of any scientific discourse organized in a society such as ours." Genealogy is an "attempt to desubjugate historical knowledges . . . to enable them to oppose and struggle against the coercion of a unitary, formal, and scientific theoretical discourse" (Foucault 2003g, 9). Thus, genealogies require the excavation and articulation of subjugated knowledges, knowledges that "have been disqualified as inadequate to their task or insufficiently elaborated: naïve knowledges, located low down on the hierarchy, beneath the required level of cognition or scientificity" (Foucault 1980b, 82). Foucault maintained that criticism performs its work by uncovering and restoring these subjugated, unqualified, and even directly disqualified knowledges, such as the knowledge of the psychiatrized individual, of the delinquent, and of the nurse. Historical ontologies (genealogies) exhume these phenomena, that is, exhume these subjugated knowledges, exhume these obsolete and even archaic discourses, events, and institutional practices, in order that the historically contingent character of the self-understandings and self-perceptions that we hold in the present can be discerned.

Racism against the Abnormal

The use to which McWhorter (2009) puts Foucault's genealogical technique in her work on racism and sexual oppression demonstrates both the subversive potential that the technique of genealogy offers feminist philosophy of disability and the ways that the technique can add theoretical complexity and political sophistication to current understandings of how disability is imbricated in other apparatuses (*dispositifs*) of power. Insofar as McWhorter adopts Foucault's thesis that modern racism is "racism against the abnormal" (Foucault 2003g; see also Tremain 2012, 2013a)—as he referred to this *dispositif* (apparatus)—racism, in McWhorter's analysis, is much more comprehensive than most other contemporary academic or popular conceptions assume it to be. For Foucault, the networks of power that constitute what in the present day is aptly called racism aim to eliminate, contain, manage, or exploit abnormality in ways that threaten, harm, and oppress the people who come to be classified as abnormal. Thus, McWhorter's genealogy of modern racism renders evident the artifactual and interactive character of current racist, sexist, ableist, antisemitic, classist, and homophobic practices by unearthing their conjoined descent through the practices that precipitated them and the power relations through which they have been mutually constitutive and reinforcing. As an example of the co-constitutive character of race and mental illness, consider these remarks that physician Pearce Bailey makes in a paper delivered to the American Neurological Association in 1921:

> [It] appears that [blacks and Native Americans] could not under any present circumstances attain the average intelligence of the cultured races . . . not because there is any detailed information as to the potentiality of the primitive mind, but because mental deficiency is so profusely distributed among [them] that their average intelligence

must be inferior to that of average European intelligence. . . . [The] existence of a mental disease implies a developed intelligence, a kind of intelligence that would possess imagination, ideas, a certain quickness in mental processes. (1922, 188–89, in Gilman and Thomas, 2016, 64–65; parenthetical remarks in Gilman and Thomas)

For Bailey, who cites statistics about mental diseases in various races, black people and members of other "inferior races" were less susceptible to madness than the European race precisely because they were racially inferior: in the nineteen U.S. states with higher deficiency rates than the national U.S. average, the insanity rate was below the national average among African Americans, Indigenous peoples, Italian Americans, and Mexican Americans. As Sander L. Gilman and James M. Thomas (2016, 64–65) point out, such associations between race and mental disease were often used as a rationale for alleging that certain races had an inherent aptitude for certain occupations (such as sharecropping) and as support for deterministic ideas about sexuality, elaborating the categories of race and mental illness and disease simultaneously and together (also see Stuckey 2017).

McWhorter follows the descent of the notion of one race—*the* Race—constituted by and through mechanisms and strategies of biopower from the early eighteenth century to the present and the inextricable linkage between that heritage and the emergence of sexuality in biopolitical and eugenic discourses on the family and the scientific management of sexualized populations (2009, 139–40, 12–13). To chart this heritage of modern racism, McWhorter weaves together insights drawn from erudite academic and archival material, articles in the popular press, and the subjugated knowledges of community organizers, neighbors, and activists. Foucault (1978, 26) noted that the forms of observation and campaigns with respect to sex and sexual conduct that emerged in the eighteenth century around the concept of population became the basis for links between sex and varieties of racism from the nineteenth century on: (im)purity of bloodlines and lineage, the birth of "monsters" and other oddities, polluted women, miscegenation, and so on (see also Stoler 1995; Roberts 1998; Shildrick 2001). As he explained it,

Evolutionism, understood in the broad sense—or in other words, not so much Darwin's theory itself as a set, a bundle, of notions (such as: the hierarchy of species that grow from a common evolutionary tree, the struggle for existence among species, the selection that eliminates the less fit)—naturally became within a few years during the nineteenth century not simply a way of transcribing a political discourse into biological terms, and not simply a way of dressing up a political discourse in scientific clothing, but a real way of thinking about the relations between colonization, the necessity for wars, criminality, the phenomena of madness and illness, the history of societies with their different classes, and so on. (2003g, 256–57)

Foucault argued that social relations that operate in the mode of biopower—that is, social relations that aim to strengthen and enhance life—require the theme of evolutionism to justify that fact that they kill people, kill populations, and kill civilizations. Modern societies that operate in the mode of biopower, Foucault wrote, appeal to evolutionism as a form of racism to justify war and other forms of state-sanctioned killing (Foucault 2003g, 254–58). "If the power of normalization wished to exercise the old sovereign right to kill, it must become racist," Foucault (256) stated. In the normalizing societies of biopower, racism is the precondition that makes killing acceptable. Within societies that operate in the mode of biopower, "killing," Foucault noted, must be understood to include indirect forms of murder in addition to direct forms of murder: exposing someone to death, increasing the risk of death for some people, political death, expulsion, and so on. He pointed out, furthermore, that within societies that operate in the mode of biopower, racism makes possible the establishment of a relationship between one's own life and the death of the other, a relationship that takes biology as its reference point. He explained this biological dyad thus:

> "The more inferior species die out, the more abnormal individuals are eliminated, the fewer degenerates there will be in the species as a whole, and the more I—as species rather than individual—can live, the stronger I will be, the more vigorous I will be. I will be able to proliferate." The fact that the other dies does not mean simply that I live in the sense that his death guarantees my safety; the death of the other, the death of the bad race, of the inferior race (or the degenerate, or the abnormal) is something that will make life in general healthier: healthier and purer. (255, punctuation in Foucault)

For Foucault, in short, modern racism is a set of power relations that produces effects referred to as "antisemitism" and "white supremacy";

however, what is at issue in modern racist regimes of power is not religion, culture, or skin color per se, but rather whether one is normal or abnormal. In his lecture course at the Collège de France in 1975–76, Foucault (2003g) described racism against the abnormal as a racism preoccupied not with attacking members of another race, but rather with protecting the boundaries of *the* race, the only race that matters, the human race embodied in its "highest" representatives (see McWhorter 2009, 139–40). Within modern racist regimes of power, nonwhite skin and non-Christian religious and cultural affiliation are marked as abnormal, but so too are (for example) low IQ test scores, seizures, cleft palates, intersex, trans identity, and same-gender coupling. Modern racism, McWhorter notes, is neither identical with, nor exhausted by, attitudes and actions that harm people of color or Jewish people, as is generally supposed: although modern racism encompasses these phenomena, it also exceeds them (2009, 34).

Indeed, McWhorter's genealogical work (and Foucault's own) demonstrates that modern racism is racism on whose genealogy can be directly mapped the biopolitical, cultural, medical, administrative, and institutional practices that philosophers of disability and disability studies scholars identify as constitutive of the history of ableism. That is, McWhorter's genealogy of modern racism indicates how the technique of genealogy can be used to show that the apparatus of disability is historically, conceptually, politically, and socially inseparable from the legacies of other apparatuses of force relations in ways that few feminist philosophers of disability and disability studies scholars have thought before. In another context, Eva Feder Kittay advances a related argument about the co-constitution of the apparatuses of racism and ableism when she writes, "Seeing racism through the prism of disability adds the insight that rather than predicated on group membership, racism is the exclusive claim to a set of desirable inherent properties—that is to say, the characteristics or intrinsic properties that those in power judge to be desirable and want for their exclusive possession" (2016, 719). Notwithstanding Kittay's appeal to inherent (or, intrinsic) characteristics and properties—an appeal that a historicist and relativist feminist philosophy of disability that draws upon Foucault would eschew—she seems to concur that modern racism is racism against the abnormal, as Foucault aptly put it. My argument in chapter 4 is designed to show how a certain feminist engagement with one of Foucault's genealogies of abnormality misunderstands the prescience of the genealogy.

Government as the Conduct of Conduct

In Foucault's 1978–79 lecture course at the Collège de France (later published in English as *The Birth of Biopolitics*), he linked his claims about the historical emergence of biopower and its objects with his approach to the theme of government (Foucault 2008). Recall that Foucault pointed out that modern power is productive rather than merely repressive: it produces objects and induces effects. Foucault argued that power is more a question of government, that is, the direction of conduct, than it is a question of confrontation between adversaries. Foucault used the term *government* in this sixteenth-century sense to refer to the art of government, that is, any form of activity that aims to shape, guide, or affect the conduct of oneself or someone else, proposing that the term be defined, in general, to mean "the conduct of conduct" (1982).

In an important 1982 interview, Foucault explained that he adopted this earlier, broad meaning of the term *government* because it encompasses both calculated modes of action that structure the field of possible action of oneself or other people and legitimately constituted forms of political and economic subjection. In other words, when the term *government* is used to refer to an activity in this way, it should be understood to concern one's relation to oneself, interpersonal relations that involve some form of control or guidance, and relations within social institutions and communities, as well as relations concerned with the exercise of political sovereignty. Analyses of force relations that construe power as government, that is, as the direction of conduct, take into consideration innumerable practices that have previously been assumed to fall outside the scope of power—including technologies of normalization that act as mechanisms for the systematic objectivization of subjects as (for instance) deaf, criminal, and mad, and techniques of self-improvement and self-transformation (technologies of the self) such as weight-loss programs and fitness regimes, assertiveness training, botox injections, breast implants, psychotherapy, and rehabilitation—in addition to recognizably power-laden procedures and practices such as state-generated prohibitions and punishments and global networks of social, economic, and political stratification, the deleterious effects of which congeal disproportionately along disabling, racialized, and gendered lines. Foucault maintained that although power appears to be merely repressive, the most effective exercise of power consists in guiding the possibilities of conduct and putting in order the possible outcomes. In his most succinct articulation of power as government, Foucault wrote,

What defines a relationship of power is that it is a mode of action which does not act directly and immediately on others. Instead it acts upon their actions: an action upon an action, on existing actions or on those which may arise in the present or the future. . . . The exercise of power . . . is a total structure of actions brought to bear upon possible actions; it incites, it induces, it seduces, it makes easier or more difficult; in the extreme it constrains or forbids absolutely; it is nevertheless always a way of acting upon an acting subject or acting subjects by virtue of their acting or being capable of action. (1982, 220)

In his summary to the 1978–79 lecture course at the Collège de France, Foucault (2008) argued that the phenomena that from the eighteenth century onward begin to appear as problems that require management emerged as such and developed their urgency within the framework of liberal governmentality. Foucault was concerned with philosophical questions that surround governmentalities—that is, rationalities of government—which he defined as systems of thinking about the practice of government that have the capacity to rationalize some form of this activity to both the people who practice it and the people upon whom it is practiced, where this capacity entails to render both thinkable and applicable or acceptable. He argued, furthermore, that the emergence of liberal governmentality evinced a transformation in political and economic thinking and the nature of the relationship between knowledge and government. From the eighteenth century forward, in fact, the government of living populations has generated specific problems for liberalism, which Foucault construed as an art of government, that is, as a principle for the rationalization and exercise of government based on a conception of autonomous legal subjects endowed with rights and individual freedoms (see also Rabinow and Rose 2003, xi). Insofar as subjects under liberal government are endowed with these allegedly inherent rights and freedoms, liberalism's capacity to continually refashion itself in a practice of auto-critique is ensured. As Foucault pointed out, liberalism (as an art of government) can be identified simultaneously, though in different forms, as both the regulative scheme of governmental practice and the theme of a (sometimes) "radical" opposition. Liberalism—as an art of government rather than an institution or ideology—Foucault explained, constitutes a tool for the criticism of reality, that is, for the criticism of (1) a previous governmentality that one tries to shed; (2) a current governmentality that one attempts to reform and rationalize; and (3) a governmentality that one opposes and whose abuses one tries to limit (1997a, 75).

The configuration of power centered on life (biopower) through which life itself becomes the ground for political struggle—in a word, biopolitics—is, in short, a strategy of liberal governmentality. Insofar as the phenomena toward whose management biopower is directed emerged as urgent within the frameworks of liberalism and capitalism, such a strategic movement of power must operate in ways that maximize the efficiency of the state and minimize its political, economic, and social costs, while at the same time guiding, influencing, and limiting people's actions in ways that seem to enhance their capacity to be self-determining. As I have indicated, biopower has made the government of people operate efficiently and economically in this way by establishing mechanisms of normalization in domains not traditionally associated with the state. This governmental transformation can be explained in terms of the growing reliance on regulatory forms of power constitutive of the very objects and subjects that they subsequently come to govern and represent. That is, the government of individuals and populations that had at one time been the jurisdiction of juridical and state institutions has been steadily assumed by apparatuses of control (medicine, the university, education, administrative discourses, and so on) that guide and manage people's actions in ways that make such actions appear to be the self-originating outcomes of their capacity to choose from an array of possible actions. As Wendy Brown explains, liberal government "acquired a new and complex relationship with freedom—it produced, organized, managed, and consumed individual freedom, all without touching the subject" (2015, 58).

Totalizing and Individualizing Power

Beginning in the 1950s, a new art of government, in the form of a new economized mode of reason, has come into existence. Liberal governmentality has transmogrified into a neoliberal mode of normative reason. As Brown explains, the transition from Keynesianism and democratic socialism to neoliberalism is the transition to a form of governmental reason through which the entire social field is economized and subjects are "responsibilized" (2015, 48–61). This management and administration of people's actions in ways that accord with the exercise of their freedom is most effectively and efficiently done from a distance through the distribution and prescription of norms and standards that people freely endeavor to approximate. Thus, Foucault observed that modern force relations are constitutive of the subject in a distinctively (neo)liberal fashion. As he explained it, a characteristic and troubling property of the practice of government in the West has been the tendency toward a form of political sovereignty "of all and of each"—*omnes et singulatim*—the effects of which are to totalize and individualize (Foucault 1982, 2003; Gordon 1991, 3; see also Simons and Masschelein 2015). To be an individual, in the modern sense of the word, is to be linked to a totality. Under modern governmental strategies, totalization and individualization do not exclude one another, but rather operate as related processes. The management and administration of individuals and populations now takes as its rationale and aim the achievement of security through neoliberalism.

In the interview "The Subject and Power," Foucault (1982, 208) explained his understanding of the relations between the processes of totalization and individualization by outlining the shift in emphasis of his work from a concentration on dividing practices and other modes of objectivization of the subject to the question of self-subjectification and technologies of the self in which the subject acts upon itself, is self-reflexive, and even self-creating. In the following chapter, I indicate that disability studies scholars who focus exclusively on the second axis of the matrix of subjectification, that is, "the second part" of Foucault's inquiry into the constitution of the subject—in particular, his writing in the first volume of *The History of Sexuality* and in *Discipline and Punish*—to critique his work do not take account of this shift. Significantly, Foucault explained the basis for the shift of emphasis in his studies of subjectivity in this way: "[The current technique of power] applies itself to immediate everyday life which categorizes the individual, marks him by his own individuality, attaches him to his own identity, imposes a law of truth on him which he must recognize and which others must recognize in him. It is a form of power which makes individuals subjects" (1982, 212). Without attention to Foucault's claims about modes of self-subjectification, disability theorists cannot adequately appreciate his approach to the constitution of the subject, including how indispensable the double bind of totalization and individualization is to an understanding of the constitution of the subject by and through force relations. Were disability theorists who criticize Foucault's approach to the subject to give greater attention to his claims about modes of self-subjectification, they would likely recognize the transformative promise that these claims hold out for work on disabled identity.

In his work on governmentality, Foucault aimed to show how the double bind of totalization and individualization that characterizes the modern nation-state is the mechanism through which the nexus between force relations and freedom is produced (Foucault 1994; see also Simons and Masschelein 2015). The power of the modern (neo)liberal state to produce an ever-expanding and increasingly totalizing web of social control of subjects is inextricably intertwined with, and dependent upon, its capacity to generate a growing array of progressively finer specifications of the individuality of subjects: by performatively differentiating and distinguishing them from each other, ranking and hierarchizing them, and categorizing and classifying them, all in accordance with a set of normalizing and homogenizing criteria, effectively producing them as identifiable and recognizable kinds of subjects while simultaneously rendering them interchangeable.

This, then, is how we should understand the incessant impetus to generate an increasing number of classifications of and distinctions between kinds of "disabilities" (e.g., physical disabilities versus cognitive disabilities; severe disabilities as opposed to moderate disabilities; attention deficit disorder rather than attention deficit hyperactivity disorder; and so on). The endless variations, classifications, and distinctions of (the apparatus of) disability that have come to be recognized and documented are strategic products of biopower, both totalizing and individualizing. Through these strategies, disabled individuals are constituted as correlative elements of power and knowledge. As Foucault noted, "The individual is no doubt a fictitious atom of an 'ideological' representation of society; but he is also a reality fabricated by this specific technology of power that I have called 'discipline'" (1977a, 194). Foucault's claim was that the very idea of the individual and the knowledge that may be derived from the individual must be understood in terms of this disciplinary production. In short, the more individualizing is the nature of the state's identification of subjects, the farther is the reach of its normalizing and totalizing apparatuses in the administration of their lives (see Rajchman 1991, 104).

Given the inexorable bind between the individual and the totality in modern (neo)liberal states, Foucault argued that analyses of subjection should not attempt to identify some centralized and overarching font of subjecting power, but rather "should try to grasp subjection in its material instance as a constitution of subjects" (1980b, 97). In another, earlier context, Foucault had remarked that in his work he had been trying to render evident the "constant articulation of power on knowledge and of knowledge on power," especially with respect to the experiences of the subject. Power—that is, its exercise—he argued, perpetually creates knowledge and knowledge constantly induces effects of power (1977a). Foucault was especially concerned to show how the emergence of the human sciences (sociology, psychology, anthropology, and so on) over the last two centuries has been entwined in the problems and practices of biopower and the social production and management (government) of subjects. Thus, Foucault's remarks on biopower, the subject, and government in his later work direct theorists to discern the multifarious ways that "subjects are gradually, progressively, really and materially constituted through a multiplicity of organisms, forces, energies, desires, thoughts, [and so on]" (1980b, 97).

Although Foucault's work is commonly characterized as centrally concerned with power, he stated in various writings that inquiry into the complicated constitution of subjects, that is, how humans are made subject, was the crux of his theoretical endeavors (see, e.g., 1982, 208). He was concerned to show that although modern governmental force relations appear to regulate political life in purely negative—that is, repressive—terms by prohibiting and controlling the subject, their logic is far more byzantine than traditional juridical conceptions of power represent. Modern force relations govern subjects by guiding, influencing, and limiting their actions in ways that accord with the exercise of their agency and freedom. As I have pointed out, Foucault maintained that the most effective exercise of modern power relations consists in guiding the possible conduct of free and autonomous subjects and influencing the possible outcomes of their actions by putting in place the courses of action from which they may choose. Relations of governmental power enable subjects to act to constrain them. In virtue of their subjection to governmental force relations, subjects are in effect formed, defined, and reproduced in accordance with the requirements of them. The production of these practices—these *limits* of possible conduct from which subjects choose their acts and hence constitute themselves—goes hand-in-hand with concealment of them, allowing the naturalization and legitimation of the discursive formation in which they circulate (see also Butler 1999).

In an interview that contains some of the most explicit and straightforward explanations of his ideas about the constitution of the subject within and through enabling constraints, Foucault asserted that the "modern state" should be considered not as an entity that "developed above individuals, ignoring what they are and even their very existence," but rather as "a very sophisticated structure, in which individuals can be integrated, under one condition: that this individuality would be shaped in a new form, and submitted to a set of very specific patterns" (1982, 214). In Foucault's terms, to be a subject is to be simultaneously subject to external control and dependence, on one side, and tied to one's own identity by a conscience or self-knowledge, on the other side. Thus, although Foucault claimed that subjectivity is a secondary phenomenon, that the subject is an effect of the nexus of power-knowledge, he did not deny that the individuation of its agency and the lived character of its experiences are real. On the contrary, he acknowledged that these aspects of subjects are very real constituents of and for them, as much of his later work shows. Nevertheless, he endeavored to underscore that such constituents of the subject are contingent and historically specific, not inherent to them, nor historically continuous. Furthermore, subjectivity itself, that is, subjectivity as a property that the subject possesses, was, for Foucault, neither eternal nor fixed, nor are free will and autonomy—concepts on which the very modern idea of subjectivity relies—inherent and immutable.

Genealogies of the Subject

Foucault's genealogical work on the subject aimed to show that concepts such as free will, autonomy, and subjectivity are not historical constants, although the dominant interpretive frames of history, philosophy, and theology (among others) represent them as such. Each of these putatively inherent and foundational properties or attributes of the subject has come into being through certain historically contingent practices, accidents, events, and interests. Thus, each of them has its own history, which it is the task of the genealogist to chart (Foucault 1977b, 153). In this regard, Foucault followed Nietzsche's naturalistic metaethics, explaining the relation between interpretive frameworks, genealogy (as a practice), and the constitution of the human being/subject in this way:

> If interpretation is the violent or surreptitious appropriation of a system of rules, which in itself has no essential meaning, in order to impose a direction, to bend it to a new will, to force its participation in a different game, and to subject it to secondary rules, then, the development of humanity is a series of interpretations. The role of

genealogy is to record its history: the history of morals, ideals, and metaphysical concepts, the history of the concept of liberty or of the ascetic life; as the stand for the emergence of different interpretations, they must be made to appear as events on the stage of historical process. (151–52)

McWhorter's (1999) genealogical work on sexual normalization further elaborates Foucault's own genealogy of sexuality, which affirmed the existence of various forms of sexual subjectivity, while showing how the very phenomenon of sexual subjectivity—that is, sexual subjectivity as a *dispositif* (apparatus)—arose within a specific historical context, out of disparate administrative and bureaucratic projects; was produced through certain institutional and individual preoccupations, in coordination with the birth of the human sciences; and complemented particular socioeconomic shifts. Although Foucault held that sexual subjectivity— including gay subjectivity—is real, he nevertheless showed that sexual subjectivity is neither timeless nor unchanging, but rather has taken shape through the action of certain historical and political forces and would cease to exist without them, to be replaced by some other way in which to organize the social and procreative world (McWhorter 1999, 30). Foucault's refusal in this way to give epistemological or methodological priority to subjectivity derives in part from the influence on his thinking of historian of science Georges Canguilhem, whose work led Foucault to have a strong sense of the discontinuities of scientific history and to understand that concepts play a historical role independent of any sort of phenomenological transcendental consciousness (see Gutting [2003] 2008). In short, Foucault's conception of the subject did not continue in the tradition of modern philosophy's *cogito*, which gives primacy to subjectivity. The subject, for Foucault, was not a sovereign or self-constituting point of origin from which knowledge and truth claims emanate. The subject was instead a life-long effect of constitutive force relations, that is, an effect of force relations continuously constituted and reconstituted through concrete and institutional practices and discourses over the course of a lifetime.

In the following chapter, I continue to sketch a genealogy of impairment, the disabled subject, and the apparatus of disability. I also respond to criticisms of Foucault's claims about subjectivity and identity (among others) that some disability theorists have directed at him (and poststructuralism more generally), indicating why these claims are unfounded or inaccurate and ought not to be accepted. In chapter 4, I consider criticisms that Foucault's work is inappropriate for feminist philosophy and theory. Once again, I address these criticisms of Foucault directly and show why their unsubstantiated character renders them unworthy of assent. In the third and fourth chapters, that is, I demonstrate that when one carefully examines Foucault's texts, most of the charges that disability theorists and feminist philosophers have directed at him seem almost indistinguishable from unsubstantiated rumor. Nevertheless, insofar as I wish to advance a feminist philosophy of disability inspired by Foucault, I am compelled to respond to these criticisms and make explicit why they ought not to be endorsed.

CHAPTER 3

Historicizing and Relativizing Philosophy of Disability

An Overview of Critical Responses

In my 2001 article "On the Government of Disability," I draw upon Foucault's claims about the productive character of power and Butler's claims about the performativity of gender to undermine the distinction between impairment and disability that conditions the BSM, the model of disability that, at the time, had dominated disability theory and anti-ableist activism for close to three decades. Even now, the BSM enjoys considerable endorsement, in part because it seems to incisively depict the social circumstances of disabled people, that is, its definition of disability seems to aptly encompass (among other things) high rates of unemployment among disabled people; discrimination against disabled people in housing, health care, and education; and their exclusion from public spaces due to physical, infrastructural, and institutional inaccessibility as the causes of the disadvantage that they experience. On the terms of the BSM, however, the distinction between impairment (construed as a prediscursive human attribute or characteristic) and disability (construed as the contingent form of social disadvantage imposed upon people with impairments) is universal and the categories of impairment and disability themselves are regarded as mutually exclusive. In the 2001 article, I assume Foucault's nominalist and historicist approach to social identities and categories in order to argue that impairment is as artifactual and as culturally and historically specific as disability; that is, I show that the distinction between impairment and disability made on the BSM collapses upon closer scrutiny.

In the years since the article's publication, several disability theorists (not all of whom are proponents of the BSM) have criticized the use to which I put Foucault in the article, as well as the implications for disability studies and disabled people that they believe my arguments to entail. These critics have been especially concerned about the implications that they perceive to follow from my arguments about the constitution of the disabled subject and my critique of identity politics. My arguments, they have variously asserted, are counterproductive for disability theory and activism (Hughes 2015; Siebers 2008b; Scully 2008; see also Catherine Mills 2011). The ensuing debates about the nature of impairment and disability and the usefulness of Foucault for critical work on disability have for the most part taken place outside of philosophy; nevertheless, philosophers ought to become informed about these debates because they provide additional reasons to doubt that the categories of impairment and disability are self-evident and hence not philosophically interesting, as well as offer insights into the performative character of identities and social categories more generally.

Some of the criticisms that disability theorists have raised about my use of Foucault dovetail with recent challenges that feminist philosophers (and theorists) direct at use of his work; that is, both disability theorists and feminist philosophers juxtapose his insights with the central assumptions of what in the humanities and social sciences are now often referred to as "the new materialism" and "the new realism." In fact, both "new" theoretical movements emerged largely in reaction to perceived excesses of Foucault's approach and of poststructuralism more generally. Some disability theorists, like some feminists, rely upon the assumptions of an earlier form of materialism—namely, historical materialism—to critique Foucault's claims and hence the claims of philosophers and theorists of disability who use his work (for instance, Erevelles 2015). Other disability theorists (like some feminists) draw upon an assortment of assumptions from both the earlier and new forms of materialism to implicitly or explicitly criticize the work of philosophers and theorists of disability who use Foucault, although in some cases doing so entails that they inadvertently undermine their own critical positions (e.g., Garland-Thomson 2011).

Disability theorists and feminist philosophers (and theorists) who endorse one or both new theoretical movements allege that two fundamental problems with Foucault's work make it unsuitable for critical theory that aims to stimulate social change. The two alleged problems can be formulated in this way: (1) Foucault offered a thin conception of subjectivity and identity by kicking away their foundations and thereby rendering them "fictive" (for instance, Alcoff 2000; Corker and Shakespeare 2002; Siebers 2008a, 2008b); and (2) Foucault (and poststructuralism) offered an account of the material body and embodiment that is tantamount to a form of linguistic idealism or, in any case, gives far too much significance to language and representation (for instance, Priestley 1998; Corker and Shakespeare 2002; Siebers 2008a, 2008b; Garland-Thomson 2011). With respect to the first problem, disability theorists who argue in this way follow many feminists who have for quite some time argued that a stable and coherent subject is required as a basis for politics. These disability theorists and feminists argue that insofar as the subject in Foucault does not provide such a foundation for politics, his work is inadequate and inappropriate for (respectively) the disabled people's movement and the feminist movement (see Siebers 2008a, 2008b; Hughes 2015; Erevelles 2015; Alcoff 2000, 2006; Fraser 1989; Haslanger 2012; Oksala 2016). The second criticism, although in circulation within some corners of disability theory for a long time now, has been given new life thanks to disability theorists who have taken up new materialist theories or aspects thereof (Siebers 2008a, 2008b; Garland-Thomson 2011). In fact, both criticisms of Foucault have, by now, become so commonplace in some corners of disability studies and feminist philosophy that they are, by and large, seldom fully elaborated and even more rarely is adequate textual support provided to substantiate them (for instance, Scully 2008; Siebers 2008a, 2008b; Haslanger 2012; Catherine Mills 2011).

In this chapter, I respond to criticisms according to which Foucault (and poststructuralism) offers a thin conception of subjectivity and denies materiality by indicating why these criticisms are unsubstantiated and misconstrue his claims. The argument of the chapter is designed in part to show how the genealogical technique—that is, practice—of investigation that Nietzsche introduced and that Foucault took up and adapted in his own work on the history of sexuality and the history of the modern prison facilitates ways to both talk back to these criticisms and elaborate a feminist philosophy of disability that goes beyond them. In general, I want to show that Foucault's historicist approach to (among other things) subjectivity, identity, experience, and the material body has greater explanatory power and transgressive potential for feminist philosophy of disability and disability theory than his critics in feminist philosophy and disability studies have thus far acknowledged.

A feminist philosophy of disability that draws on Foucault's historicist and relativist insights can better account for historical contingency and cultural differences than can disability theory that unquestioningly assumes disabled subjectivities, identities, and experiences to be self-evident, transhistorical, and foundational. Furthermore, a feminist philosophy of disability that employs Foucault's technique of genealogy (as well as other elements of his work) avoids the ahistorical, teleological, and transcultural notions that beleaguer much work done in disability studies. Feminist philosophy of disability that uses Foucault's genealogical technique (among his other techniques and tools) assumes that the notions of (for instance) disabled subjectivity, disabled identity, and the disabled body that currently circulate in disability theory are historically contingent and culturally specific, as are the very concepts of subjectivity, identity, materiality, and body themselves. None of these notions should be regarded as universal, as a fact-of-the-matter, or as sacrosanct. Each of them is a product of social history, a history that genealogy can trace, and thus each is open to reassessment and transformation.

The argument that I elaborate in the chapter proceeds in this way: First, I provide more detailed explanations of the first two theoretical conceptions of disability that I sketched in the introductory chapter and, in addition, elaborate some of the assumptions on which my own historicist and relativist understanding of disability as an apparatus relies. Next, I examine one influential critique within disability studies of the poststructuralist (and hence, Foucault's) account of subjectivity, experience, the material body, and identity. My aim is to show how this critique misconstrues and misrepresents poststructuralism in general and Foucault's approach to subjectivity, experience, the body, and identity especially. In this context of the chapter, I point out the epistemic limits that uncritical acceptance of current ways of thinking about subjective experience and identity imposes upon philosophy of disability and disability theory. In turn, I introduce feminist insights about the binary thinking that has structured dominant forms of Western thought in order to consider various ways in which disability theorists have argued that the account of the body that Foucault's work and poststructuralism more generally provide is inadequate and inappropriate for disability theory. On the terms of these arguments in disability theory, the articulation of experiences, knowledges, and claims to entitlement that purportedly follow from the presence of a naturally impaired body is taken as the impetus and rationale for disability theory and practice. By contrast, the historicist and relativist approach to disability that I aim to advance eschews the assumption on which these argumentative claims implicitly, and in some cases, explicitly, rely, according to which there exists a prediscursive material body that disability theory can identify, articulate, and accurately represent. A feminist philosophy of disability that is circumspect about its own historicity and cultural specificity construes the conceptual objects of impairment and disability as elements of a historically contingent apparatus in Foucault's sense.

Conceptions of Disability

In the introductory chapter, I note that the assumption according to which force relations are productive of (the apparatus of) disability contravenes the conceptions of disability that feminist philosophies and theories of disability commonly assume. In that context, I identify three such conceptions. The first conception construes disability as the functional manifestation of an intrinsic characteristic, a biological, corporeal, or some other difference, or an attribute or property (such as an impairment) that certain people have that gives rise to distinct forms of social discrimination against them. The second conception construes disability as the form of discrimination and oppression imposed upon people who have an intrinsic characteristic, attribute, or property (namely, an impairment). The third, hybrid, conception of disability may be a combination of the other two conceptions, though it need not be. It is here, that is, as hybrid conceptions, that I categorize various disability theories that assume a new materialist approach to disability. I focus on two of these materialist approaches to disability in the latter part of this chapter. In a moment, I shall consider the first and second conceptions more closely to distinguish them from the historicist and relativist understanding of disability that motivates the argument of this book; however, I want first to explain certain epistemological and ontological assumptions of a fourth conception of disability. It is opposition to this fourth conception that has precipitated the emergence of all three other conceptions.

In the literature of disability studies, and indeed on the terms of the first three conceptions of disability that I broadly outline in chapter 1, this fourth understanding of disability is (as I indicated) referred to as "the medical model of disability." I variously refer to this understanding of disability as the "conventional," "medicalized," or "individualized" conception of disability, to take account of the fact that this approach shifts within limits, that is, to account for the capacity of this fourth conception to be continuously refashioned in response to critique of its terms and its strategies, technological change, social conditions, and so on. The conception is not static, although many (if not most) of the conceptual objects that emerge from it are naturalized as such. On this fourth, bipartite, conception, disability is, in effect, assumed to be equal to, or the inevitably detrimental consequence for human functioning of, an objective biological characteristic (i.e., a naturally detrimental human attribute), namely, an impairment. As biological human attributes (or characteristics), impairments are assumed to possess transhistorical and transcultural properties that exist before and independent of social norms, practices, and policies. In short, on this conception of disability, impairments are the objective, biological precursors to disability, that is, the intrinsic characteristics (pathologies or abnormalities) of individuals that manifest in remarkably uniform kinds of "disabilities" (construed as abnormal functioning). That a "person with an impairment" has a lower quality of life and fewer opportunities for the future than a person without an impairment is taken to be the self-evident and inevitable consequences of an impairment's intrinsically negative character. Hence, this conventional, medicalized, and individualized conception of disability recommends that social resources be directed to the development of scientific and medical research and interventions that promise to correct, eliminate, and prevent impairments that entail disabilities and their attendant restrictions on people's life prospects. It is this fourth conception of impairment and disability that is generally presupposed in mainstream (and some feminist) bioethics, cognitive psychology, ethics, and theories of justice (among other areas of philosophy and cognate disciplines).

Theorists and researchers in disability studies and disabled activists have responded to some of the aforementioned assumptions made on this fourth understanding of disability—this medical model of disability—by developing a sociopolitical interpretation of the phenomena of disability that locates their genesis not in human biology alone, or even necessarily, but rather in the interaction between certain people and the social, economic, and political structures and processes of the environment in which they are situated. This interpretive frame can be identified as a social model of disability in the broad and loose sense to which I referred in the first chapter. Two conceptions of this sociopolitical interpretation of disability—one that emerged in the United States and the other, namely, the BSM, that emerged in the United Kingdom—have been predominant in disability scholarship and anti-ableist activism in their respective nations of origin and abroad. The conception that emerged in the United States is an example of the first of the three conceptions of disability that I describe at the outset of this section. The BSM is an example of the second of the three conceptions that I describe there.

Disability theorists and activists in the United States, spurred on by the successes of the women's movement and the black civil rights movement, as well as by the ideological assumptions of liberal individualism, fought long and hard for legislation that would institutionalize a tripartite conception of disability into U.S. domestic policy. This conception, which also underlies a classification system once used by the World Health Organization (WHO), makes roughly the same epistemological and ontological assumptions about the categories of impairment (i.e., as biological deficit) and disability (i.e., as functional limitation) as the conventional, medicalized conception, but adds a third category—initially termed "handicap"—to represent the social disadvantages (e.g., discrimination, prejudice, and forms of exclusion) predicted to accrue to individuals who meet the criteria for either or both of the other categories. Despite their initial efforts, disability theorists and activists in the United States nevertheless came to reject the term of reference—handicap—that was originally used to designate this third category before the conception's institutionalization in the Americans with Disabilities Act (ADA) of 1990. Rejection of the term *handicap* was based upon a contemporary myth, once widely accepted in the disability studies community and disability rights movement[1] in the United States and elsewhere, according to which in the past the term was associated with the social practice of public begging. Leaders in the U.S. disability movement and authors in American disability studies believed that by using the term, they implicitly demeaned disabled people. Although this association has since been shown to be unfounded, the term *handicap* has never been revived in American disability studies or the U.S. disability rights movement.[2] The third category, concerned with disadvantage and exclusion, is nonetheless preserved in the ADA (and the Americans with Disabilities Amendment Act of 2008) through its broad definition of "disability discrimination."

Harlan Hahn's "sociopolitical definition of disability" (as he referred to it) also played a role in early articulations of the first conception and indeed in the early days of disability studies in the United States, influencing the formulation of the categories of disability and disability discrimination that eventually became entrenched in the ADA. Hahn's definition assumes that disability stems from the failure of a structured social environment to adjust to the needs and aspirations of "citizens with disabilities" rather than from the inability of a given individual with a disability to adapt to the demands of society. The devaluation of people with disabilities, Hahn argues, is due to the reluctance of society to recognize their dignity and worth as human beings and grant them civil rights as members of a political community. Hahn claims that his sociopolitical definition of disability provides a foundation for the development of a "minority-group model of disability" that would enable a major change in the direction of research on disability (1985, 93). As he explains it, research that assumes the minority-group model of disability would not concentrate on the economic or functional implications of disability, but rather would focus on the attitudinal and behavioral significance of perceptions attributed to visible and permanent characteristics. On the terms of Hahn's minority-group model, "disabilities" are among the many other bodily attributes (such as skin color, gender, and age) that have historically been used as means with which to differentiate between people and to discriminate against some of them. Thus, the minority-group model (roughly, a token of the first conception) has precipitated the emergence of the idea that "people with disabilities" constitute a historically disenfranchised group and should be recognized as such under the law.

Let me point out that within disability studies circles and disabled people's communities, the term *people with disabilities* is increasingly regarded as dated and oppressive, as a legacy of ableism (see Titchkosky 2001). The term is the signature locution of "people-first" language, an artifact of the late twentieth-century self-advocacy movement and the Normalization Movement, the latter of which I referred to in the previous chapter. Members of these movements developed people-first language to counter and resist the stigma and prejudice that they perceived to be embodied in the term *disabled*. The term *disabled*, they argued, implies that their disabilities consume them, are essential characteristics of them, and thus define them. The motto of many proponents of people-first language is "See the person, not the disability." Self-advocates and other proponents of people-first language maintain that the term *people with disabilities*—which gives priority and centrality to the term *people*—renders a given person's disability as merely one among many of the person's characteristics, simply another human difference. Due to the social circumstances and historical context in which self-advocates and their allies advanced these arguments for people-first language, the arguments have had noticeable rhetorical force, gaining significant momentum and harnessing noteworthy institutional and legislative influence internationally, as the entrenchment of the ADA demonstrates.

Nevertheless, as I have noted, an increasing number of disabled people and disability studies scholars internationally eschew the term *people with disabilities*. For instance, the internationally renowned disabled media expert and activist Lawrence Carter-Long has asserted that "If you 'see the person, not the disability,' you're only getting half the picture. Broaden your perspective. You might be surprised by everything you've missed." Carter-Long thinks that if one "sees the person, but not the disability," then one "misses perspective." As he explains it, "In 2016, anyone who would dare to assert that race 'doesn't matter' or that they 'see the person, not the gender' would instantly, and I think rightfully, be called out as either naïve or ignorant." For Carter-Long, the term *people with disabilities* is a euphemism that obscures the unemployment, inaccessibility, violence, poverty, and other forms of oppression and disenfranchisement that most disabled people confront. Carter-Long argues that, equally, "to suggest disability is simply a 'difference' and has no impact on a person's life is a very privileged position to take. Most disabled people don't have that luxury. The assertion flies in the face of reality and minimizes the very real discrimination disabled people face" (qtd. in King 2016). Despite the efforts of Carter-Long and other disabled activists, as well as some disability studies scholars, the term *people with disabilities* nevertheless lives on in government legislation and public policy, administrative classifications and regulations, disability theory, the popular press, academic discourses, and even some activist organizations worldwide.

Since the 1970s, a growing number of disability theorists in the United Kingdom and internationally have adopted the terminology and epistemological and ontological commitments of the BSM, the conception of disability to which the second, strict sense of the term *social model* refers. The BSM uses the same terms of reference as the bipartite medicalized conception—namely, *impairment* and *disability*—though it redefines the concept of disability in important ways (for instance, Oliver 1990, 1996). Proponents of the BSM claim that their model also redefines impairment. They argue that impairments are not intrinsic defects that demand to be corrected or eliminated (as the "medical model" assumes), but rather are descriptively neutral human characteristics that are fundamental to human existence and on which social disadvantages are imposed. As Oliver (one of the first proponents of the BSM) has put it, "The social model insists [that] disablement is nothing to do with the body. It is a consequence of social oppression" (1996, 24).

Indeed, the claim that there is no causal connection between impairment (construed as a neutral human characteristic) and disability (construed as a form of social oppression) has been widely regarded in disability studies and activist circles as the most important innovation of the BSM. The authors of the BSM's key principles, as well as many of its more recent leading proponents, have more or less endorsed historical materialism; thus, they variously argue that the restricted opportunities that disabled people confront are not the inevitable consequences of their impairments, but rather are created by social and economic arrangements and conditions that can be transformed. For example, Oliver explains that the "cultural production of disability" is dependent on a variety of factors, including the type of economy in a cultural context, the size of the economic surplus, and the values that influence the redistribution of this surplus. In more concrete terms, disability comprises the innumerable aspects of social life that impose restrictions on "people with impairments," including personal prejudice, inaccessible public buildings, unusable public transportation systems, segregated education, exclusionary workplace arrangements, and so on. Proponents of this model of disability argue that the most effective way for governments to increase the opportunities available to disabled people and improve their quality of life is to supply the resources required to reorganize environments in ways that ensure their inclusion in social life rather than allocate huge sums of money and other resources to the development of technologies that aim to correct and eliminate impairment (and hence, people with impairments).

The Subject of Impairment

Later in this chapter, I introduce criticisms of the BSM that other disability theorists have advanced. In this context, however, I am primarily concerned to explain the key principles of the BSM and show that proponents of the model have misunderstood the assumptions about causation on which their model of disability relies, as well as subsequently to distinguish the BSM from my own claims about the apparatus of disability. Let me begin by noting that epistemological and ontological assumptions on which both the BSM and the minority-group model rely bear a remarkable resemblance to assumptions made on the conventional, medicalized, conception of disability used in the subfields of bioethics and medical ethics, cognitive science, mainstream ethics, and mainstream theories of justice. For although proponents of the BSM and the minority-group model may not agree with the assumption that the medicalized conception (the fourth conception) makes about the disvalue of an impairment, both models assume with the latter conception that impairments are intrinsic properties (attributes) of individuals that exist before, and independent of, social norms, practices, and policies. As disability theorist Lorella Terzi (2004, 141) puts it, people with accredited impairments have always existed, in all societies. Insofar as disability theorists have assumed that impairment is a transhistorical and universal phenomenon in this way, they have been concerned to formulate arguments about (among other things) why social responses to impairment vary between historical periods and cultural contexts, that is, why people with impairments are included in social life in some places and periods and excluded from social life in some places and periods. Notice that impairment is represented in these claims as nonhistorical (biological) matter of the body, which is molded by time and class, is culturally shaped, or on which culture is imprinted. In other words, the category of impairment has remained the passive, politically neutral foundation of disability on both the BSM and minority-group model, as well as the conventional, medicalized conception of disability. To be sure, the BSM and minority-group model seem to improve upon the medicalized conception of disability insofar as they do not assume with this fourth conception that the social disadvantages that disabled people confront are a direct consequence of impairment. Proponents of the BSM err, nonetheless, by denying a causal connection between impairment and disability altogether. The relation of entailment between impairment and disability is more complicated than either the medicalized conception or the BSM suggests. Let me elaborate these important claims.

Recall that the BSM was articulated to counter individualized, or medicalized, models of disability that represent its phenomena as equal with, or the inevitable consequences of, a detrimental personal attribute or characteristic (impairment). On the terms of the BSM, however, impairment is not conceived as equal to or synonymous with disability, nor is impairment believed to cause disability. Rather, the BSM construes disability as a form of social disadvantage that is imposed "on top of" one's impairment. In addition, impairment is represented as a natural entity whose identity is distinguishable from the identities of an assortment of other human attributes or characteristics, such as gender, age, and sexuality. Thus, proponents of the BSM make two assumptions: (1) disability is not a necessary consequence of impairment; and (2) impairment is not a sufficient condition for disability. Nevertheless, an unstated premise of their model is that (3) impairment is a necessary condition for disability. On the terms of the BSM, that is, one must "have" or be presumed to "have" an impairment to be regarded as a disabled person. Proponents of the BSM do not argue that people who are excluded or discriminated against due to (say) skin color are, in virtue of that fact, disabled, nor do they argue that racism is a form of disability. Equally, intersexed people who are socially stigmatized and may have been surgically "corrected" in infancy or childhood do not seem to qualify as disabled. On the terms of the BSM, only people who "have" or are presumed to "have" an impairment get to count as disabled. Thus, the strict division between the categories of impairment and disability that the BSM is claimed to institute is in fact a chimera.

Foucault argued that modern force relations are constitutive of the subjects that they subsequently come to represent insofar as these forms of power put in place the limits of possible conduct for subjects. Notice that if this insight is combined with the foundational (i.e., necessary) premise of the BSM (impairment), then it seems that subjects are produced who "have" impairments because this identity meets certain requirements of contemporary political arrangements. As my discussion below of the U.K. government's Disability Living Allowance (DLA) shows, to make individuals productive and governable within the juridical constraints of that regime, the policy in fact contributes to the production of the "person with an impairment" that it is claimed to merely recognize and represent. It would seem, then, that the identity of the subject of the BSM ("people with impairments") is formed in large measure by the political arrangements that the model was designed to contest. Consider that if the identity of the subject of the BSM is produced in accordance with these political arrangements, then a social movement that grounds its claims to entitlement in that identity will inadvertently extend these arrangements in new ways.

If the constitution of the "impairments" that are alleged to underlie disability sustains and even augments current social arrangements, then philosophers of disability and disability theorists should not continue to conceive of impairment as a politically neutral, biological (i.e., natural) characteristic, or attribute, of a prediscursive body upon which recognizably disabling conditions are imposed. Instead, the putatively natural impairments that allegedly underlie disability should themselves be identified as products of knowledge-power that are incorporated into the self-understandings and self-perceptions of certain subjects and elaborated in administrative policies, medical and legal discourses, cultural representations, and so on. This, then, indicates that impairment is *performative*. A relatively recent style of reasoning—namely, the diagnostic style of reasoning—has emerged that materializes impairments as universal attributes (properties) of subjects through the iteration and reiteration of rather culturally specific regulatory norms and ideals about (for example) human function and structure, competency, intelligence, locomotion, and ability. The diagnostic style naturalizes impairment as an interior identity or essence on which culture acts to camouflage its contingency, that is, the contingency of the style of reasoning and the productive force relations that materialized impairment as "natural" in the first place.

In short, impairments are indeed implanted; that is, impairment has been disability—or rather, an element of the apparatus of disability—all along. Practices of the apparatus of disability into which the subject is inducted and divided from others produce the illusion that they have a prediscursive, or natural, antecedent (impairment), one that in turn provides the justification for the multiplication and expansion of the regulatory effects of these practices. The testimonials, acts, and enactments of the disabled subject are performative insofar as the allegedly natural impairment that they are purported to disclose or manifest has no existence prior to or apart from these very constitutive performances. That the apparent universality of the discursive object called "impairment" is assumed to be evidence for its prediscursive existence obscures the fact that the constitutive power relations that define and circumscribe impairment have already put in place broad outlines of the forms in which that discursive object will be materialized, for whom it will be materialized, and in the service of what interests. The shifting limits and borders of the classification of impairment demonstrate its historicity and cultural specificity. The artifactual character of the category is also displayed through its steady expansion as an increasing number of ever more finely tuned deformities, disorders, and syndromes are brought into being, materializing the category, elaborating its representation, and rendering it knowable (see Tremain 2001). Thus, insofar as proponents of the BSM claim that disability is not an inevitable consequence of impairment, they misunderstand the productive constraints of modem power. For the category of impairment emerged and in part persists to legitimize the disciplinary practices and associated style of reasoning of the apparatus of disability that generated it in the first place.

Christine Overall (2006) has used my analysis of the discursive constitution of impairment to argue that old age is also socially constituted rather than an entity existing in nature, prior to culture, and independent of human agency. Most philosophers and feminists, Overall notes, will agree with the claim that age identity, like gender identity and racial identity, is created, reinforced, and sustained through normative conventions, relations, and practices, albeit not consciously or with intention. She argues, however, that the so-called biological substratum of age, too, is a social construction. How is it possible for age and old age to be social constructions? Age theorists, Overall observes, grant that the ageing process itself—that is, the rate at which one ages, how one ages, and how ageing people are regarded—is to some extent socially generated evaluation. Yet most age theorists, she points out, take for granted that this cultural process is superimposed upon an immutable and objective biological foundation of years lived and life stage attained. Overall thinks that this assumption is mistaken. As she explains it,

> Years lived and life stages attained are also socially constructed and interpreted, and there is no definite, biologically given number of years lived that, by itself, constitutes being old or that provides an immutable and inevitable foundation on the basis of which social ageing processes are built. Years lived do not, of themselves, constitute one's age—whether young age, middle age, or old age. Ageing is not a "natural" process; that is, it is in no way outside of culture. (2006, 129)

As Overall remarks, there is a great deal of cultural and historical variability and flexibility with respect to the designation of the number of years that constitute old age, youth, or middle age. Cultures, she notes, "pick out" a certain number of years and attribute to that number a certain biological and cultural significance—for example, that one is worn out, no longer in one's prime, near the end of one's life, and so on. Nevertheless, Overall points out that so-called old age, like impairment, can be redefined in a host of new ways by choosing new numbers and new features that constitute oldness, youth, and middle age (also see Overall and Tremain 2016).

Eventalization and Examination

The artifactual character of impairment and disability (and other social categories such as old age) could be recognized and acknowledged if philosophers of disability and disability theorists were to conceive of inquiry about disability as problematization, taking up what Foucault referred to as "eventalization" (2003d, 249). Foucault used the term *eventalization* to refer to a procedure of analysis that amounts to a "breach of self-evidence," one that puts into relief the *singularity* of a given practice or state of affairs where otherwise there would be a tendency "to invoke an historical constant, an immediate anthropological trait, or an obviousness that imposes itself uniformly on all" (249). Eventalization aims to show that things are not as necessary as they seem. As Foucault remarked, "It wasn't as a matter of course that mad people came to be regarded as mentally ill; it wasn't self-evident that the only thing to be done with a criminal was to lock him up; it wasn't self-evident that the causes of illness were to be sought through the individual examination of bodies; and so on" (249). Foucault illustrated his idea of eventalization with reference to the context of punishment, explaining that to analyze the practice of penal incarceration as an "event," rather than an as institutional fact or ideological effect, involves the determination of the "penalization" of already-existing practices of internment—that is, of their progressive insertion into the form of legal punishment—and of the "carceralization" of practices of penal justice, that is, the movement by which imprisonment as a form of punishment and technique of correction became a central component of the penal order.

Eventalization is just the sort of analytical procedure that should be put in the service of a historicist and relativist philosophy of disability that aims to establish the historical contingency and cultural specificity—that is, the singularity—of the apparatus of disability by identifying how elements of this apparatus are naturalized, rendered ahistorical and universal, and encompass a steadily expanding segment of the population. Analysis of the apparatus of disability through "this procedure of causal multiplication" (Foucault 2003d, 249) would involve consideration of how a multitude of processes constitute the apparatus of disability and its naturalized and naturalizing mechanisms. To analyze disability as an event, that is, would involve determination of the processes of (what we might call) "disableization," whereby the apparatus of disability variously incorporates a growing number of people's lives, through a multiplying number of means and techniques, in order to distinguish certain subjects from others, identify them, improve them, render them more productive, eliminate them, and govern them in a host of other ways (see also Puar 2009). When disability is analyzed through the procedure of eventalization, subjects are understood to be produced as disabled and impaired (rather than "have" disabilities and impairments), that is, are made disabled and impaired through innumerable elements of the apparatus of disability, including an accelerating array of social policies, administrative decisions, medical and scientific classifications and examinations, techniques of surveillance and registration, cultural representations, aesthetic practices, and academic research.

The procedure of eventalization can thus be used to identify how the public and private administration and management (in a word, government) of impairment contribute to its naturalization, materialization, and objectivization. In an early adoption of Foucault's insights for the study of disability, Margrit Shildrick and Janet Price explain how impairment has been naturalized and materialized in the context of a particular piece of social policy—the United Kingdom's DLA—that was designed to distribute resources to people who need assistance with "personal care" and "getting around." The official rationale for introduction of the policy was to ensure that the particularity of certain individuals does not cause them to experience undue hardship that the welfare state could ameliorate. Shildrick and Price argue, however, that the questionnaire that prospective recipients of the benefit are required to administer to themselves abstracts from the heterogeneity of their own bodies to produce a regulatory category—impairment—that operates as a homogeneous entity in the social body. The definitional parameters of the questionnaire and indeed the motivation behind the policy itself posit an allegedly preexisting and stable entity (impairment) based on regulatory norms and ideals about (for example) function, utility, and independence. In virtue of responses to the questions posed on the form, every prospective recipient of the benefit is in turn enlisted to elaborate individuated specifications of this entity—that is, this impairment. To do so (and to produce the full and transparent report that the government bureaucrats demand), potential recipients are required to document the most minute experiences of pain, disruptions of a menstrual cycle, lapses of fatigue, and difficulty in operating household appliances and to associate these phenomena in some way with this abstraction.

Through a performance of textual confession ("the more you can tell us, the easier it is for us to get a clear picture of what you need"), potential recipients are made subjects of impairment (in addition to their constitution as subjects of the state) and rendered "docile," that is, are rendered as subjects who can be used, enabled, subjugated, and improved. Although the questions on the DLA form seem intended to extract very idiosyncratic detail from subjects/recipients, the differences that the questions produce are highly coordinated and managed ones. Indeed, the innumerable questions and subdivisions of questions posed on the form establish a system of differentiation and individuation whose totalizing effect grossly restricts individuality (Shildrick and Price 1996, 101–2).

In short, impairment is not a natural, value-neutral, universal, and objective human characteristic or aspect of human existence that certain people possess, but rather is the naturalized and materialized outcome of a classification initially generated in medical, administrative, and juridical contexts (among others) to facilitate normalization. In other words, technologies of normalization—and the discourses that embody them—have been complicit in the historical emergence of the category of impairment and contribute to its persistence. Impairment is in fact a new conceptual object of the diagnostic style of reasoning that emerged with biopower in the late eighteenth century. Since the thirteenth century, the term *impaired* has been used to refer to any obstacle or impeding force. In the late seventeenth century, the term *impairment* appeared as a noun related to the general state (health, well-being, and so on) of an individual. It was not until the late eighteenth century (the historical context in which biopower emerged), however, that the term *impairment* came to refer to a specific physiological deficit, that is, a specific attribute or property of an individual (*Oxford English Dictionary*, s.v. *impairment*). Recall Hacking's claim that styles of reasoning materialize objects, individuated with the style, that were not previously noticeable among the things that exist. In addition, recall Foucault's insight that force relations are productive of and immanent in the entities and states of affairs that they manage and control. Political theory, Foucault wrote, "must cease once and for all to describe the effects of power in negative terms: it 'excludes,' it 'represses,' it 'censors,' it 'abstracts,' it 'masks,' it 'conceals.' In fact, power produces; it produces reality; it produces domains of objects and rituals of truth" (1977a, 194).

Until their formation in and articulation by and through the diagnostic style of reasoning at the close of the eighteenth century, impairments—as properties or attributes of individuals—did not exist. Prior to the late eighteenth century, the belief that currently prevails, according to which impairments should be prevented or corrected, would have been unintelligible or incoherent inasmuch as it could not cohere with the style of reasoning that prevailed in that earlier historical context. Before the late eighteenth century, that is, surgical, chemical, and genetic correction of impairment were not only technologically impossible, they were also conceptually impossible. Statements about impairment (and its correction and prevention) came to be candidates for true and false only with the articulation of the discursive space associated with the diagnostic style of reasoning; that is, impairment emerged as a possible object for clinical inquiry and examination only because of this distinctive, historically specific form of reasoning. The normalizing, disciplinary role of the diagnostic style of reasoning, whose techniques are both individualizing and totalizing, should not be overlooked. In *Discipline and Punish*, Foucault connected the forms of knowledge and power that emerged by and through practices of observation and surveillance in prisons to the disciplining role of the examination more generally:

> The examination combines the techniques of an observing hierarchy and those of a normalizing judgment. It is a normalizing gaze, a surveillance that makes it possible to qualify, to classify, and to punish. It establishes over individuals a visibility through which one differentiates them and judges them. . . . In it are combined the ceremony of power and the form of the experiment, the deployment of force and the establishment of truth. . . . The superimposition of the power relations and knowledge relations assume in the examination all its visible brilliance. It is yet another innovation of the classical age that historians of science have left unexplored. (1977a, 184–85)

Who, Foucault asked, will write the history of the examination, the history of "its rituals, its methods, its characters and their roles, its play of questions and answers, its system of marking and classification" (185)? In the "slender technique of the examination," he asserted, is to be found a whole domain of knowledge and thus a whole type of power. The introduction of the examination opened up two correlative possibilities: first, the individual was constituted as a describable, analyzable object in order to permanently capture her supposedly natural abilities under the gaze of a body of knowledge; second, a comparative system was constituted that made possible the measurement of overall phenomena, the description of groups, the characterization of collective facts, the calculations of the gaps between individuals, and their distribution in a given population. The disciplinary and regulatory knowledge-power of the diagnostic style of reasoning that produces information about the subject in the context of the examination is, in short, simultaneously individualizing and totalizing: individualizing insofar as the information produced by and through the examination ties the subject to an individuality, a personal identity, and a sensibility that are made objects of knowledge; and totalizing insofar as the subject is situated within more encompassing socially significant categories and designations on the basis of perceptions and interpretations of the information produced.

Making Up People with Impairments

Notice that both personal identities and social categories are constituted through practices such as the examination. In numerous discussions designed to show how medical, juridical, and psychiatric classifications, statistics, and other social scientific information create and cause to emerge new kinds into which people can be sorted (e.g., Hacking 1991b; 1995), Hacking, who acknowledges his debt to Foucault, has used the term *human kinds* to refer to the social groups whose initial composition can be attributed to knowledges that the human sciences have engendered. In an early incarnation, Hacking (1992a) called this composition of human kinds "making up people." In his early discussions of making up people, that is, Hacking had argued that the human kinds that human sciences such as psychology, psychiatry, and sociology supply are distinct from the natural kinds that physics, astronomy, and other natural sciences claim to discover insofar as, in many cases, the people who are classified as members of a kind come to have knowledge of the relevant kind, which changes their self-perceptions and behavior, motivates them to forge group identities, and often forces changes to the classifications and to the knowledge produced about the people of the kind. Hacking came to refer to this form of "strategic reversibility" (to use Foucault's term) as "the looping effects of human kinds" (Hacking 1995, 351), articulating these arguments to explain the historical emergence and revision of the categories of (among others) autism, madness, child abuse, and multiple personality disorder.

Hacking (2007) has, nevertheless, rejected his earlier idea that there is a distinct notion of human kinds, or even the vaguer class of kinds that he once referred to as "interactive kinds." Hacking's former *human kind* terminology was patterned on the philosophical notion of a natural kind. Thus, one might think that an understanding of what natural kinds are would hasten an understanding of his (earlier) notion of human kinds. Rachel Cooper (2004) has pointed out, however, that such an understanding of natural kinds seems elusive. Although multiple accounts of natural kinds—essentialist, nonessentialist, realist, and so on—have been proposed, each one of them is controversial: it is unlikely that any of these candidates will be given general acceptance. Thus, Cooper asks if it can be determined whether human kinds are distinct from natural kinds in the absence of an agreed upon account of natural kinds. She remarks that, thankfully, this is not a problem: paradigmatic examples of natural kinds can in fact be identified, including chemical elements, fundamental particles, and biological species (75–76). Cooper argues that to know whether human kinds are distinct from natural kinds one could, therefore, consider whether human kinds are fundamentally like or unlike kinds such as chemical elements, fundamental particles, and biological species. Cooper claims, furthermore, that human kinds are not fundamentally unlike (distinct from) these paradigmatic natural kinds. Hacking has subsequently remarked that he "does not protest [Cooper's] argument," but rather, "goes further back." As Hacking explains it, "There is, if possible, even less of a class of human kinds than there is of natural kinds" (2007, 234). Hence, Hacking has returned to his old friend the phrase *making up people*, using the generic term *kinds* to articulate the co-constitution of personal identities and social groups and the categories that identify them.

These reflections on making up people are implicitly a form of philosophical nominalism that Hacking (1992a) has referred to as "dynamic nominalism," explaining that he elaborated this form of nominalism to correct what he regards as the excesses of traditional nominalism. Nominalism in the grand tradition of Thomas Hobbes, Locke, J. L. Austin, and others, he argues, is wholly static. A "static" nominalist, he writes, thinks that all categories, classes, and taxonomies are given by human beings rather than by nature and are timeless, that is, are essentially fixed throughout the existence of humankind. A dynamic nominalism, by contrast, accounts for the interaction between names and people. In the case of making up kinds of people, Hacking says, the names alone do not tell the whole story. In addition to the names of the classifications— that is, the names by which certain people are identified—making up kinds of people, he notes, involves the people who are classified; the experts who classify, study, and presume to help them; and the institutions within which the experts and the people classified are in contact and through which authorities exercise control. Hacking has attributed this species of nominalism to Foucault, who famously pointed to the historical and cultural specificity of homosexuality. Many gay historians, theorists, and activists have claimed (and some continue to claim) that homosexuals have always and everywhere existed. Foucault argued, however, that homosexuality as a way to be a subject came into existence—that is, became a problem through its problematization—only in a certain historical and cultural location, namely, in recent times in the West. Although Foucault agreed that there were many people in ancient Athens who engaged in plenty of highly codified same-gender acts, he argued that the homosexual as a kind of person did not exist in that time or place. In the first volume of *The History of Sexuality* he wrote,

> As defined by the ancient civil or canonical codes, sodomy was a category of forbidden acts; their perpetrator was nothing more than the juridical subject of them. The nineteenth-century homosexual became a personage, a past, a case history, and a childhood, in addition to being a type of life, a life form, and a morphology, with an indiscreet anatomy and possibly a mysterious physiology. Nothing that went into his total composition was unaffected by his sexuality. . . . The sodomite had been a temporary aberration; the homosexual was now a species. (1978, 43)

My argument is that the diagnostic style of reasoning that brought into being the medical and psychiatric classifications of homosexuality, the homosexual, and impairment—and hence their administrative, juridical, economic, and other articulations—also created and caused to emerge another new kind of person, namely, the "person with an impairment." Although both the classification of impairment and the person said to embody this attribute achieved general notoriety only with the widespread promulgation in the twentieth century of the WHO's diagnostic tool, the *International Classification of Impairments, Disabilities, and Handicaps* (and to some extent its rudimentary predecessors), these phenomena—that is, impairment and the person with an impairment—actually emerged in tandem in the late eighteenth century and from that time forward were mutually constitutive. Prior to the emergence of the diagnostic style, beings such as the one-headed monster with two bodies to which the Renaissance philosopher Michel de Montaigne devoted an essay in the sixteenth century were variously regarded as revelations of divine will, omens of moral significance, or supernatural. Beings such as this child out of whose chest seemed to grow another child were not, however, regarded as "people with impairments" (nor conjoined twins), that is, they were not regarded as people in need of improvement, correction, elimination, care, or political organization. Indeed, people with impairments as a kind did not exist in that historical context, which is to say that people did not experience themselves in this way, nor were they perceived by or did they interact with legal authorities, medical experts, and each other in this way. In short, it was not possible to be this kind of person until the diagnostic style of reasoning that began to emerge in the late eighteenth century made it so. Hence, the significance of nominalism for my historicist approach to the conceptual objects that the apparatus of disability produces, including the conceptual object called "impairment." Before the articulation and elaboration of the classification of impairment in these contexts, by and through these technologies of normalization, neither impairments nor people with impairments existed. This, then, is the problematization—that is, the eventalization—of the categories of impairment and disability.

Experience as Evidence

In the opening remarks of this chapter, I indicate that Foucault's ideas about subjectivity, subjection, and the constitution of the subject constitute one aspect of his work that some disability theorists (and some feminist thinkers) have criticized. Tobin Siebers has been quite critical of Foucault's ideas about the subject, experience, identity, and subjection (among other things). In "Disability Experience on Trial," Siebers (2008a) objects to the argument that feminist poststructuralist historian Joan W. Scott (1991)—who draws on Foucault—makes about the shortcomings of historical inquiry that relies upon experience as evidence, extending the conclusions that he extrapolates from these objections to criticize a position on minority identities that, he claims, is characteristic of poststructuralism in general. To be sure, Siebers—who aligns himself with both the new realist and the new materialist movements—does not explicitly or directly attribute to Foucault the problems that he perceives in Scott's argument; however, inasmuch as Scott draws upon Foucault's claims, and insofar as Siebers claims that there seems to be "uniformity" on such matters among theorists "in the poststructuralist tradition" (Siebers 2008a, 305n6), it is fair to say that the general remarks about poststructuralism that he makes in the article are meant to apply to Foucault, if not especially to him, given his notoriety as one of its initiators, despite the fact that he himself eschewed the designation of "poststructuralist."

Siebers (2008a), as the provocative title of his influential article might suggest, set out to show why the articulation of "disability experience" is an important and valuable enterprise for disability studies scholars, whose pursuit the claims of Scott and poststructuralists threaten to confine and restrain. In contrast to what Scott and poststructuralists assume, Siebers writes, disability experience has the potential to both augment social critique and advance emancipatory political goals. He argues, furthermore, that insofar as Scott and poststructuralists in general do not acknowledge, and indeed dismiss, the importance and value of "experience as evidence," their claims have limited potential as tools with which to enlarge and enrich the social critiques of disabled people (and other minority groups) and to advance their emancipatory political goals. Scott, he says, "attacks" feminists and cultural historians who argue that history must be rewritten to include the perspectives and experiences of women, people of color, and victims of class discrimination, accusing them of falling prey to foundationalism. Noting that Scott (1991, 779) states that "it is not individuals who have experience, but subjects who are constituted through experience," Siebers (2008a, 294) sardonically remarks that, apparently, individual experience cannot serve as an origin of explanation or authoritative evidence because it is socially constructed, that is, experience is threatened as a basis for knowledge claims due to its social construction. For Scott, Siebers claims, even when experience is used to create alternative histories or to correct prevailing misinterpretations, it becomes, if given the status of evidence, "merely another brick in the foundationalist discourse of history." Siebers argues that although Scott and others in the poststructuralist camp argue that experiences of minority identity "have no critical value," he hopes that knowledge gained from disability experience renews the incentive to reclaim and retheorize experiences of minority identity (292–93). He therefore urges disability theorists and other minority thinkers to take up realist accounts of minority identity rather than poststructuralism. Unlike poststructuralism, which "discounts" the knowledge claims of minority identities insofar as it assumes that identities are little more than socially constructed fictions, realism, Siebers asserts, recognizes both the social construction of identities and that identities constitute epistemologies about the world in which we live. Siebers avers that although poststructuralism has always held that "the more radical and absolute the critique, the greater is its potential for emancipation," the proof for acceptance of this dictum seems less and less apparent. Does the desire for absolute critique always work in the interest of politically progressive goals? Is the banishment of experience radical? Or is it reactionary (293; see also Oksala 2016; Alcoff 2006)?

No other disability theorist has explicitly challenged the arguments that Siebers directs at Scott in his article; that is, disability theorists seem for all intents and purposes to have implicitly accepted the criticisms that Siebers makes about Scott (and poststructuralism more generally), according to which she (and poststructuralist approaches) dismisses the critical value of subjective experience, given its social construction. Anything other than acceptance of Siebers's views in this context seems to be out of the question. After all, what could be more vital to the recognition and elevation of the histories, perspectives, interests, and emancipatory goals of disabled people and members of other historically marginalized and stigmatized populations than the articulation, documentation, and acceptance (as evidence) of their personal accounts and narratives? These stories have been hidden from history and continue to be ignored or discredited, obfuscation and dismissal that reinforce and reproduce the narrow picture of (among other things) the human that has been produced and disseminated by and within mainstream society. What disability theorist would deny that, and why?

My argument is that there is very good reason to dissent from Siebers's criticisms of Scott and poststructuralism in this context and, furthermore, that doing so does not require one to take the position that minority identities "have no critical value," nor that they are "little more than socially constructed fictions," both of which claims Siebers attributes to Scott (and to poststructuralists in general), but which she seems not to assume. I submit that in addition to the fact that Siebers seems to misunderstand the philosophical underpinnings of realism, he misconstrues Scott's position (and poststructuralism more generally), providing an uncharitable, very selective, and textually unsubstantiated exegesis of Scott's claims and of poststructuralist assumptions in general, as he does in his 2008 book with respect to Foucault (see Siebers 2008b, especially 54–59). Siebers ignores one dimension of the double bind—"twin politics" (M. Lloyd 1996, 243)—of the subject for Foucault (and poststructuralists such as Scott), that is, by focusing exclusively on Foucault's work on how force relations act upon subjects, Siebers ignores that, for Foucault, the constitution of the subject involves self-subjectification, self-creation, and potentially, self-transformation (see also Scully 2008). Contra Siebers, Scott's stated position is that experience, although it offers an important element for critique, should not be regarded as self-evident, as the "bedrock of evidence" on which explanation is built, nor as "uncontestable evidence" from which explanation is derived, but rather should be regarded as a starting point for questions about (for instance): the constructed nature of experience; how one is constructed as a minority subject in the first place; how that subject-position is established by and through discursive practices; how that subject-position operates; and how it constitutes subjects who understand and act in the world in the way in which they do (Scott 1991, 777). As Scott explains,

> We know [minority identities] exist, but not how they have been constructed; we know their existence offers a critique of normative practices, but not the extent of the critique. Making visible the experience of a different group exposes the existence of repressive mechanisms, but not their inner workings or logics; we know that difference exists, but we don't understand it as relationally constituted. For that we need to attend to the historical processes that, through discourse, position subjects and produce their experiences. It is not individuals who have experiences, but subjects who are constituted through experience. (779)

Notice that, contra Siebers, Scott's claim is not that experience, because of its social construction, has no epistemic value, but rather that there is no Cartesian *cogito* or ready-made subject that encounters, confronts, and experiences the world. The subjects who have experiences come into being by and through the experiences themselves; that is, the constitution of the subject takes place hand-in-hand with the experiencing itself. Notice, furthermore, that Scott, contra Siebers, acknowledges that the existence and experiences of minority identities afford us a means with which to critique extant practices and uncover repressive mechanisms of force relations. Since subjectivities are secondary phenomena, however, we do not and cannot know in advance the extent of the critique that the experiences of minority identity offer; that is, we do not and should not assume that we know from the outset of our investigations of minority identities what their existence and experience of them can tell us about (for instance) how they came into being and why, nor what interests or whose interests their lived existence serves, nor whether, instead, this information will tell us things about the existence and experience of minority identity that we never would have otherwise imagined. Notice, then, that on this understanding of experience our investigations into minority identities and the experiences that constitute them are not conceived as finite, teleological, or, as Siebers puts it, "absolute" projects, but rather as ongoing practices. For, as Kwame Anthony Appiah (2016) argues, all identities are created through practices rather than beliefs, as philosophers and other intellectuals usually assume. Identity, Appiah points out, is an activity, not a thing.

Scott recommends that we assume something like Teresa de Lauretis's redefinition of experience to engage in this sort of open-ended critical undertaking. De Lauretis defines experience as the process by which subjectivity is constructed and through which one places oneself in social reality, or is placed in it, and thus perceives and comprehends as subjective material, economic, and interpersonal relations that are in fact social and, in a larger perspective, historical (1984, 159, in Scott 1991, 782). On such a redefinition, experience becomes that for which explanation is sought and about which knowledge will be produced rather than the origin or authoritative evidence that grounds what is already known. When we think of experience in this way, we historicize it, as well as historicize the identities to whose constitution experience contributes. Indeed, a historicist examination of experience critically scrutinizes all the explanatory categories associated with experience that are ordinarily taken for granted as self-evident, transparent, and foundational, including subjectivity, identity, agency, nature, body, and biology, and continues to study categories such as gender, race, and sexuality that are already recognized as socially constituted.

Historicized understandings of experience are critical ontologies of ourselves whose aims include the identification of both the historically contingent limits of who we are now and the epistemic limits that uncritically thinking of experience and identity in accepted ways can impose upon us. Hence, these historicized understandings of experience—that is, these critical ontologies of our minority identities—do indeed rely in part, but only in part, on the insights drawn from subjugated knowledges, such as the recovered knowledges of the incarcerated lunatic and ridiculed hunchback and the subjugated epistemologies of the disenfranchised cripple, empowered disability activist, and politicized autistic student. Historicized understandings of experience also require that we consider how these subjugated knowledges themselves are products of and conditioned by the historical a priori of the epoch within which they were constituted. Foucault, writing under the pseudonym Maurice

Florence (1994), defended the historicist conception of experience and demotion of the subject in this way:

> Refusing the philosophical recourse to a constituent subject does not amount to acting as if the subject did not exist, making an abstraction of it on behalf of a pure objectivity. This refusal has the aim of eliciting the processes that are peculiar to an experience in which the subject and object "are formed and transformed" in relation to and in terms of one another. The discourses of mental illness, delinquency, or sexuality say what the subject is only in a certain, quite particular game of truth; but these games are not imposed on the subject from the outside according to a necessary causality or structural determination. They open up a field of experience in which the subject and the object are both constituted only under certain simultaneous conditions, but in which they are constantly modified in relation to each other, and so they modify this field of experience itself. (3–4)

The impetus for this sort of historicized understanding of experience is not, as Siebers claims, "the desire for absolute critique," but rather the desire to show that our current subjective experience is not a decontextualized and inherent property or manifestation of our (minority) identities; that our current identities are not the self-evident, inevitable, and predetermined outcomes of our past subjective experiences and identities; and that our current subjective experiences of minority identities are not necessary predictors of the future. In short, a historicized understanding of the experience of impairment, disability, and disabled identity can demonstrate that these phenomena are the products of arbitrary and contingent constraints (including self-imposed constraints) rather than natural, prediscursive, prior to culture, or biologically determined. In this way, historicized understandings of the disabled subject, minority identity, and experience open conceptual conditions of possibility for resistance and personal and social transformation that should animate a feminist philosophy of disability.

I want to turn to consider the second charge that some disability theorists variously direct at Foucault (and poststructuralism more generally), namely, that his work offers an inadequate account of corporeal reality and materiality that amounts to a form of linguistic idealism, or at least confers too much significance upon language and discourse or language and representations. The motivational assumptions of these disability theorists differ; however, they agree with each other insofar as they reject the idea that the body is merely a social construction of language and representation ("a fiction"), an idea that they (unanimously) attribute to Foucault and poststructuralism more generally (see, for instance, Siebers 2008b, 54–59). The broad argument of disability theorists who criticize Foucault in this way can be summed up thusly: (1) Foucault eliminates the fundamental materiality of the body in ways that are idealist—that is, his claims imply that everything is a linguistic construction or representation; (2) contra Foucault, disabled people's corporeality and experience of it cannot be reduced to the level of mere linguistic constructions and representations, nor do "signs" precede the embodied experiences of disabled people; (3) disabled people's bodies and, more exactly, their bodily differences, make a real, lived difference for disabled people who encounter architectural barriers, systemic prejudice and bias, and lack of opportunities on a daily basis due to prevalent restrictive and uninformed beliefs about what a body should do, what form it should take, how it should appear, how it feels, what can be learned from it, and so on; (4) disabled people, by virtue of their corporeal differences from normative bodies, could produce a wealth of knowledge about embodiment (including about its variations, fluctuations, and inconsistencies) were their insights not suppressed, discounted, and ignored due to the persistence of these very norms; and (5) since a central—if not *the* central—purpose of disability theory should be to take into account and elaborate the moral, political, social, and epistemological differences that the bodily differences between disabled and nondisabled people make, Foucault's work (and the work of other poststructuralists) is inadequate, if not counterproductive, for disability theory because it undermines the authoritative status of disabled people's knowledge about their own bodies and experiences (Hughes 2015; Siebers 2008a, 2008b; Scully 2008).

Binary Thinking and the Sexed Subject

Before I address these criticisms, let me introduce claims about the body and materiality (among other things) that feminist philosophers and theorists have made. Just as some disability theorists persistently charge Foucault with neglect of the body and its materiality, so, too, some feminist philosophers and other feminist theorists criticize him in this way. In fact, some of these feminist philosophers and theorists have directly influenced and even precipitated the recent emergence, or rather resurgence, of materialist approaches in disability theory, as well as other approaches—such as phenomenology—in disability theory that give primacy to the body. Some feminist philosophers and theorists who critique Foucault's approach to the body and materiality argue that his neglect of the body is of a piece with the long history of somatophobia in the tradition of Western philosophy, even though he himself distinguished his analytical tool (genealogy) from "the philosopher's method" because of the latter's refusal to acknowledge the body (see Foucault 1977b). If we wish to develop a feminist philosophy of disability that employs genealogy, we must take account of this legacy in Western philosophy, for it may indicate how the conceptions of materiality and embodiment that many disability theorists hold in the present reinstate that history.

Since the Enlightenment, dominant strains of Eurocentric, Western philosophy have assumed as their fundamental premise that for a given entity, state of affairs, or relation to be worthy of philosophical investigation, it must be universal, objective, and immutable. Thus, Western ethics, metaphysics, philosophy of language, and political philosophy have concerned themselves with an ostensibly universal subject who allegedly transcends the vagaries of contingency and subjectivity through an unyielding faculty of reason, pledges allegiance to no tribe, is born of no mother, and can be found nowhere, but nevertheless is every man existing everywhere (see Benhabib 1987).

Over the past several decades, feminist philosophers (among others) have endeavored to show both that sexism and other systemic relations of power have generated and conditioned many of the foundational claims of Western philosophy and that the allegedly universal and unencumbered subject of the Western philosophical tradition has always been situated, reflecting the assumptions, biases, and perspective of that social positioning. Feminist philosophers (and others) have also endeavored to demonstrate that the set of cultural, theoretical, discursive, and institutional practices that constitute this philosophical tradition have, each in their own ways, contributed to the constitution of the social and political categories (such as sex and race) into which subjects in the West have been divided (see Harding 1986; Haraway 1991).

The identification and critique of a set of interrelated dualisms that have historically structured (and continue to structure) Western intellectual thought have been at the heart of these feminist arguments. Some of the dualisms that feminists have identified are: nature-culture; reason-emotion; mind-body; objectivity-subjectivity; form-content; public-private; male-female; masculine-feminine; subject-object; impartiality-partiality;

and fact-value. In the terms of this dichotomous thinking, feminists have argued, the former term of each respective pair is privileged and assumed to provide the form for the subordinate latter term (content) of the given pair, whose very recognition is held to depend upon (indeed, require) the transparent and stable existence of the former term. On this dichotomous thinking, the significance of anything—including, and indeed especially, the latter term of a given pair—that threatens to undermine the transparent and stable existence and dominance of the former term of a given pair, or to reveal its artifactual character— and hence the artifactual character of the opposition itself—must be marginalized, obscured, or nullified. Thus, women are both depreciated and disqualified within the terms of the binary thinking that has conditioned Western philosophy, while men are elevated within it. Feminist theorists have pointed out, furthermore, that given the interrelations between the terms on each side of these dualisms, women have, since time immemorial, been tendentiously associated with the already depreciated body, emotions, the feminine, the private realm, partiality, and subjectivity, while men have been associated with the venerated mind, reason, the masculine, the public realm, impartiality, and objectivity (see Harding 1986; Benhabib 1987; Lloyd 1993). Binary thinking has been so gripping in Western intellectual thought that Western feminists themselves have inadvertently engaged in it, deriving the distinction between sex and gender that conditioned more than three decades of feminist scholarship from both the opposition between nature and culture that was foundational to Claude Lévi-Strauss's structuralist anthropology and early research on intersex.

Johns Hopkins psychologist John Money and his colleagues, the psychiatrists John and Joan Hampson, introduced the term *gender* in the context of research on intersex to refer to the psychosocial aspects of sex identity. Money and his colleagues, who at the time aimed to develop protocols for the "treatment" of intersex, required a theory of identity that would enable them to determine which of two sexes to assign to their clinical subjects. The concept of gender (construed as the psychosocial dimensions of sex), they believed, would enable them to make these designations. In 1972, Money and Anke Ehrhardt popularized this idea that sex and gender constitute two separate categories. The term *sex*, they claimed, refers to physical attributes that are anatomically and physiologically determined. By contrast, the term *gender*, they wrote, refers to the subjective, internal conviction that one is either male or female—one's gender identity—and the behavioral expressions of that conviction. As Money and Ehrhardt explained it, gender identity is "the sameness, unity, and persistence of one's individuality as male, female, or ambivalent" (1972, 257). Money and Ehrhardt claimed that their theory of gender identity enabled medical authorities to understand the experience of a given subject who was manifestly one sex but wished to be its ostensible other. Nevertheless, in the terms of their sex-gender paradigm, "normal development" was defined as congruence between one's "gender identity" and one's "sexual anatomy" (Fausto-Sterling 2000, 4). Although Money and his colleagues concluded from their studies with intersexed people that neither sexual behavior nor orientation as "male" or "female" has an innate or instinctive basis, they did not recant the foundational assumption of their theory, namely, that there are only two sexes. To the contrary, they continued to maintain that intersex results from fundamentally abnormal processes; thus, they insisted that their patients required immediate treatment because they ought to have become either a male or a female (Fausto-Sterling 2000, 46).

Despite the prescriptive residue of the sex-gender formation, it appealed to early "second-wave" feminists because of its motivational assumption that everyone has a gender identity that is detachable from each one's so-called sex. Without questioning the realm of anatomical or biological sex, feminists took up the sex-gender paradigm to account for culturally specific forms of an allegedly universal oppression of women. The distinction between sex and gender that feminist theorist Gayle Rubin articulated in 1975, through an appropriation of structuralist anthropology and Lacanian psychoanalysis, has arguably been the most influential in feminist discourse. By drawing on Levi-Strauss's distinction, Rubin cast sex as a natural (i.e., prediscursive) property (attribute) of bodies and gender as its culturally specific configuration. "Every society has a sex-gender system," Rubin wrote, describing a sex-gender system as "a set of arrangements by which the biological raw material of human sex and procreation is shaped by human social intervention and satisfied in a conventional manner." On the terms of Rubin's structuralist distinction, sex is a product of nature as gender is a product of culture (Rubin 1975, 165).

Historicizing and Relativizing Sex-Gender

The structuralist nature-culture distinction on which Rubin's sex-gender distinction relies was purportedly invented to facilitate cross-cultural anthropological analyses; however, the universalizing frame of structuralism obscures the multiplicity of cultural configurations of "nature." Insofar as structuralist analysis presupposes that nature is prediscursive (i.e., prior to culture) and singular, it cannot interrogate what counts as nature within a given cultural and historical context, in accordance with what interests, whose interests, and for what purposes. In fact, various feminist philosophers have pointed out that the theoretical device known as the nature-culture distinction is already circumscribed within a culturally specific epistemological frame. Harding (1986) has remarked, for example, that the way in which contemporary Western society distinguishes between nature and culture is both modern and culture bound. The culture-nature distinction is also interdependent on the field of other binary oppositions that have structured Western modes of thought. To be sure, some feminists criticized the nature-culture distinction early on and identified binary discourse as a dimension of the domination of what inhabits "natural" categories (women, people of color, animals, and the nonhuman environment). These early feminist critiques of the nature-culture distinction did not, however, extend to a derivative of the distinction: namely, the sex-gender distinction. Donna Haraway (1991) asserts that feminists did not question the sex-gender distinction because it was too useful a tool with which to counter arguments for biological determinism in "sex difference" political struggles. By ceding the territory of anatomical "sex," Haraway states, feminists encountered massive resistance and renewed attack on the grounds of biological difference from the domains of biology, medicine, and significant components of social science.

The category of gender has been historicized and relativized in most mainstream feminist theory at least since Rubin articulated her version of the feminist sex-gender distinction in the mid-1970s. Due to the epistemic authority that feminists conferred upon the sex-gender distinction, however, the category of sex remained an inert fact of the matter within feminist discourse, conceived as prediscursive, prior to culture, and hence devoid of political import until the 1990s, when, thanks to the groundbreaking work of Butler, Haraway, Anne Fausto-Sterling, Hazel Carby, and other feminist philosophers and theorists, sex, too, became an object of critical inquiry. Many feminist philosophers and theorists now argue that the political and explanatory power of the category of gender depend precisely upon relativizing and historicizing the category of sex, as well as the categories of biology, race, body, and nature (among others). They acknowledge that each of these categories has, in its own way, been regarded as foundational to gender; yet, they point out that none of these categories is an objective entity with a transhistorical and transcultural identity. In this regard, Oyèrónké Oyěwùmí, has criticized European and Euro-American feminists for their proposition that all cultures "organize their social world through a perception of human bodies as male or female." Oyěwùmí's criticism of Western feminists puts into relief how the imposition of a system of gender can alter how racial and ethnic differences are understood. In Yoruba culture, Oyěwùmí explains, relative age is a far more significant social organizer than sex. Yoruba pronouns, for example, indicate who is older or younger than the speaker; they do not refer to "sex" (Oyěwùmí 1998, 1053). In short, the category of sex (like the category of impairment) must be considered in the specific historical and cultural contexts in which it has emerged as salient (see also Oudshoorn 1994).

In *Gender Trouble*, Butler (1999) argues that if the category of sex is itself a gendered category—that is, politically invested and naturalized, but not natural—then there really is no ontological distinction between sex and gender. As Butler explains it, the category of sex cannot be thought of as prior to gender, as the sex-gender distinction assumes, since gender is required to think sex at all (143). In her now-famous formulation, Butler argues that the stylized performance of gender is the means through which "sexed nature" (sex) is materialized as natural, as prior to culture, and as a politically neutral surface on which culture acts (10–11). In other words, Butler reverses the accepted feminist understanding of the relation of entailment between sex and gender, a reversal of causation that, as I point out in the following chapter, Foucault had already motivated in the first volume of his history of sexuality series (see Foucault 1978, 154–56). Foucault's insight that power is productive can be used to argue that the impairment-disability distinction that grounds much disability theory is also performatively structured in this way.

As I note above, the association of the body with women and its subordination to the mind with which men have been associated, as well as the exclusion of both the body and women from political and public discourse, the civic realm, and indeed history, were central to early feminist critiques of dualistic thinking. Thus, feminist philosophers (and others) have regarded the promotion and elevation of women as inextricably interwoven with the reevaluation of the body and embodiment, endeavoring to bring the body to the center of critical discussion from the excluded social position it has hitherto occupied. They have done so by variously focusing their efforts on events and embodied experiences of the body that had previously been omitted from philosophical and critical discourse, events and experiences such as menstruation, pregnancy, having breasts, and menopause. In other words, these feminist efforts have tended to assume that sex and sexual difference are foundational, universal, and prediscursive, assumptions that Butler's work on gender performance was designed to undermine. Nevertheless, in recent years, some feminists have argued that Butler (and other poststructuralist feminists) has placed too much emphasis on gender, at the expense of attention to sexual difference, and (like Foucault) lends far too much significance to language and discourse as constitutive of corporeal reality. Feminists who argue in this way have been responsible for the emergence of the recent materialist feminisms and feminist materialisms, as well as recent feminist uses of phenomenology.

Materializing Disability

Some of the latest innovations in disability theory with respect to the (impaired) body mirror these conceptual shifts in feminist philosophical and other theoretical discourses on the body. Throughout the last decades of the twentieth century, that is, some disability theorists have called for greater attention to be paid to impairment, largely in reaction to the dominance of the BSM, whose distinction between impairment and disability has installed its own version of the nature-culture distinction within disability theory. Some critics of the BSM, who are nevertheless sympathetic to it, have argued that due to its (almost) exclusive focus on structural and institutional factors that cause disability, the BSM neglects the lived experience of impairment—including the lived experience of pain—thus presenting an incomplete picture of disabled people's lives. For example, Kittay has argued that "while the [BSM] has been useful in all sorts of ways, the distinction between the [medical model and the BSM] is too simplistic." As Kittay explains it, "There are aspects of disability that no one really wants that are part of the impairment, like pain, caused by impairment itself" (qtd. in Picciuto 2015; see also French 1993; Crow 1996; Morris 1996; Hughes and Patterson 1997; Thomas 1999).[3]

In Carol Thomas's materialist-feminist effort to revise the BSM, she introduces the term *impairment effects* to refer to pain and other dimensions of living with impairment that she and other sympathetic critics of the BSM have argued that it ignores. Some disability studies scholars have claimed that Thomas's materialist-feminist approach to disability also eschews the foundational status that the BSM confers upon the category of impairment. For Thomas writes that a materialist perspective on impairment would explain how pathologized, morphological, anatomical, and genetic differences, bodily variations that are defined in Western medical discourses as "impairments," are shaped and changed temporally and spatially through the dynamic interrelationship between human bodies and social and physical environments (1999, 33). Thomas agrees with disability theorist and activist Paul Abberley (1996) that what is assigned to the category of impairment is neither transhistorical nor universal in character, but rather is "historically and spatially specific: "what *is* and what *counts as* impairment is always socially located, situated in time and place" (Thomas 1999, 132–33; emphasis in Thomas). Notice, however, that with these remarks, Thomas implies that the category of impairment itself is transhistorical and transcultural, recuperating the ahistorical foundationalism of the BSM that, to some readers, she had seemed to avoid.

Proponents of the BSM claim that their version of the impairment-disability distinction enables disability theory and activism to account for cultural variation; however, the derivation of the distinction from a conception of nature and culture formulated within a culturally specific epistemological frame limits the scope of the cross-cultural and transnational application of the distinction. A historicist and relativist feminist philosophy of disability that uses genealogy would, by contrast, investigate the singularity of the categories of impairment and disability and how their respective epistemological and ontological statuses have been achieved, including how the belief has taken hold that impairment is a transhistorical and transcultural property or characteristic of the subject that exists prior to culture, is prediscursive, and indeed is somehow part of the fabric of the universe. Thus, I want to advance an argument about the discursive constitution of impairment according to which the idea of impairment is historically specific and performative, providing the justification for the expansion and multiplication of disabling practices. Impairment is not a "natural" (i.e., biological), value-neutral, and objective human characteristic or aspect of human existence that certain people possess or embody, the signification and significance of which may vary from one historical era to the next and from one culture to another. Again, once one acknowledges that the category of "normal" does not identify an ahistorical and universal internal state or characteristic, one should concede that the identity of a category—such as impairment—

that is defined in terms of its departure from the normal is also a historically contingent construction. Impairment cannot be thought of as prior to disability because disability—construed as either a functional limitation or a socially instituted disadvantage—is required to think of impairment at all. Even the idea of pain and the experience of it are historically and culturally relative and interpreted. Prinz, who has written at length about the influence of culture on cognition, argues that the causes, effects, and embodiment of every one of our emotions and drives—"fear, anger, disgust, even hunger, thirst, and sexual desires"— are culturally conditioned. As Prinz explains it, "We may have brain circuits [with] homologues in other creatures, but we are also far more susceptible to social learning than other creatures are." Thus, "our biological machinery is co-opted from the start" (Prinz and Tremain 2016).

Even if critics of my historicist and relativist approach to impairment and (apparatus of) disability concede that the experience of pain and interpretation of it are historically specific and culturally relative, they might raise an additional objection to the approach. Such critics might argue that even if the experience of pain (and interpretation of it) is in some way a historically conditioned and culturally relative event, there remain aspects of at least some impairments that are objectively detrimental, that is, would be detrimental within any conceivable historical and cultural context. Many such critics in fact make this sort of argument by appealing to blind people and aesthetic values; that is, these critics argue that insofar as blind people do not experience (say) the aesthetic values of visual art—in particular, they cannot appreciate the beauty of these works of art—they are objectively disadvantaged. A life without this experience of (say) da Vinci, Van Gogh, and O'Keeffe is an impoverished one, these interlocutors claim. Notice, however, that this objection attributes transhistorical and transcultural properties, that is, intrinsic values, to the works of da Vinci, Van Gogh, and O'Keeffe themselves and indeed to artworks in general. Although the theory of art and aesthetics according to which beauty can be objectively defined has dominated discussions of art and aesthetics throughout the history of Western philosophy, some philosophers of art and aesthetics challenge the assumptions of the theory. Prinz argues, for instance, that there can be no objective evaluation of art because artworks do not have intrinsic values that exist apart from other social and political values and influences. Beauty has plasticity, Prinz asserts, pointing out how perceptions of beauty in art have changed over time. In short, aesthetic values are neither transhistorical nor transcultural; rather, every artwork and every art movement is a reflection of its time and place and intentionally so (Prinz and Gelonesi 2016). If there is no objective, intrinsic value in a work of art, that is, if there is no objective value of art, there can be no objective experience of art's value nor any objectively valuable experience of art from which blind people are precluded. The same sort of argument can be made about disabled people and allegedly objective experiences of other aesthetic values.

It is useful to bear Prinz's remarks in mind when one considers that disability theorists who assume phenomenology to argue that the BSM fails to account for the body and impairment also direct phenomenological arguments at Foucault to assert that he, too, fails to appropriately and adequately acknowledge embodiment. To argue against the use of Foucault in disability studies, these authors have invariably drawn upon the work of Maurice Merleau-Ponty, which they take to be the philosophy of embodiment par excellence. Almost without exception, these authors appear to think that the mere fact that Foucault issued criticisms of phenomenology is sufficient to demonstrate that his work ignores the lived body and embodiment. Seldom has adequate textual support been supplied to substantiate these charges. For example, in her efforts to show why Foucault's work has limited use for disability studies, Jackie Leach Scully notes disapprovingly that in Foucault's *Remarks on Marx* he described phenomenology as "unfolding the entire field of possibilities connected to daily experience" (Foucault 1991, 31, in Scully 2008, 12). Scully seems to think that this brief and rather cryptic remark shows both that Foucault eschewed phenomenology and that he denied the materiality and lived experience of the human body from which phenomenology putatively derives its impetus. Hence, she follows up her appeal to Foucault's remark by noting that he "didn't mean it as a compliment" (Scully 2008, 12).

To be sure, Scully might also be familiar with the derisive remarks that Foucault made about phenomenology in *The Order of Things* and *The Archaeology of Knowledge*. Recall that (as I noted in the previous chapter) phenomenology gives primacy to subjectivity, which, by contrast, Foucault regarded as a secondary phenomenon. In the foreword to the English edition of *The Order of Things*, therefore, Foucault rejected phenomenology by arguing that it "places its own point of view at the origin of all historicity—which, in short, leads to a transcendental consciousness" (1970, xiv). In *The Archaeology of Knowledge*, furthermore, he famously indicted phenomenology for its "transcendental narcissism"

(1972, 203). Perhaps these remarks have prompted Scully (among others in disability studies) to conclude that Foucault scorned the existential phenomenology of Merleau-Ponty. Gary Gutting ([2003] 2008) has argued, however, that Foucault directed the latter remark at Jean-Paul Sartre (not Merleau-Ponty) due to the centrality that Sartre gave to the subject. Other commentators have argued that Foucault's remarks in these contexts are almost certainly directed at the transcendental phenomenology of Edmund Husserl, not the existential phenomenology of Merleau-Ponty (see, e.g., McQuillan 2011, 39–49; Gutting [2003] 2008; cf. Oksala 2005). Indeed, Gutting ([2003] 2008), in an entry on Foucault in *The Stanford Encyclopedia of Philosophy*, writes that Foucault was enthralled by the French avant-garde literature of authors such as Georges Bataille and Maurice Blanchot, in which he found the experiential concreteness of existential phenomenology.

Bill Hughes and Kevin Patterson, who draw heavily upon Merleau-Ponty in their 1997 phenomenological study of disability, acknowledge that an approach to disability that incorporates Foucault's insights would be a worthwhile way to map the constitution of impairment and examine how regimes of truth about disabled bodies have been central to government of them. These authors have claimed, nevertheless, that such an approach would entail the "theoretical elimination of the material, sensate, palpable body" (Hughes and Patterson 1997, 330). Scully, too, in the 2008 book to which I refer above, criticizes Foucault in this way. For example, after citing the first edition of the collection of essays on Foucault and disability that I edited, Scully asserts that "Foucauldian poststructuralism's" "exclusive commitment to uncovering discourses carries the epistemological risk of missing the stubbornly prediscursive body. (Bodies *are* before they speak or are spoken about.)" (2008, 12; emphasis in Scully). Scully remarks that although attention to the normalizing and naturalizing representations of discourse about disability has been a powerful resource for disability studies, the concentration on discourses becomes problematic "when the idea that there is a biological substrate to embodiment slides out of sight entirely." If this were to happen, she cautions, there would be "nothing to stop theory from becoming untethered from materiality, forgetting that bodies have real constraints (including anatomical and biochemical ones) that limit their redescription or transformation" (7). Absent a biological substrate on which to hang disability, disability theory would, apparently, float free-form in the realm of linguistic idealism.

Historicizing and Relativizing the Disabled Body

The arguments that Hughes and Patterson and Scully articulate in these contexts seem to ignore what Foucault says about the body in the first volume of *The History of Sexuality*, the point of which remarks is

> to show how deployments of power are directly connected to the body—to bodies, functions, physiological processes, sensations, and pleasures; *far from the body [being] effaced, what is needed is to make it visible through an analysis in which the biological and the historical* . . . are bound together in an increasingly complex fashion in accordance with the development of the modern technologies of power that take life as their objective. (1978, 103–4; emphasis added)

Foucault was concerned to historicize the body rather than to eliminate it. Just as Prinz argues that each of our moral values has a history (2007) and that the cause, effects, and embodiment of our drives and emotions are historically and culturally conditioned (Prinz and Tremain 2016), so, too, Foucault argued that conceptions of our bodies, their materiality, their biology, and the significance that we give to these phenomena are bound with the historical conditions of possibility for their constitution. As the aforementioned passage from the history of sexuality series indicates, furthermore, the charge that Hughes and Patterson and Scully direct at Foucault according to which he denies or obscures the sensuous, material character of the body variously begs the question, for the materiality of the body per se (and of impairment, race, sex, and biology in particular) is precisely what philosophy of disability and disability theory must examine rather than straightforwardly assume to be the basis from which inquiry should proceed.

The idea that there is an ahistorical and prediscursive materiality of the body—that is, the very idea of a natural, material human body that exists apart from, and prior to, history and linguistic and social practices and policies, a body that can be immediately and transparently experienced—is itself the product of a certain historically specific discourse about the human being (itself a construction). A historicist and relativist approach to the impaired and disabled body that considers both its materiality and the experience of its materiality as the effects of certain historically specific material conditions—including the contingent force relations immanent to these conditions—can identify, resist, and transform the ways in which these phenomena have material-*ized* it, that is, can identify, resist, and transform the way that these conditions and the force relations immanent to them have materialized the impaired and disabled body as a certain kind of body and, in addition, have materialized impairment and disability as certain kinds of "pathology." To put the point another way, the impaired and disabled body (and its materiality) cannot be dissociated from, nor is it ontologically or temporally antecedent to, the historically contingent discursive practices that have brought it into being—that is, brought it into being as that kind of thing.

In short, the notion that there exists a prediscursive material body that itself is what constrains the redescription and transformation of disabled people's bodies is an idea that philosophers of disability and disability theorists ought to contest. The material "constraints" (including anatomical and biochemical ones) that Scully cautions may go unrecognized if theory were to become detached from materiality have themselves been brought into being as constraints on bodies only within the terms of a culturally and historically specific conception of the body, its materiality, longevity, biochemical composition, appearance, anatomical structure, and so on. Though a truth discourse may seem to innocently describe the phenomena of the human body (its constraints, composition, vulnerabilities, and so on), it significantly contributes to the constitution of that body, its materiality, bodily constraints, corporeal vulnerabilities, and so on. In other words, the redescription and transformation of bodies are not determined by their putatively "prediscursive" material constraints per se; rather, the extent to which, in what ways, and even whether redescription and transformation of material bodies can take place is always already circumscribed and delimited by the historically contingent conception of the body (and the style of reasoning from which that conception emerged) that effectively brings into being the facts, laws, and norms about its material constraints, restrictions, strengths, and so on in the first place.

The materiality of the body is not the antecedent a priori of the body's categorization; rather, in this historical context, the materiality of the body is its regulative consequent. As Butler points out in an oft-quoted remark, "there is no reference to a pure body which is not at the same time a further formation of that body" (1993, 10). Scientific facts about the human body are not beyond the reach of the genealogical approach that I recommend. Insofar as there is no reference to a pure body that is not itself constitutive of that body, scientific facts materialize the body that they are claimed to (merely) discover and represent. The articulation of scientific accounts about the anatomy and biochemistry of human beings is an embedded and value-laden human enterprise that can be appropriately addressed only if "scientific" discourses are understood as performative and intertwined with other ("nonscientific") historically contingent and shifting discourses in a complex matrix of force relations that generate institutional practices; asymmetries of social power; modes of subjectivity, experience, and identity; social policy decisions; instruments of medical knowledge; administrative models and classifications; intersubjective relations; and so on.

Let me underscore that our self-perceptions and self-understandings, behavior, habits, and so on, as well as courses of possible action from which we may choose, are not independent of the descriptions available to us under which we may act; nor do the available descriptions occupy some vacuous discursive space. In another context, Joshua Knobe (2017) has pointed out that experimental studies in cognitive science show that redefinition of the distinction between normal and abnormal, for example, can change the possibilities of what information people take into consideration and even what actions they take on the basis of this information. Indeed, it is by now a truism in some philosophical quarters that intentional action always takes place under a description. Furthermore, descriptions, ideas, and classifications combine to work in a cultural matrix of institutions, practices, power relations, and material interactions between people and things. Although some philosophers dismiss the critique of ableist language in philosophy by arguing that the critique is a distraction from more urgent moral and political issues that surround disability, they do not seem to understand or appreciate the performative character of this ableist language and its embeddedness in concrete practices. Concepts, classifications, and descriptions are never "merely" words and representations that precede what they come to represent, but rather are imbricated in the constitution of (among other things) institutional practices, social policy, intersubjective relations, and medical instruments in ways that structure, that is, *limit*, the field of possible action for humans, including what possible self-perceptions, behavior, and habits become available to them in any given historical moment.

Ideas, descriptions, and classifications are integral elements of modern government. Thus, it is politically hazardous to claim, as proponents of the BSM do, that the category of impairment is prior to, and can be dissociated from, the cultural matrix of contingent governmental practices that bring it into being as that sort of thing—that is, that generate certain phenomena *as* impairment to limit the possible responses to these phenomena. In chapter 5, I show how the materialization of impairment in discourses that surround prenatal testing and screening practices and embryonic stem cell (ESC) research, as well as the technologies themselves, puts in place the productive limits of the field of possible actions—including the behavior of prospective parents, self-perceptions of disabled people, and professional practices of clinicians—that are available to subjects in our present.

Performative Materiality

Rosemarie Garland-Thomson (2011) has in recent years recommended the term *misfit* to refer to what she claims is a new "feminist materialist disability concept." As Garland-Thomson explains it, the idea of a misfit and the situation of misfitting "elaborate a materialist feminist understanding of disability by extending a consideration of how the particularities of embodiment interact with their environment in its broadest sense, to include both its spatial and temporal aspects." "Material feminism," she asserts, "expands the idea of social construction of reality toward a materialist-discursive understanding of phenomena and matter" (592). Such a material feminism, Garland-Thomson writes, emphasizes what Barad calls "interactive becoming" (Barad 2008, 146, in Garland-Thomson 2011, 592), which is a kind of becoming that understands the fundamental units of being not as words and things or subjects and objects, but rather as dynamic phenomena produced through entangled and shifting forms of agency that are inherent in all materiality (Garland-Thomson 2011, 592). Referring to Barad's work, Garland-Thomson states that this sort of materialist-discursive understanding is a "corrective move" that "shifts concepts such as Butlerian performativity toward the material and away from the linguistic-semiotic-interpretive turn in critical theory according to which every thing tends to be understood as (in Barad's words) 'a matter of language or some other form of cultural representation'" (Barad 2008, 120, in Garland-Thomson 2011, 592). In other words, Garland-Thomson says, the concept of misfit reflects the shift of emphasis within feminist theory from the discursive to the material, whereby analytical focus centers on the co-constituting relationship between flesh and the environment (594).

In order to elaborate this materialist concept of misfit, Garland-Thomson makes three arguments: (1) "the concept of misfit emphasizes the particularity of varying lived embodiments and avoids a theoretical generic disabled body that can dematerialize if social and architectural barriers no longer disable it"; (2) "the concept of misfit clarifies the current feminist critical conversation about universal vulnerability and dependence"; and (3) "the concept of misfitting as a spatial and perpetually temporal relationship confers agency and value on disabled subjects at risk of social devaluation by highlighting adaptability, resourcefulness, and subjugated knowledge as potential effects of misfitting" (592). In the terms of misfitting, Garland-Thomson asserts, "the materiality that matters involves the encounter between bodies with particular shapes and capabilities and the particular shape and structure of the world" (594).

Garland-Thomson's term *misfit* has become a widely cited addition to the toolbox of disability theory insofar as it seems to aptly capture the experiential reality and circumstances in which disabled people often find themselves. Introduction of the idea of misfit has sparked renewed interest in materialist approaches within philosophy of disability and disability studies, encouraging other influential disability theorists to elaborate their own "post-poststructuralist" approaches. Nevertheless, it is not at all clear that Garland-Thomson's claims about misfitting, nor that the work of disability theorists (such as Siebers and Scully) with whom she associates these claims, "fit" in any recognizably coherent way with the assumptions that underlie Barad's material-discursive feminism; that is, although Garland-Thomson aligns her recent work in feminist disability theory with Barad's material-discursive feminism, it is by no means self-evident that Garland-Thomson's feminist disability theory relies on the presuppositions that a feminist material-discursive conception of disability that draws upon Barad requires. In fact, the assumptions that Garland-Thomson makes in this context run counter to the material-discursive feminism that Barad articulates and are in fact incompatible with what a feminist material-discursive philosophy of disability would promote.

These problems, I want to point out, stem primarily from the fact that Garland-Thomson's materialist-feminist disability theory (like Thomas's) uses a binary distinction between impairment and disability that is analogous to Rubin's sex-gender distinction, as well as a binary distinction between the embodied self and "the world." These distinctions, which are in effect extensions of the age-old nature-culture distinction, require precisely the sort of exclusionary foundationalism that Barad eschews; that is, Barad's (for instance, 2007, 26, 32, 60, 67, 150–51) materialist-discursive feminism leaves no place for binary thinking or for prediscursive substrates (such as sex, impairment, and material body) that putatively provide epistemological and ontological foundations (for, respectively, gender, disability, and the environment). Despite Garland-Thomson's appeal to Barad's concept of material-discursivity, her remarks in this context in effect recuperate the materialism and binary thinking of the BSM, a materialism that leaves no place for the performative character of discourse, as Barad's material-discursive feminism clearly does. Indeed, on Garland-Thomson's understanding of Barad's material-discursive feminism, discursive practices seem to fall out of the equation; that is, Garland-Thomson does not seem to appreciate the performative character that Barad attributes to discursive practices, nor does she seem to understand the important role that the performative character of discursive practices plays in Barad's agential realism. Hence, I want to point out that, contra Garland-Thomson, the actual targets of Barad's critique with respect to the "undue influence" that language has had on critical theory are representationalism and correspondence theories of truth, not "Butlerian performativity" (as Garland-Thomson refers to it). In "Posthumanist Performativity," Barad writes,

> A *performative* understanding of discursive practices challenges the representationalist belief in the power of words to represent pre-existing things. Performativity, properly construed, is not an invitation to turn everything into words; on the contrary, performativity is precisely a contestation of the excessive power granted to language to determine what is real. Hence, in ironic contrast to the misconception that would equate performativity with a form of linguistic monism that takes language to be the stuff of reality, performativity is actually a contestation of the unexamined habits of mind that grant language and other forms of representation more power in determining our ontologies than they deserve. The move toward performative alternatives to representationalism shifts the focus from questions of correspondence between descriptions and reality (e.g., do they mirror nature or culture?) to matters of practices/doings/actions. (2008, 106; emphasis in Barad)

Garland-Thomson allows that the binary distinctions that she draws are unsatisfactory ("limited"); rather than bite the bullet with respect to the foundationalism of these distinctions, however, she takes recourse in an appeal to consequentialist considerations in order to justify her endorsement and advancement of the impairment-disability distinction and its incorporation into her materialist feminist disability theory, describing the distinction between impairment and disability as "theoretically groundbreaking" and the feminist sex-gender distinction that influenced the articulation of the impairment-disability distinction in some circles as "useful" (Garland-Thomson 2011, 591–92). Such a theoretical move, while expedient for the advancement of Garland-Thomson's argument, nevertheless renders the argument conceptually incoherent. Indeed, my own claims about the materialization and naturalization of impairment by and through technologies and strategies of the apparatus of disability, claims that do not rely on the matter of a prediscursive substrate of impairment, are more compatible with a materialist-discursive feminism of the kind that Barad recommends than the social constructivist conception of disability that Garland-Thomson has produced.

Historicizing and Relativizing Materiality

Nevertheless, when we adopt a historicist and relativist approach to the phenomena (including the materiality) of the body in general and the disabled body in particular, we can recognize that a materialist-discursive understanding is neither the fact of the matter about bodies, nor a true story or more accurate description about them, but rather another chapter in the history book of how this, here, now, was once possible. To put the point another way, the materiality of the body and, indeed, the very idea of materialism and recognition of materiality are historical artifacts. In short, the concept of a material body is a historically specific production whose contextual and cultural significance is variously dependent upon an array of historically contingent scientific, social-scientific, medical, legal, popular, and administrative discourses. Although in this historical and cultural context the body is thought of primarily in developmental and material terms, in another historical and cultural context, in earlier contexts, in non-Western contexts, and, presumably, in subsequent historical contexts, it was, is, and will be thought of quite differently, be investigated quite differently, be described quite differently, and so on. A historicist and relativist genealogical approach to the body shows that the concept of the body—the mechanical body in one historical moment, the normalized body in another moment, and the developmental body in yet another moment—has not been stable, not even over the last two centuries, nor have practices to observe, understand, manipulate, and control the body, nor subjective experiences of it, remained invariable. On the contrary, conceptions of the body and experiences of it have varied tremendously (McWhorter 2007, 4–5, 17). As McWhorter writes,

> Foucault the Nietzschean genealogist never says there is no body; he simply looks at the historical record to see how the concept "the body" has functioned in relation to the political, social, and economic forces in which it appeared. Nietzsche never found a time before evil; Foucault does not find a time before the body, but he does discover that the concept has altered a great deal over the centuries and has functioned very differently in different contexts. This fact . . . *tends* to upset the notion that the body exists somehow beneath language as a biological given, but it does not refute it. What it does do is undermine claims to definitive knowledge of the body by creating awareness—some might say a suspicion—that current claims are no more "untainted" by power relations than the claims of previous generations and that they, too, may pass away. (4–5; emphasis in McWhorter)

Historically speaking, significant shifts and changes in perceptions and theories about the body go hand-in-hand with momentous shifts and changes in styles of reasoning (Hacking 1992b, 1; 2002). Recall that, as Hacking (1992b, 10–11) points out, styles of reasoning bring into being new types of objects, individuated with the style, which had not previously been noticeable among the things that exist. New clinical discourses that emerged with the diagnostic style of reasoning in the late eighteenth century created the modern body as a product of medical examination and disciplinary power and continue to have direct (and indirect) implications for the classification of certain people as abnormal and in need of repair and transformation. For example, the concept of "medical police," which emerged in Germany in 1764, instituted a system for the observation of pathology and standardization of medical knowledge and practice, as well as standardization of medical education and instruction. This standardization of medicine, which spread to all of Europe, was imperative, for beginning in the eighteenth century (the historical moment in which biopower began to emerge), human existence, human behavior, and the human body were brought into an increasingly dense and important network of medicalization that allowed fewer and fewer things to escape its attention. Disease, for instance, came to be considered a political and economic problem for social collectivities, and they sought to resolve it as a matter of policy (Foucault 2003d, 320–29).

Urban medicine from the mid-eighteenth century on was nothing more than an improvement on the politico-medical schema of the quarantine at the end of the Middle Ages in which medicine's power consisted of distributing individuals side-by-side, isolating them, individualizing them, observing them, monitoring their state of health, checking to see whether they remained alive or were dead, and in this way maintained society in a compartmentalized space, closely observable and controllable, by means of a painstaking record of all events that occurred. Gone were the bad old days when, to purify the common city space, the discovery of a case of leprosy would result in the diseased subject's immediate expulsion from that city space and exile to a gloomy place inhabited only by other polluted and defective individuals. Driven by the diagnostic style, the public hygiene schema that appeared, especially in France, from the second half of the eighteenth century onward replaced the previous religious model of medicine with a military model that depended on a meticulous diagnosis, analysis, and inspection of the city, that is, on a continuous surveillance and recording of it (Foucault 2003d, 320–29).

A mechanism of biopower, the diagnostic style of reasoning introduced new modes of perceiving and understanding that have effectively brought the modern Western body and its materiality into being, that is, have brought the modern Western body into being as that type of thing. The clinical and administrative discourses that were introduced by the diagnostic style have formulated, categorized, and delimited this body, in turn subjecting it to new laws, measurements, and causal relations that demarcated divisions between normal and abnormal, sick and healthy, sane and insane to ensure the stability of the body's state of health, promote its longevity, and improve its productive success. Hence the diagnostic style has created and caused to emerge new objects of knowledge and information with respect to this body—among which impairment, development, and materiality are only a few—as well as new sentences ("I have a disability") about the body's functions, its characteristics, forces, elements, and capacities, and new evidence such as "symptoms" with which to evaluate these candidates for truth and falsehood. Indeed, the new clinical discourse about the body articulated by and through this style of reasoning introduced new, inescapable rituals into daily life, all of which were performative insofar as they became indispensable to the self-understandings and self-perceptions of the participants in this new discourse. When we adopt Hacking's insight that styles of reasoning are self-authenticating, we can understand how the belief took hold that the descriptions elaborated in the course of these examinations truly grasped and reflected reality, that is, we can understand how the diagnostic style—and the medical, juridical, and scientific authorities who employ it—has become the arbiter of the truth and knowledge about the modern body that the style itself brought into being—including the new objects, sentences, laws, and evidence with respect to it—settling what it is to be objective about it. This, then, is how Hacking's idea of styles of reasoning provides robust epistemological scaffolding for Foucault's genealogical approach to subjectivity and the body's materiality.

In this chapter, I showed how genealogy can be used as a tool with which to elaborate a historicist and relativist approach to feminist philosophy of disability. In doing so, I situated genealogical work on disability squarely in philosophical debates that have shaped intellectual thinking in the West, as well as positioned the work in ongoing discussions that have conditioned (Western) academic feminism and disability theory for more than three decades. The relativist and historicist stance on disability that I have sketched has far-reaching implications for claims that moral and political philosophers, cognitive scientists, and bioethicists (among others) advance about disability, as well as for discussions within philosophy about the field's homogeneity, including discussions about the virtual exclusion of disabled philosophers (and disabled philosophers of disability especially) from its ranks. Thus, my discussion in the chapter has advanced the arguments that I aim to unravel in both the reconstructive-conceptual and metaphilosophical spheres of my enquiry. Insofar as the historicist and relativist approach that I have offered can better account for cultural, political, religious, national, generational, social, and moral differences (to name only several) than can alternatives to it, the approach suggests ways to move forward with interventions designed to improve the professional status of disabled philosophers and members of other underrepresented groups, as well as ways to elevate the status of non-Western and Indigenous philosophies in the discipline, in addition to the evident work that such an approach accomplishes at more abstract and theoretical levels.

CHAPTER 4

Foucault, Feminism, Disability

———— ᲈᲐᲐ ————

Feminist Criticism of Foucault

In the previous chapter, I address the main charges that disability theorists direct at Foucault, namely, that he did not offer a conception of subjectivity that could serve as the basis of a disabled people's movement, nor did he provide an account of human corporeal materiality that would enable disability theorists to articulate the differences that disabled embodiment entails. My arguments in the chapter demonstrate that these charges are unsubstantiated, misconstruing some of Foucault's key ideas. I show, for example, that disability theorists commonly misunderstand Foucault's conceptions of the subject and identity and, thus, fail to appreciate their subversive potential. I also show that some disability theorists misrepresent Foucault's claims about the body, characterizing them as idealist rather than as historicist. My arguments in the chapter oppose the ahistorical and universalist foundationalism of the charges that disability theorists direct at Foucault. Indeed, my reconstructive-conceptual argument in the chapter is designed to demonstrate that Foucault's historicism and nominalism can be used to explain how the apparatus of disability has naturalized and materialized impairment in historically specific and culturally relative ways.

As I note in the third chapter, some charges that feminists direct at Foucault resemble the charges that disability theorists direct at him. I point out, furthermore, that to a great extent my arguments against these charges from disability theorists could therefore be regarded as implicit responses to such charges from feminist philosophers and theorists. In this chapter, I consider additional charges that feminists direct at Foucault and the authors who draw upon his insights, charges according to which his work is sexist, androcentric, and exemplifies male biases. Feminist charges that Foucault's work in general and his history of sexuality in particular are masculinist, sexist, and reflect male biases vex feminist philosophers of disability who believe that his claims about (for instance) the constitution of subjects, genealogy, discipline, and regimes of truth imbue their feminist analyses of disability and ableism with complexity and richness, as well as inspire theoretical sophistication and intellectual rigor in the fields of philosophy of disability and disability studies more generally. Nevertheless, a feminist philosophy of disability would ignore these feminist criticisms of Foucault at its own peril.

In this chapter, therefore, I address what I take to be the main source of these critiques. Then, I narrow the focus of the chapter to concentrate on Foucault's treatment of the nineteenth-century case of an itinerate farmhand, Charles Jouy, who came to be accused of rape and sexual abuse. Various feminists claim that Foucault's treatment of the Jouy case demonstrates the masculinism and sexism that condition his corpus of writing in general and his work on the history of sexuality especially. I argue that these criticisms are unsubstantiated, relying in some cases upon readings of Foucault that a great deal of textual evidence contradicts. I end the chapter by considering the conditions of possibility for discussion of the Jouy case in feminist philosophy and indeed for the momentum that the discussion has gained in the field, as demonstrated by the number of articles about the incident involving Jouy and Adam that have appeared in highly esteemed venues in the field.

Foucault and Gender

A principal argument—if not the principal argument—that feminists direct at Foucault is that his history of sexuality disregarded the significance of ("social") gender. The first volume of *The History of Sexuality* has been the main target of these criticisms. In the final chapter of this book, Foucault introduced a reversal of the causal relation between sex and sexuality that the feminist sex-gender distinction institutes.[1] Whereas the feminist sex-gender distinction assumes that the category of "sex" is a self-evident fact of nature and biology from which gender and sexuality follow, Foucault argued that "sex is the most speculative, most ideal, and most internal element in a deployment of sexuality organized by power in its grip on bodies and their materiality, their forces, energies, sensations, and pleasures." "The notion of 'sex,'" he claimed, "made it possible to group together, in an artificial unity, anatomical elements, biological functions, conducts, sensations, and pleasures, and it enabled one to make use of this fictitious unity as a causal principle, an omnipresent meaning." With this innovative reversal of the terms of debate about sex, gender, and sexuality, Foucault posited sexuality as the "real historical formation [that] gave rise to the notion of sex" (1978, 157), that is, as the apparatus of force relations that produces the ideal of "sex" as the foundational property that sexuality seeks to evoke or express. For Foucault, in other words, "sex" was an *effect* of force relations that comes to pass as the *cause* of a naturalized human desire. Sex, though it initially emerged as a mechanism of the apparatus of sexuality, has itself become an apparatus of force relations with which the apparatus of sexuality (among other apparatuses) is mutually constitutive and reinforcing.

Foucault's seemingly counterintuitive intervention into discussions about sex and sexuality presented a challenge to conventional understandings of these terms, a challenge that one might have expected feminists to welcome. Indeed, Foucault's reversal of the causal relations between sex and sexuality seemed to anticipate Butler's transformative claims about these categories. Regardless, one might have expected feminists to applaud the way that Foucault historicized and relativized the category of sex. Some feminists argue, however, that a significant and troubling result of this reversal of sex and sexuality is the separation of gender from both these terms. E. L. McCallum explains this feminist objection to the reversal thus: "By refocusing the foundation of the debate around the reversal of the order of sex and sexuality, Foucault seem[ed] to place an inordinately narrow emphasis upon the relation of these two terms at the expense of considering any others—most notably 'gender'" (1996, 79). De Lauretis argues, for instance, that insofar as Foucault relied upon the conceptual premise that sexuality is a technology of sex, but not gender, "[his] theory, in fact, excludes, though it does not preclude, the consideration of gender" (1987, 3). Foucault's "critique of the technology of sex," de Lauretis writes, "does not take into account its different solicitation of male and female subjects, or the conflicting investments of men and women in the discourses and practices of sexuality" (ix). In Foucault, de Lauretis states, sexuality is not understood as gendered, that is, "as having a male form and a female

form, but [rather] is taken to be one and the same for all—and conse-
quently male" (14). De Lauretis argues, furthermore, that even when
Foucault located sexuality in women's bodies—as he did by pointing out
that women's bodies have historically been regarded as "thoroughly saturated with sexuality"—he perceived sexuality as an attribute or property
of the male (14). One implication of de Lauretis's criticisms is that Foucault, in keeping with the Western philosophical tradition, made allegedly universal claims and adopted a purportedly neutral stance, while
advancing an androcentric position that assumes males to be the norm.
In another context, Margaret McLaren, noting that several feminists
have responded to Foucault's "neglect of sex and gender issues" (2002,
92) by extending his ideas to discuss these feminist concerns, states that
this extension of his ideas for feminist purposes "helps to remedy the
gender gap" (97) in his work (also see Koopman 2017a).

To assess these accusations of androcentrism and masculinism, I want
to introduce remarks that Foucault made in the closing pages of *The
History of Sexuality*, volume 1 (1978). In part 4 of this introduction to his
history of sexuality series, Foucault identified "four great strategic uni-
ties which, beginning in the eighteenth century, formed specific mechanisms of knowledge and power centering on sex" (103). One of the
"four great lines of attack" (146) that Foucault identified was "the hysterization of women's bodies," which he described as a threefold process
whereby the feminine body was analyzed and understood as thoroughly
saturated with sexuality, was integrated into the sphere of medical practices, by reason of a pathology intrinsic to it, and was placed in "organic
communication" with: (1) "the social body (whose regulated fecundity
it was supposed to ensure)"; (2) "the family space (of which it had to
be a substantial and functional element)"; and (3) "the life of children
(which it produced and had to guarantee, by virtue of a biologic-moral
responsibility that extended through the entire period of the children's
education)." He pointed out, furthermore, that the archetypal Mother,
embodied in actual women who supposedly instantiate her negative
image of the "nervous woman," constituted the most visible form of this
hysterization (104). Through the process of the hysterization of women
(and their bodies), "sex" became defined in three ways, Foucault wrote:
first, as an intrinsic property that men and women have in common;
second, as an intrinsic property that men possess par excellence and
that women lack; and third, as that property which, by itself, constitutes
woman's body, ordering it entirely in terms of its reproductive functions

and keeping it in a state of constant agitation with respect to the effects of that function (153).

Notice that Foucault's remarks with respect to the threefold process of women's hysterization precisely describe what feminists who assume the sex-gender distinction would identify as women's gendering in a specific historical moment and cultural context, in this case, late eighteenth-century France. In that eighteenth-century context, Foucault pointed out, women became subjected to a distinct medical-psychiatric discourse and to a discourse on motherhood that rendered them responsible for the lives of their own children and the life of society at large, that is, a discourse on motherhood that was both individualizing and totalizing. Thus, it seems evident that Foucault did account for the epistemological space that feminist discourse refers to as "gender," even though he did not actually use the term *gender* in his analyses. In addition, it seems evident that his transposition of sex and sexuality laid the groundwork for both the reversal of the causal relation between the categories of sex and gender and the pathbreaking argument about gender performativity that Butler makes some years later. Indeed, it seems as if feminists who argue that Foucault fails to account for gender in his history of sexuality, that is, who argue that his history of sexuality incorporates masculinist and androcentric biases, disregard the substance of his remarks about women in the first volume of the history of sexuality series.

Now, an interlocutor could, of course, acknowledge that Foucault addressed women and gender in the first volume of the history of sexuality series yet argue nevertheless that his treatment of women, gender, and sexuality in the book and elsewhere in his histories of sexuality was inadequate. I maintain, however, that the general remarks that I cite above seem both adequate and appropriate, given that Foucault intended the first volume to be only the introduction to a projected series of texts, that is, intended it to simply introduce themes that he subsequently would develop in later works. It is well known that prior to his untimely and unexpected death in 1984, Foucault had planned to write a volume in the series on the history of sexuality that would specifically concern the issue of "the hysterization of women's bodies." In a widely read interview whose English translation appeared in 1977 under the title "Power and Sex," Foucault remarked,

> For a long time [doctors] tried to pin women to their sex. For centuries they were told: "You are nothing but your sex." And this sex, doctors

added, is fragile, almost always sick and inducing illness. "You are man's sickness." And towards the 18th century this ancient movement ran wild, ending in a pathologization of woman: the female body became a medical object *par excellence*. I will try later to write the history of this immense "gynecology" in the broad sense of the term. (1977c, 115)

These remarks indicate that Foucault had a keen understanding of the social constitution of illness (an element of the apparatus of disability) and its imbrication in the differential gendering of women and men in the West and that he aimed to devote future work to the articulation of this natural- izing and gendered history. In short, there seems to be ample reason to refuse to endorse the claim that Foucault's history of sexuality in general is androcentric, masculinist, and relies upon sexist biases. Nevertheless, I shall now turn to examine the charge that Foucault's treatment of the case of the nineteenth-century farmhand Charles Jouy acutely exemplifies his male biases and sexism. No one aspect of Foucault's oeuvre has been more con- sistently and vehemently subjected to the charges of masculinism and male bias than his reference to Jouy, who, at the age of about forty, engaged in "sexual" activity with a girl, Sophie Adam, was reported to juridical authori- ties, in turn was handed over to medical and psychiatric experts, and sub- sequently was incarcerated in Maréville (the location of the main insane asylum of the Nancy region at the time) for the remainder of his life.

The Case of Charles Jouy

In the first volume of *The History of Sexuality*, Foucault described the encounters between Jouy and Adam and the repercussions of these events in this way:

> One day in 1867, a farm hand from the village of Lapcourt, who was somewhat simple-minded . . . obtained a few caresses from a little girl, just as he had done before and seen done by the village urchins around him; for, at the edge of the wood, or in the ditch by the road leading to Saint-Nicolas, they would play the familiar game called "curdled milk." . . . What is the significant thing about this story? The pettiness of it all; the fact that this everyday occurrence in the life of village sexuality, these inconsequential bucolic pleasures, could become, from a certain time, the object not only of a collective intol-

erance but of a judicial action, a medical intervention, a careful clinical examination, and an entire theoretical elaboration. (1978, 31)

Feminists have been virtually unanimous in their condemnation of
Foucault's "sexist" interpretation and flippant treatment of the incidents
involving Jouy and Adam; that is, they largely agree about the following:
(1) insofar as these sexual encounters took place between a female child
and a male adult, they involved a fundamentally coercive and threaten-
ing power differential whereby the male adult occupied a position of
dominance and control relative to the girl; (2) the incidents amounted
to the sexual abuse and rape of a female child by a male adult; and furthermore (3) Foucault's "casual" use of the incidents and their consequences in order to mark the consolidation of a new regime of sexuality evinces an arrogant "male and adult" insensitivity to the impact that
sexual abuse and rape have in the lives of girls and women. My aim is
to show that this accepted feminist interpretation of the Jouy case and
Foucault's use of it (hereafter referred to as the AFI) relies upon misunderstandings of his remarks about the case. I argue that this misinterpretation of the case does not support the broader claim that his work
in general and his history of sexuality in particular are masculinist and
rely upon sexist male biases. To argue in this way, I provide an account of
Jouy's identity and the incidents involving Jouy and Adam that takes seriously insights derived from philosophy of disability and critical disability
theory and history, as well as draws upon nominalist assumptions that I
outlined in earlier chapters. When Foucault's treatment of the Jouy case
is carefully considered through a nominalist approach to philosophy of
disability and critical disability theory and history, the AFI unravels and
should be recognized as textually unsubstantiated, theoretically misguided, and politically limited (and limiting).

Linda Alcoff (1996) has articulated the most impassioned critique of
Foucault's presentation of the case of Jouy. Alcoff designed her discussion of the Jouy case and Foucault's use of it to enable a broader critique
of his "incorrect, politically dangerous" position on sex with minors,
which position on "pedophilia," she maintains, puts into relief the problematic character of the relations among power, discourse, knowledge,
and pleasure in his more comprehensive work on sexuality (101). Alcoff,
who refers to the case of Jouy as a case of "child molesting," claims that
there are two reasons why Foucault included it in the introduction to his
history of sexuality: first, to suggest that, historically, the designation *pedo*-

phile was the paradigm category of "dangerous individuals," and second, to mark the moment in the history of sexuality when sex was brought under the jurisdiction of expert discourses in the human sciences, that is, when previously mundane behaviors and acts, extracted orally in and through the confessional, became "the business of the law," and the sexuality of children came into view as an urgent problem (102–3). Alcoff emphasizes that Foucault used the Jouy case in order to show that the medical and legal responses to the sexual activity between Jouy and Adam were peculiar and inappropriate, exceeded its significance, and were generated through and by discursive structures of domination. To substantiate this claim, she points out that Foucault underscored what he regarded as the exaggerated character of these responses to the sexual activity between Jouy and Adam by describing the "expert" medical examinations, done to identify signs of degenerescence, that Jouy was forced to undergo— including measurement of his "brainpan," inspection of his anatomy, and study of his facial bone structure—and the invasive and detailed psychiatric questioning about his "thoughts, inclinations, habits, sensations, and opinions" (Foucault 1978, 31) to which he was subjected. This account has led Alcoff (1996, 106) to contend that although Foucault was concerned to stress that the farmhand Jouy was eventually incarcerated for the rest of his days, he was evidently unconcerned about the consequences of the incidents for the young girl Adam. Indeed, Alcoff claims that Foucault's account of the incidents between Jouy and Adam and their aftermath seems designed to elicit sympathy for Jouy.

Alcoff asserts that Foucault's narrative encourages the view that adults who engage in sexual activity with children are motivated by sexual needs that they cannot satisfy with their peers, and moreover, that the children who participate in these acts do so willingly, are not coerced, and may even initiate the acts themselves. Foucault's narrative, she claims, replicates and reinforces most of this culture's mistaken beliefs about the nature and character of sexual practices between adults and children. Foucault's readiness to make these assumptions about the incidents between Jouy and Adam manifests, in Alcoff's words, "typical male and adult patterns of epistemic arrogance," for, as she puts it, he "lacked sufficient evidence to warrant his claims about the girl's participation in or feeling about" the incident (1996, 108). She asserts, furthermore, that Foucault both rejected the view that sexual relations between adults and children are always harmful for the children involved and argued against legal interventions in adult-child sexual relations and the "consensus" position of psychiatry that such relations, in whatever form they take, will, inevitably, produce trauma for children and, invariably, indicate pathological problems in the adult. Noting that Foucault mentioned that Jouy "decently" gave Adam "a few pennies" after one encounter, Alcoff asks, if these sexual relations were reciprocally desired and pleasurable for both Jouy and Adam, then why was money exchanged to ensure the girl's participation? "Whose point of view is silently assumed when one determines that the prostituting of small girls is a petty and trivial event?" (100, 108). Alcoff readily acknowledges that, to be sure, children can have a variety of sexual feelings and that some children may even act on them; she emphasizes, however, that adult-child sex is, nevertheless, wrong because children occupy different social positions than adults and are more vulnerable than them, regardless of whether the children have acted on their sexual feelings. This "ubiquitous inequality," she states, will always structure the interpretation by adults of children's behavior and expression. As Alcoff explains,

> It is obvious that children are disempowered relative to adults in both discursive and extradiscursive ways. Their discourse is subordinate and subjugated, and their actions are constrained within systems of possibility set out beforehand without their participation. . . . Their position vis-à-vis adults can therefore be characterized by its dependency, vulnerability, and relative powerlessness. . . . This results not simply from the fact that children are usually smaller and physically weaker but because they are economically dependent on adults for their livelihood, and for a thousand other things. (122–23)

The influence of Alcoff's critique of the Jouy case (and Foucault's use of it) is evident in Jana Sawicki's discussion of the case in an online review of *Abnormal* (Foucault 2003a), the 2003 English translation of a lecture course that Foucault gave at the Collège de France in 1974–75. Sawicki explains that she devotes a large portion of her review to Foucault's treatment of the case of the "proto-sex offender Jouy" in his March 19 lecture of the course for two reasons: first, because the more condensed example of the case that Foucault used in *The History of Sexuality*, volume 1, has led some feminists to be skeptical about the value of his history of sexuality; and second, because the case played a central role in Foucault's thinking about sex during this period of his work. She points out that although Foucault professedly used the case of Jouy in the first volume of his history of sexuality as an example of "the spread of social control over sex as an omnipresent and constant danger," feminists have reacted skeptically to this use of the case, which they believe exemplifies, as she puts it, "a gender-blind insensitivity to the real danger that Jouy's pleasures may have posed for [Adam]" (Sawicki 2005). As I have indicated, feminists also use the case to demonstrate Foucault's general failure to account for gender in his work on the history of sexuality more broadly.

Sawicki points out that in the 1974–75 lectures (which were situated between the publication of *Discipline and Punish* and *The History of Sexuality*, volume 1) Foucault offered more detailed analysis of themes central to the books than he did in the books themselves. In these lectures, Sawicki remarks, "Foucault claims that the abnormal individual represents a synthesis of three figures (only two of which receive treatment in these lectures): the monster, the onanist and the incorrigible individual, each of which is the correlate of different sciences and each of which has a distinct history." Forms of abnormality, which came into view with the spread of disciplinary techniques, offered an inexhaustible domain of intervention to psychiatry, whose original function, she says, was to oversee public hygiene and protect society from illness. In its early stage, Sawicki writes, psychiatry occasionally intervened in legal settings to assess the degree of madness in rare and monstrous crimes; she notes, however, that the emergence in the second half of the nineteenth century of the abnormal individual whose actions are subject to involuntary and spontaneous natural impulses enabled these psychiatrists to explain the motiveless crime that the theory of delirium of earlier alienists had been unable to do. In the same historical context in which this transformation in the medico-legal realm took place, Sawicki remarks, abnormality was also sexualized. The adolescent masturbator became the basis for the expansion of medical control within the family insofar as seemingly endless causal power to produce illness was attributed to the act of masturbation. In other words, childhood sexuality became accorded tremendous potential for pathology (Sawicki 2005).

Once Sawicki has outlined what she perceives to be the general structure of Foucault's approach in the 1974–75 lecture course, she introduces her discussion of the Jouy case. Like Alcoff, Sawicki is troubled that Foucault minimizes the serious nature of the sexual activity between Jouy and Adam and the impact that these incidents would have had on the latter. She points out, for instance, that although Jouy was a man of forty (albeit, she says, "one whom adult women couldn't take seriously"), Foucault nevertheless concluded, "We have here a village infantile sexuality of the open air, the side of the road, and the undergrowth that legal medicine is cheerfully psychiatrizing" (2003d, 295, in Sawicki 2005). Like Alcoff, furthermore, Sawicki draws attention to the remarks that Foucault made about the Jouy case in *The History of Sexuality*, volume 1, to ask, were these sexual exchanges really "inconsequential" and "petty," let alone pleasurable for Adam, as Foucault would have us believe?

Sawicki allows that the discussion of the Jouy case in *Abnormal* is instructive insofar as it captures the historical transformation from a criminal psychiatry that is oriented toward identification of transient psychological illness to a criminal psychiatry that is oriented toward identification of a permanent, congenital condition of abnormality, an arrested development that, in Jouy's case, was manifested in his inability to control his sexual tendencies, permanently deformed sexual instincts that were themselves signified externally on and by his deformed anatomy. She argues, nevertheless, that Foucault's tendency to dismiss the incidents as "inconsequential," taken together with both his suggestion that Jouy may have been the victim of Adam (implied by his repeated references to the fact that Adam had previous sexual liaisons with adolescent boys on the edge of the field) and his suggestion that she appeared not to mind (she didn't report the incidents to anyone) "smacks of masculinist incredulity about the seriousness and reality of rape." Indeed, Sawicki asserts that Foucault's account implies that there was one victim of the incidents between Jouy and Adam and that victim was Jouy. Adam's fate is not an issue at all for Foucault, Sawicki states, though he does, she observes, mention that members of the village recommended that Adam be sent to a house of correction for her "bad behavior." Johanna Oksala, who agrees with Sawicki that Jouy is the only victim in Foucault's story, has remarked that whereas the consequences for Jouy of the sexual interactions with Adam demonstrate that in the late nineteenth century the adult experience of pedophilia was effectively medicalized as a structural abnormality, the suggestion that Adam should, until she came of age, be confined to a house of correction for her indecent behavior indicates that a corresponding psychiatrization of the child's experience of pedophilia was not yet conceivable (Oksala 2011, 2016).

Should we conclude from Foucault's apparent insensitivity to the actual gravity of rape that the incidents between Jouy and Adam were genuinely innocent? Should we believe that the sexual lives of adolescents were perfectly acceptable before the introduction of the corrective and protective measures of the new form of knowledge-power that Foucault identified? Was Jouy harmless? Sawicki contends that Foucault's use of the Jouy case prevents us from asking these questions. She claims that the genealogical function of the case is, for Foucault, to highlight a transformation in the discursive practices about abnormality, a transformation that marks the emergence of an intensification of the interest in infantile sexuality and abnormal sexual tendencies and of policing sexual behavior. In other words, Foucault's use of the Jouy case is part of a "history of the present" (to use his terminology) in which he historicized our preoccupation in the present with the development, that is, the psycho-sexual development, of children. Thus, to appeal to present-day concerns about Adam's choices, about the effect on her development of the exchange of sexual caresses for money or the fact that she may even have been raped, would beg one of the questions that Foucault raises. In any case, Sawicki, like Alcoff, contends that Foucault's failure to address Adam's fate, in combination with his suspicion that she was, in some sense, not even rapeable, undermines the critical effect of his discourse on abnormality. Sawicki grants that these "bucolic" pleasures may have been more pleasurable, or less damaging, in an earlier era, that is, before they became the intense focus of this particular normalizing power-knowledge; she argues, however, that the purpose of genealogy is not to endorse the past but rather to interrogate the present (Sawicki 2005). Nor, I would add, is the purpose of genealogy to eliminate the specificity of the past by generalizing the specificity of the present.

Against the AFI

Recall that Alcoff claims that Foucault used the Jouy case in his history of sexuality in part to indicate that the designation *pedophile* comprised the paradigm category of "dangerous individuals." Recall also that Sawicki describes Jouy in similar, though more general, terms as the "proto-sex offender" and suggestively asks whether we should regard him as "harmless." As my remarks in the previous section show, furthermore, Oksala (like Alcoff) describes Jouy's experience of the sexual activity with Adams as "pedophilia," a consequence of which was its medicalization as a structural abnormality (Oksala 2011, 2016). In this section, I want to show why both the claim that Jouy was a "pedophile" and the claim that the sexual activity between Jouy and Adam represented "pedophilia" to the experts, who examined him, and to Foucault, who wrote about him, ought not to be accepted. If my arguments are compelling, then there is further reason for feminists to relinquish the belief that Foucault's work is infused with masculinist and sexist biases. To make a convincing case, I shall first consider the etymology of the relevant terms, namely, *pedophile* and *pedophilia*.

In the introduction to his history of sexuality, Foucault pointed out that in the nineteenth century certain sexual acts became characterized as perversions. Within the same historical moment, as his work showed, sexuality came to be regarded as the key to the subject's identity. In other words, perverse acts (perversions) came to be regarded as the manifestation of a perverse sexuality performed by a certain type of subject, namely, a pervert. Since perverse acts (perversions) were regarded as the products of a certain type of subject (namely, perverts), the identification of perversions (perverse acts) required the identification of these subjects, these perverts, who performed them. Indeed, the identification of perversions, it was believed, would enable an understanding of the pervert himself and hence enable an understanding of the motivation to commit perverse acts (see C. Taylor 2009). Chloë Taylor, in her provocative discussion of the Jouy case and the criminology of rape, explains that "just as the offender became a delinquent, so the sexual agent became a pervert, an individual with a determining sexuality, a being whose very existence was defined by sexual acts that he desired or performed, and whose existence, like that of the delinquent, was constituted as an object of scientific knowledge" (2009, 8). The experts who investigated the Jouy case regarded the acts in which Jouy had engaged not as the result of his social position or circumstances, but rather as the inevitable consequences of his being, body, and self. As Taylor explains it, Jouy provided these doctors and scientists with the opportunity to gain a clinical understanding of the nature of pedophiles in general. In Foucault's terms, Taylor writes, Jouy was individualized—as a "pedophile"—by power in the process of their interrogations of him. He had not been a pedophile before he began to confess; however, he took on this identity, she writes, because scientists viewed him in this way and made him speak in these terms. Taylor remarks that although we in the modern West did not invent sadism, sex with children, or any of the other acts identified as perversions, we have constituted these acts as identities; that is, we have invented pedophiles, rapists, and other sexual identities (8–9).

Foucault was a nominalist about kinds of people; that is, Foucault held that people do not come naturally—that is, universally and transhistorically—sorted into kinds in accordance with ontologically preexisting categories such as race, gender, sexuality, and disability, or with ontologically predetermined characteristics such as size and color. Rather, as I note in chapter 1, kinds of people come into being because we make them that way by and through the discursive practices that we use to describe them and in which they are inserted. As Hacking has asserted, furthermore, practices constitutive of the subject have "looping effects" (1995, 351–83): people become aware of how they are perceived and classified and the awareness in turn changes their self-perceptions and self-understandings. This theme of the constitution and self-constitution of subjects runs throughout Foucault's writing. Recall that although many people misconstrue Foucault's work, understanding it to be centrally concerned with power, he himself regarded inquiry into the constitution of subjects (how subjects are made up) as the focal point of his theoretical pursuits. In the second chapter of this book, I noted that Foucault often described his genealogical approach to the constitution of subjects as "historical ontologies of ourselves." As a kind of genealogy, historical ontologies excavate subjugated knowledges, social discourses, and institutional practices of the past to show how these knowledges and practices have molded the self-understandings and self-perceptions that we hold in the present. In one respect, Foucault's historical ontologies of deviants such as the modern prisoner, the homosexual, and the pervert represent theoretical elaborations of his nominalist stance. When we take account of the important role that the constitutive effects of bio-power's classifications of deviance especially played in Foucault's thinking, that is, when these aspects of Foucault's nominalism are taken into account and applied to the case of Jouy, the AFI begins to unravel.

The term *paedophilia erotica* was coined in 1886 (close to twenty years after Jouy was apprehended) by Krafft-Ebing in a typology of psychosexual perversion that he used in *Psychopathia Sexualis* (the leading medico-legal textual authority on sexual pathology at the time). A "cerebral neurosis," pedophilia was, according to Krafft-Ebing, a rare form of "paraeasthesia," that is, a form of "misdirected sexual desire" ([1886] 2011). The *Oxford English Dictionary* defines *paedophilia* as "an abnormal, esp[ecially] sexual, love of young children" and attributes the first recorded usage of the word in the English language to the psychiatrist Havelock Ellis in 1906. It indicates, furthermore, that the first recorded use of the word *paedophile* occurred forty-five years later, that is, in 1951. In the following year, 1952, "pedophilia" was included in the first edition of the *Diagnostic and Statistical Manual of Mental Disorders* (*DSM*). Foucault, whose archival erudition was exemplary, would have been well acquainted with the etymologies of these terms. For the nominalist Foucault, therefore, the scientists who examined Jouy could not have treated him as a case of "pedophilia," nor could they have gotten Jouy to recognize himself as a "pedophile." For the nominalist Foucault, when Jouy was apprehended in 1867, pedophiles did not exist, nor was "pedophilia" yet a way to describe the sexual relations that Jouy engaged in with Adam. Hence, it is therefore not at all likely that Foucault would have used the case of Jouy to advance claims about how the experience of "pedophilia" became medicalized as a structural abnormality.

Proponents of the AFI might argue that although the term *pedophile* did not enter the psychiatric lexicon until the mid-twentieth century, adults who desire and engage in sexual activity with minors existed before this time: before this time, there were adults with a pathological sexual desire for children that characteristically led them to use their positions of relative social dominance and personal power to coerce or force children to engage in sexual relations with them. Indeed, proponents of the AFI might challenge my position by pointing out that Foucault's own work, in *The Use of Pleasure* (1985) especially, attests to this historical fact. In other words, proponents of the AFI might argue that even before the term *pedophile* was used to designate the "kind" of adults who desire and engage in sexual relations with children, there were pedophiles (adults who desire and engage in sexual relations with children). They might argue, furthermore, that insofar as the adult Jouy used his position of adult male dominance relative to the girl-child Adam to repeatedly coerce her to masturbate him, used his physical power over her to rape her, and subsequently used his access to financial means to appease her for what he had done, he was a pedophile. In short, one could argue that Jouy's behaviors and actions with respect to Adam were the paradigmatic behaviors and actions of someone who, only eighty-four years later, would be recognized as a pedophile, even if, at the time that the behaviors and actions took place, there was no word to designate him (and his behaviors and actions) as such. I shall now indicate why one ought not to accept these arguments, regardless of whether one refuses Foucault's nominalism in this way or endorses it.

Why did Foucault use the Jouy case in *The History of Sexuality*, volume 1, and *Abnormal*? I contend that no single answer to this question should be offered because Foucault used the Jouy case in the March 19 lecture for a different purpose than he subsequently did in *The History of Sexuality*, volume 1, though ultimately, in both contexts, he aimed to articulate the techniques and mechanisms of a racism of normalization. Remarks that François Ewald and Alessandro Fontana make in the foreword to *Abnormal*, according to which the lectures should not be read as preliminary sketches of the books but rather have "their own status," lend support to my identification of a discrepancy in the uses to which Foucault put the Jouy case (Ewald and Fontana 2003, xiii). That this discrepancy has gone unnoticed and unappreciated by proponents of the AFI is, I maintain, one of the chief reasons why they have misunderstood and hence misrepresented Jouy and his relationship with Adam.

By the time that the English translation of the 1974–75 Collège de France lectures appeared in print (in 2003) under the title *Abnormal,* English-language readers of Foucault were already familiar with the example of the Jouy case that he had used in the first volume of *The History of Sexuality* (published almost three decades earlier) to show the expanding control of sexuality and the intensification of interest in childhood sexuality. By the time *Abnormal* appeared in 2003, furthermore, many feminist philosophers and theorists had also already read Alcoff's scathing feminist critique of Foucault's first use of the case published in English, including her identification of Jouy as a "pedophile" and "dangerous." Nevertheless, remarks that Monique Plaza (1981) earlier made, according to which Foucault (allegedly) said that rape is on par with a punch in the face and advocated the decriminalization of adult-child sexual relations, almost certainly established the milieu for the misapprehension of the case that conditions the AFI and feminist reception of Foucault's work more generally.

Sawicki, Oksala, and other proponents of the AFI assume that Foucault used the case as an example in the lectures to make claims about the widening juridical and medical control over sexuality and the discovery and proliferation of perversions by and through the human sciences, as he (subsequently) did in the first volume of his history of sexuality. Sawicki understands Foucault's 1974–75 lectures to have detailed a historical transformation within forensic psychiatry, that is, a transformation from a forensic psychiatry whose object of inquiry was a transient psychological illness that resulted in rare and monstrous crimes (such as the crime of Henrietta Cornier, who decapitated her neighbor's infant) to a forensic psychiatry whose object was a permanent, congenital condition of abnormality (pedophilia) that gives rise to actions that are involuntary and spontaneous, exemplified in Jouy's inability to control his sexual tendencies; in other words, Foucault used the Jouy case to show how the congenital abnormality that came to be regarded as characteristic of the "sex offender" was psychiatrized. As Sawicki (2005) puts it in her review: Jouy was the prototypical sex offender. Oksala, too, thinks that Foucault used the Jouy case to demonstrate the medicalization, in the second half of the nineteenth century, of pedophilia as a structural abnormality.

Materializing Abnormality

At the outset of the 1974–75 course, Foucault stated that his goal for the course was to study "the emergence of the power of normalization, the way in which it has been formed, the way in which it has established itself without ever resting on a single institution but [rather] by establishing interactions between different institutions, and the way in which it has extended its sovereignty in our society" (2003a, 26). Psychiatry's identification of abnormalities was one (but only one) means through which normalization could be enacted and enforced. Hence, Sawicki and Oksala are correct insofar as they recognize that in the March 19 lecture, Foucault had used the Jouy case to illustrate psychiatry's "discovery" of a permanent abnormality; however, the nineteenth-century psychiatric discovery that Foucault used the case to illustrate was not pedophilia, as they claim, but rather imbecility. Recall that in her review of *Abnormal* Sawicki states that in his 1974–75 lectures Foucault claimed that "the abnormal individual represents a synthesis of three figures (*only two of which receive treatment in these lectures*): the monster, the onanist and the incorrigible individual" (Sawicki 2005; emphasis added). This remark by Sawicki, which at first glance seems to be an equivalent paraphrase of the statement that Foucault makes at the beginning of the March 19 lecture, notably evinces the way that she (and Oksala) misunderstands the form of abnormality that he introduces in the lecture. For at the beginning of the day's lecture, Foucault said something quite different about the third of the three figures and the shape that the lecture itself would take. What he said is this:

> I began [the course] by promising a genealogy of the abnormal individual on the basis of three characters: the great monster, the little masturbator, and *the recalcitrant child.* The third figure is missing from my genealogy and I hope you will forgive me for this. *You will see its outline appear in today's exposition.* I have not had time for its genealogy, *so we leave it in outline.* (Foucault 2003a, 291; emphasis added)

In turn, Foucault explained his use of the Jouy case in this way: "By looking at a particular case, today I want to show the quite precisely compound and mixed figure of the monster, the little masturbator, and, at the same time, the recalcitrant individual, or anyway, the individual who cannot be integrated within the normative system of education" (291). Later in the lecture, Foucault remarked that "with someone like Charles Jouy, who has been subjected to this kind of psychiatrization, the three elements or three characters are brought together: the little masturbator, the great monster, and then the individual who rejects all discipline" (306). In short, Jouy, as an "imbecile," is the culmination of Foucault's genealogy of the abnormal individual, for he is the archetypal abnormal individual: the composite of the monster, whose actions are spontaneous ("rise up") and involuntary; the masturbating child, whose infantile sexuality reflects his arrested development; and the recalcitrant child/individual, who cannot be taught right from wrong, or at least not in the standard way.

Foucault argued that it was only by establishing that Jouy remained extremely close to and almost fused with his own childhood and the child with whom he had relationships that he could be psychiatrized. For Jouy to be psychiatrized, that is, it was necessary to show that he and Adam were of the same grain, at the same level. Their profound identity gave psychiatry its hold on Jouy: he could be psychiatrized because he shared with Adam the features of childhood and infancy. For childhood, as a historical stage of development and a general frame of behavior, had become the principal instrument of psychiatrization, the principle for the generalization of psychiatry (2003a, 304). With the (adult) child Jouy, but not the child Adam, psychiatry was afforded the opportunity to study how imbecility and idiocy halted or slowed an individual's progression along a continuum of normal development, whereby the given imbecile or idiot remained captive to infantile, amoral instincts. Imbecility and idiocy represented a cessation or delay of development, that is, a quantitative difference from normality, though, in various historical moments and in various ways, "imbeciles" and "idiots" have also been perceived as creatures apart from the rest of us, qualitatively different, creatures of a different kind.

In the January 16 lecture of the 1973–74 course that Foucault taught at the Collège de France (later published in English as *Psychiatric Power*), he had offered a detailed account of the emergence and vicissitudes of imbecility (and its sibling, idiocy). As I have indicated, in the March 19 lecture of the 1974–75 course, however, he offered only a sketch ("outline") of the imbecile, citing examples of the psychiatric and physical examinations that Jouy was forced to undergo, examples that he believed would enable recognition of the new way in which certain behavior came to be understood as pathological and on what organic bases. For throughout the nineteenth (and twentieth) century, imbeciles, idiots, and other mental defectives were subjected to an array of strategies of classification, observation, and registration that effectively constituted and materialized their impairments through: the elaboration of scientifically structured norms that emerged within the diagnostic style of reasoning; the accentuation of the imbecile's, idiot's, or other mental defective's life; and a stress on the potential danger that the person posed to the general population. Among the strategies that Jouy and his fellow mentally defective inmates were forced to endure was cranial measurement, for the early and mid-nineteenth century was, in France at least, the heyday of phrenology, whose proponents regarded the brain as the sum of different organs, each of which corresponded with independent intellectual, moral, and affective faculties. Proponents of phrenology believed that the form, size, and length of the skull represented its encephalic development. One branch of phrenology, craniology, which was both widely applied in the domain of criminal justice and instrumental to the birth and expansion of scientific racism, held that the results of a geometric investigation of the skull could predict a given person's moral character and level of intelligence (see Gould 1996; McWhorter 2009, 117–20). The theory of phrenology also provided support for emerging claims according to which idiots and imbeciles could be educated. The presupposition of independent and autonomous faculties in the human mind provided a way to circumvent the thesis of incurability that underpinned the work of two of France's leading alienist psychiatrists, Philippe Pinel and Jean-Étienne Esquirol, who were experts in the treatment of imbecility and idiocy: although education could not create a normal person, nor create new faculties, it could be used as a tool to improve a situation, to strengthen a person's existing strategies (see Verstraete 2005, 130–31; Carlson 2009, 2015).

Information gathered from anatomical investigations complemented the findings of cranial examinations. "There is the way in which adult genital organs are described," Foucault said in the March 19 lecture, in turn citing H. Bonnet and J. Bulard, two of the scientists who examined Jouy: "Despite the very small size [of the accused: M.F.] and his marked arrested physical development, his [genital: M.F.] organs are normally developed like those of an ordinary man. This phenomenon is found in imbeciles" (Bonnet and Bulard 1868, 9–12, cited in Foucault 2003a, 300). Thus, the interrogations that Jouy was forced to undergo confirmed the knowledge about imbeciles that the experts who examined him claimed to already possess. As Foucault wrote, in the report of their analysis of Jouy, Bonnet and Bulard state that Jouy was not wicked and was even "gentle," but "the moral sense has failed" (Bonnet and Bulard 1868, in Foucault 2003a, 300). They remark, furthermore, that

> [Jouy] does not have sufficient mental self-possession to resist by himself certain tendencies that he may . . . regret later, without this however allowing us to conclude that he will not start again. . . . These bad instincts . . . are due to his arrested development and we know that sometimes their irresistibility is greater in imbeciles and degenerates. . . . Fundamentally affected by arrested development, lacking the benefit of an education . . . he does not possess what is needed to counterbalance the tendency to evil and to resist successfully the tyranny of the senses. (Bonnet and Bulard 1868, 9–12, cited in Foucault 2003a, 300)

This expert psychiatric report confirmed what Béchet, the village doctor and first medical expert to examine Jouy upon his arrest, had already concluded. In a letter that he attached to his report on the matter to the investigating magistrate, Béchet was reluctant to assign guilt to Jouy, pointing out that Jouy's "moral sense . . . is insufficient to resist animal instincts" and that he was a "dimwitted person who can be forgiven because of his abstruseness" (Béchet, in Bonnet and Bulard 1868, 5–6, cited in Foucault 2003a, 296). Indeed, Foucault pointed out that after word spread about the findings of the psychiatric experts' report, Jouy was acquitted of any crime and "the entire population of Loupcourt, the name of the village, keenly desired that little Sophie Adam [be] confined in a house of correction until she came of age" (2003d, 296, cf. 319n9). When the account of the expert reports is taken together with these details about Adam's confinement, one begins to glimpse a picture of Jouy and his relationship with Adam that is very different from that which proponents of the AFI have presented thus far.

It is true that the medical and psychiatric experts who examined Jouy noted that he had bad instincts and a tendency to evil. As Foucault indicated in his January 16 lecture of the 1973–74 course, however, these sorts of associations between mental defect and danger or badness were, initially at least, economically driven, as was the generalization of psychiatric power itself. Prolonged or life-long confinement was prohibitively expensive. The 1838 French law that defined the terms and conditions of confinement and assistance to poor inmates, according to which the financial responsibility for the board and lodging required to confine an individual fell to local communities, applied to the confinement of imbeciles and idiots. For years, local authorities hesitated to confine people identified as mentally deficient due to the financial burden that doing so imposed on their collective purses. For the council of a *département*, a prefecture, or a town hall to accept and support someone's confinement, Foucault explained, the local doctor had to guarantee to the authority in question that the person not only was an idiot unable to provide for his own needs and had no family that could do so, but was dangerous, that is, would commit arson, masturbate in public, rape, murder, or commit some other violent act. Doctors complained that they were required to give false reports to get care and assistance for individuals, to exaggerate the gravity of a situation, and to depict the idiot or mental defective as someone who was dangerous. In short, danger became a vital element for enabling the procedures of confinement and assistance to be put in place. Though at one time the association between idiocy (and imbecility) and danger was essentially a paternalistic trope used to ensure that certain members of the public received care and assistance, a medical literature nevertheless gradually developed that increasingly took itself seriously, stigmatizing imbeciles and idiots and making them into people who were dangerous, or more often into people who were potentially dangerous (Foucault 2006, 219–20; Davidson 2003, xxiii). This association between idiocy (or imbecility) and danger, which enabled the expansion of psychiatric power and which, to this day, continues to fuel discrimination against certain disabled people, looms large in feminist discussions of the Jouy case, that is, in the AFI. Here, then, is a history of the present.

Searching for Charles Jouy

Most proponents of the AFI seem to assume that the meanings attributed to and associated with sexual practices (such as mutual masturbation) and sex crimes (such as rape), as well as how these events are experienced, have a transhistorical and transcultural character. In her discussion of sex crimes, however, Chloë Taylor traces the changing character of rape in the West to show that the current understanding of rape as one of the most heinous of crimes is historically and culturally specific. In the Renaissance, Taylor writes, "Rape was common, permissible, and even socially useful so long as the woman raped was either the man's future or present bride or poor, and so long as no transgression of blood (incest; rape 'up' the social scale) or excessive bloodshed was involved" (2009, 11).

I want to argue that the ways in which masturbation is perceived, understood, and experienced, too, are discursively constituted and historically shifting, and that this historical fact further undermines the AFI. That the masturbatory activity of children became a serious public health concern beginning in the nineteenth century and on into the early twentieth century, as Foucault showed in the first volume of *The History of Sexuality*, itself goes some distance toward demonstrating that social, political, and personal perceptions, understandings, and experiences of masturbation are neither historically continuous nor consistent. Although masturbation is no longer believed to cause degeneracy and insanity, as it once was, it continued to be a morally fraught, much-deliberated arena of human sexuality long after it ceased to be regarded as a cause of real physical harm. As Thomas Laqueur has noted, the rhetoric of masturbation as either beneficial or harmful worked as a covert and overt mechanism to control sexual behavior throughout the twentieth century (2003, 16, cited in Gill 2012, 477). Like the beliefs about and experiences of rape, moreover, the beliefs about and experiences of masturbation often vary within the same historical moment, depending on the social station of the subject who engages in it. The regulatory apparatuses established to control and monitor the masturbation of certain populations offer a case in point.

The practice of masturbation is steadily regarded as indicative of "normal and healthy" sexual desire and thus is encouraged for members of the general population; however, disabled people, prisoners, and other people living in institutions continue to be subjected to intense surveillance and other disciplinary practices designed to manage their masturbatory practices. That disabled people who variously pose challenges to standards and norms of rationality, intelligence, and competence, as well as to conventions of propriety and modesty—that is, disabled people "with cognitive impairments"—will masturbate in public and engage in mutual masturbation with multiple partners has been a special concern for professionals who wish to train this sector of the disabled population in socially appropriate sexual practices or to discourage their sexual practices altogether. In the 1970s, for instance, professionals advocated the use of lemon juice to correct masturbation behavioral issues (rather than the electric shock therapy that had been used for this purpose in the past). In one such intervention, parents and teachers carried portable containers of lemon juice to squirt into a given disabled individual's mouth if the individual masturbated in a public setting or masturbated "excessively" (Gill 2012, 474).

Indeed, masturbation training in sexology and sex education represents one of the few sanctioned approaches to the sexuality of disabled people with cognitive impairments. As Michael Gill explains, masturbation training for these disabled people teaches them how to masturbate in "safe, appropriate, and effective" ways (473). A range of such training materials are available, many of which promote sexuality for disabled people with cognitive impairments as nonreproductive, solitary, and heteronormative, whereby "effective" masturbation offers a release of tension and curbs "disruptive" behavior that otherwise threatens institutional routines and discipline. Some of the newest training and education materials available, however, are designed to teach these disabled people that they have the same rights to sexual pleasure and enjoyment—with both themselves and others—and the same rights to choose the orientation of their sexual expression and practices as do nondisabled people. Furthermore, some sex educators and trainers enable "safe" (noninjurious) and "effective" (to ejaculation or orgasm) masturbation for these disabled clients through a variety of techniques, including film, video, and life-size models of genitalia (473–79; see also Desjardins 2012).

How should we understand the "sexual" activity, including the masturbation, in which Jouy engaged with Adam? Proponents of the AFI depict the incidents between Jouy and Adam as sexual abuse and assault, the impact of which would have been traumatic for Adam. Given the historically shifting constitution of the character of sexual practices and sex crimes, however, this representation of these incidents is by no means self-evidently true. Alcoff has argued that "it is obvious" (1996, 122) that adults occupy positions of social, personal, economic, and institutional power over children and that this asymmetrical relation conditions their interactions, including supposedly consensual sexual interactions between them. With respect to Jouy and Adam, however, the textual evidence suggests otherwise. As Foucault and the medical and psychiatric experts who examined Jouy described him, Jouy was about forty years old, poor, marginal, underpaid, without friends or family, small in stature, gentle, a slow learner, illiterate, and homeless: he slept in stables. He was removed from school, the other boys at school had excluded him from their games and activities, and the older village girls and women his own age mocked him. By all accounts, Jouy is the predecessor of the (post)modern-day isolated, disenfranchised, and unwanted disabled person. I submit, therefore, that when Jouy asked Adam to masturbate him, as he had seen her do with other boys with whom she played the game of "curdled milk," he did so to secure a sense of belonging and recognition, to be included in the game. On one occasion, after the deed was done, Adam and her friend laughingly boasted about the incident to an adult, who responded by saying, "Oh, you little horrors!" (Foucault 2003a, 294). As Foucault explained, the psychiatrists who examined Jouy noted that this game was "part of the social landscape" of the village and was tolerated, regularly played by children in the region "whose bad tendencies [were] not [sufficiently: M.F.] restrained" (295, 319n9).

Thus, I think we should ask this question: When Adam masturbated Jouy, that is, played the game of "curdled milk" with him, was she in fact teaching him how to masturbate "effectively"? On the occasion for which Jouy was apprehended, after he and Adam seem to have engaged in intercourse, he gave her four *sous* and she ran to the local fair to buy a bag of almonds. Both Alcoff and Sawicki express disdain that Foucault referred to this act as a "decent" gesture on Jouy's part. Foucault's stance on the incident, Sawicki (2005) retorts, "smacks of masculinist incredulity to the seriousness and reality of rape." Alcoff and Sawicki agree that, given her age, Adam could not have had sufficient agency to give full-fledged consent to the sex, regardless of whether she had negotiated this payment. Notwithstanding the fact that neither Foucault's text nor the reports of the medical and psychiatric experts state whether Adam was seven years of age or fourteen years of age, I want to suggest, to the contrary, that the exchange of money might indicate either that Jouy gave Adam remuneration for her instruction or, more disturbingly, that she had exploited his gentle nature and his desire for social recognition.

Proponents of the AFI reprimand Foucault for his failure to attend to Adam's experience of the incidents, while concentrating almost exclusively on the outcomes of them for Jouy. This failure, they argue, exemplifies the masculinist bias that underpins his work on the history of sexuality more generally. My argument in this chapter has been designed to show why such claims are textually unsubstantiated and misleading. Indeed, feminist discussion of Foucault's remarks about rape have been both textually selective and skewed. As my consideration of the Jouy case above indicates, discussion in feminist philosophy and theory about Foucault's views on rape has to a large extent focused on his treatment of the case in *The History of Sexuality*, volume 1, and the March 19, 1975, lecture that was subsequently published in *Abnormal*. Thus, I have concentrated my analysis on these texts to demonstrate that they do not support the argument that Foucault trivialized the effects of rape on women and girls, nor do they support the broader argument that his work on sexuality in general is masculinist and sexist. Nevertheless, I am cognizant that the remarks that Foucault made about rape in the context of the Jouy case are not the only remarks that he made about rape. In fact, remarks that Foucault made in at least three other contexts—remarks that recent feminist discussion of his stance on rape have disregarded—lend additional support to my conviction that he did not trivialize the impact of rape on women and girls. In Foucault's discussion of "monsters" in his January 29 lecture of the 1974–75 course at Collège de France, he offered these examples:

> Some years later there is the case of Léger, whose solitude produced a regression to the state of nature. He killed a young girl, raped her, cut out her sexual organs and ate them, and tore out her heart and sucked it. Then, around 1825, there is the case of the soldier Bertrand who, in the Montparnesse cemetery, opened the graves and took out corpses of women, sexually violated them, and then cut them open with a knife and hung their entrails like garlands on the crosses of the graves and the branches of the cypresses. These figures of monstrosity, of sexual and cannibalistic monstrosity, were the points of organization, the starting points, of all legal medicine. (2003a, 102)

Although Foucault's aim with these examples was to show how the figure of the "monster" emerged in juridical-medical discourses, his descriptions cannot be said to have diminished the sheer horror of the acts, including the aspects of them that concerned sexual assault and rape. In the January 16 lecture of the 1973–74 course, Foucault (2006, 220) offered another example of an incident of rape, describing how in 1895 the psychiatrist Bourneville, to prove that idiots are dangerous, told this story: On the Eure *départment*, a man called Many raped a young girl who was both an idiot and a prostitute. As Foucault explained, the case was at the time used as evidence that idiots are dangerous. That is, the case, he wrote, was used in such a way "that the idiot prove[d] the danger of the idiot 'at the very moment *she was a victim*'." These last remarks can hardly be described as dismissive and do not trivialize the seriousness of rape. Remarks that Foucault made in an interview entitled "Sexual Choice, Sexual Act" cast further doubt on the claim that he minimized the impact of rape on women and girls. In response to a question about the self-understandings and political organization of lesbians and gay men, Foucault stated, "There is the question of freedom of sexual choice which must be faced. I say 'freedom of sexual *choice*' and not 'freedom of sexual *acts*' because there are sexual acts like rape which should not be permitted whether they involve a man and a woman or two men" (1988b, 289; emphasis in Foucault). Indeed, in a 1981 interview that Jean François and John De Wit conducted with Foucault, Foucault defended himself against accusations that he minimized the gravity of the act of rape. In the course of the interview, François and De Wit asked Foucault this question: "During the reform of the penal code in France, you commented on the question of rape and argued that it should no longer be considered a crime. What exactly is your position on this question?" (Foucault 2014, 263). I quote Foucault's response at length:

I was never part of any commission on penal reform, but there was such a commission and some members asked that I be heard as a consultant on legal problems of sexuality. I was surprised by how interesting the discussions were. During the discussions, I tried to pose the following problem. On the one hand, can sexuality truly be structured through law? Shouldn't everything that has to deal with sexuality be taken out of the legal realm? But in that case, if anything of a sexual order is to be removed from law, what should be done about rape? That was the question I posed. During a dialogue with [David] Cooper, I simply said that there was a problem that had to be discussed and to which I did not have an answer. I am discomfited, that's all. But, perhaps because of the difficulties of translation or lack of real understanding, an English journal screamed that I wanted to decriminalize rape, that I was some sort of *phallo*. . . . No, excuse me, these people didn't understand a thing. I simply said what kind of dilemma we could find ourselves in. And it is not by throwing out violent condemnations against those who pose problems that they can truly be resolved. (263)

The dialogue that Foucault mentions in the passage above is the context in which, as Plaza (1981) explains it, he said that rape is on a par with a punch in the face and argued for the decriminalization of adult-child sexual relations (see Foucault 1990). When one reads the remarks that Foucault actually made in the context of this dialogue, one can see the extent to which Plaza subsequently skews them, giving them a highly contestable and contentious interpretation. Nevertheless, some feminist thinkers reproduce Plaza's insinuations (see Hengehold 1994; Cahill 2000; Henderson 2007).

Conditions of Possibility for the AFI

In the spirit of Foucauldian genealogy, I want to consider the conditions of possibility for the discussion of the Jouy case that has taken place in feminist philosophy: How has it been possible that neither the editor of *Feminist Interpretations of Foucault* who published Alcoff's paper in 1996, nor the editors of *Hypatia: A Journal of Feminist Philosophy*, nor the several reviewers that the journal enlisted to peer review two articles on the Jouy case, nor the editor of the *Notre Dame Philosophical Reviews* has paid any critical attention to the social positioning of Charles Jouy and considered whether assumptions and prejudices currently held about disabled people played a part in the prevailing interpretation and reception of the case? How has it been possible that none of the many feminist philosophers internationally who have read the four published articles in three different high-profile venues over the course of almost two decades has questioned, let alone challenged, the epistemology of dominance that seems to have conditioned feminist philosophical accounts of the case of Jouy and Foucault's use of it? What structural, institutional, social, political, ethical, and professional influences, investments, and mechanisms have enabled and even encouraged feminist philosophers to perpetuate a misleading representation of the case, to write and publish about it in this way, and to teach it in this way?

My argument is that four factors enabled the AFI to go unchallenged until I published an article in 2013 in which I dispute it (see Tremain 2013a). These factors have combined to produce discussion of the Jouy case in feminist philosophy (and Foucault scholarship) as a local center of the apparatus of disability through which impairment has been constituted. The four factors are:

First, and perhaps most evidently, even feminists who have done a great deal of work on the ways that gender variously colludes and intersects with race, class, ethnicity, and sexuality (among other apparatuses) can succumb to ahistorical and universalistic assumptions about gendered power relations. In this instance, these sorts of assumptions precluded examination of the ways that the constitution and materialization of impairment through the apparatus of disability occurred amid and even propel certain historically and culturally specific social, juridical, and medical events of the past that have contributed to the shape of discriminatory personal and public perceptions of and beliefs about disabled populations in the present. The AFI is, in short, another example of feminist analysis that unquestioningly and uncritically assumes that male supremacy and sexism are the predominant (if not sole) forms of power operative in social interactions and exchanges between women/ girls and men/boys, and does so by concealing the complicated character of power relations, that is, obscuring apparatuses of power with which (binary) gender has historically colluded and been entwined, leaving these networks of power unexamined and enabling them to persist, reconfigure, intensify, and expand.

Second, there is a persistent lack of knowledge and understanding about disabled people, their lives, histories, and social subjection in feminist philosophical circles and in philosophy more broadly, in part because disabled feminist philosophers and specialists in (feminist) philosophy of disability remain scandalously underrepresented in the profession of philosophy. If, for example, enough feminist philosophers and Foucault scholars had read the work of (feminist) philosophers and theorists of disability and thus knew that, contrary to pervasive and harmful stereotypes, disabled people are the victims of sexual abuse and other violence at the hands of nondisabled people many times more often than the other way around, the momentum that discussion of the Jouy case has gained in feminist philosophy, over the last decade especially, might never have developed nor indeed have accelerated. Furthermore, if more feminist philosophers (and Foucault scholars) read the work of philosophers of disability and disability theorists and thus were familiar with the genealogies of cognitive impairment and the apparatus of disability, they likely would have recognized the product of the scientific and medical examinations that Jouy was forced to endure—namely, imbecility—rather than have dismissed the attention that Foucault paid to these medical and scientific examinations as apologia for Jouy's actions and for the sexual victimization of women and girls in both the past and the present.

Third, many nondisabled feminist philosophers seem to assume that, given their own relationship with and experiences of oppression, they possess the requisite knowledge to understand (or are poised to understand) ableism and disability in ways that would enable them to adjudicate when the phenomena that these forms of power produce are pertinent to a situation or state of affairs, how much significance these phenomena should be given, and under what circumstances these phenomena are insignificant. Too often, nondisabled philosophers situate themselves as "experts" who can determine what gets said about disability and ableism, how much gets said, who gets to say it, in what form it will be said, and whether to engage with what is said—and they occupy the discursive, institutional, and professional spaces to ensure that they can make these determinations (see Tremain 2013b). Yet, few nondisabled philosophers seem to know what ableism is, nor do they seem to reflect upon how their own theoretical, interpersonal, professional, and other practices recapitulate it, confirming their privileged social position vis-à-vis disabled people and reinforcing the naturalizing impulses of the apparatus of disability.

A fourth factor that has enabled the epistemological domination that heretofore has compelled feminist philosophical discussion of the Jouy case is the continued production in feminist philosophy of disabled people as the individual bearers of a politically neutral form of bad luck (recall Fricker) rather than as disadvantageously subjected to the apparatus of disability; that is, the continued refusal on the part of philosophers to conceive of disabled people as the subjects of a complicated and complex configuration of power that is inseparable from other apparatuses of subjecting power rather than as recipients of a prediscursive form of personal misfortune and thus the quintessential subjects of care. I doubt very much that the feminist philosophical community would uncritically engage in the sort of unreflective, concerted vilification of a member of any other oppressed social group the way that it has done with the disabled man named Charles Jouy. I hope that my genealogical treatment of the Jouy case in this chapter (and indeed that this book in its entirety) serves as a beacon to the feminist philosophical community, a beacon that inspires at least one feminist philosopher to challenge the ableism of the subfield of feminist philosophy and of the discipline and profession of philosophy in general.

CHAPTER 5

Bioethics as a Technology
of Government

———— ᭣᭤ ————

Bioethics and Its Objects

The preceding chapter elucidates how a certain discussion in feminist philosophy has been one local center both around which the apparatus of disability has coalesced in philosophy and from which this apparatus has expanded and been transfigured. In addition, the argument of the chapter forms part of the genealogy of impairment that this book traces insofar as it indicates how this discussion in feminist philosophy contributes to the constitution of impairment. This discussion in feminist philosophy, I note, relies upon a misinterpretation of how the problematization of disability in a specific geopolitical and historical context constituted impairment through new practices of surveillance, examination, and segregation. In the chapter, I point out that Foucault, in his Collège de France lectures of 1974–75, sought to explain how this problematization of disability in a certain historical context occurred through the naturalization, classification, and materialization of an impairment that required management and manipulation. Thus, the previous chapter concentrates primarily on the critical work required for the reconstructive-conceptual aspect of the book, offering a defense of Foucault for this purpose against charges that feminist philosophers (and theorists) have directed at him. Nevertheless, the overall argument of the chapter—and especially my identification at the end of the chapter of the historical conditions of possibility for the continued articulation and persistence of this discussion in feminist philosophy internationally—conjoin the reconstructive-conceptual claims of the chapter with the metaphilosophical thread that runs throughout the book.

In this chapter, I show how moments in the genealogy of the apparatus of disability and its naturalized foundation (impairment) can be identified in discourses that circulate within and indeed are central to the identity and subject matter of the subfield of bioethics, especially discourses about the use of genetic technologies. These technologies and the subfield of bioethics, through which they garner remarkable currency, are local centers that force relations of biopower have created and caused to emerge, that is, they are centers of biopower through which the apparatus of disability is continually reinforced, elaborated, and enlarged. Mainstream bioethicists generally assume that their task is to apply the universalizing and ahistorical principles of deontology, utilitarianism, or virtue ethics to situations that arise in biomedical contexts, that is, they presuppose that medical encounters provide opportunities for the expression and application of extant values such as autonomy, well-being, and liberty (see Beauchamp and Childress, 2012). In what follows, I assume Foucault's insight that power is productive to show that the very articulation and practice of these values through (for instance) the use of technologies and the decision-making procedures that surround them effectively generates and configures the values (see also Hall 2015, 169; Hall 2016).

A neoliberal governmentality of security—in support of which the apparatus of disability and other apparatuses of (for instance) racialized and gendered force relations have amalgamated—undergirds the academic field of bioethics and has motivated its emergence and expansion, including the incessant production within some areas of the field of questions and concerns about impairment and the refinement of positions that rationalize its prevention and elimination. Consider Foucault's remarks about the three major forms that technologies of government take in their development and history: first, a given technology of government takes the form of a dream or utopia; then, the dream of the technology of government develops into actual practices or rules to be used in real institutions; finally, the practices and rules of the technology of government become consolidated in the form of an academic discipline (Foucault 1988c, 145–62; see also Hall 2015, 166–69; Hall 2016). My argument is that the academic discipline of bioethics relies on an epistemology of domination and is an institution-alized vehicle for the biopolitics of our time, that is, bioethics is a technology of government that provides intellectual resources designed to facilitate the "strengthening" (read: fitness) of a certain population and the elimination of others. I submit, furthermore, that the implicit and explicit governmental tenor of bioethical inquiries and discussions contributes substantially to the hostile environment that disabled philosophers confront in philosophy. Thus, both the thread that articulates the reconstructive-conceptual sphere of my research and the thread that articulates the metaphilosophical sphere of my work extend through the argument in this chapter. As a product of biopower, bioethics, I contend, implicates the discipline and profession of philosophy in the apparatus of disability and the subordination of disabled people in ways that, and to a degree that, no other subfield of the discipline does, although cognitive science and cognate fields continue to gain considerable ground in this regard.

In this final chapter, I indicate that these forms of biopolitical intimidation have by no means gone unchallenged by disabled people, including disabled philosophers. Recall that an apparatus, as Foucault defined that notion, responds to an "urgent need" in a historical moment. I have asserted that the requirement to which the apparatus of disability has served as a response is normalization that facilitates the expansion of neoliberalism as a form of governmental reason. In the previous chapters, to substantiate this claim, I offer examples of how biopower and biopolitical normalization have operated through the apparatus of disability in the context of disability theory and disabled people's movements, in medicine and law in nineteenth-century France, and in feminist philosophy. In this chapter, I aim to further substantiate the claim by showing that the field of bioethics—both a product and a mechanism of biopower—has enabled the intellectual and popular acceptance of normalization in certain contexts: biopolitical normalization that disabled people and members of other stigmatized social groups increasingly oppose.

The consolidation of the field of bioethics (as both product and mechanism), which works in the service of forms of normalization whose goal is security, operates especially through the neoliberal touchstones of autonomy (construed as self-governance) and freedom (construed as individual choice), that is, it operates effectively by guiding and limiting subjects in accordance with their capacity to choose from a highly circumscribed set of possible actions. Within bioethics and elsewhere, (neo)liberal values and ideals, articulated and generated through the "doctrine of informed consent," govern medical encounters in accordance with a juridical representation of power as external to autonomy and freedom. Nowhere have the ideals of autonomy and freedom been more effective tools for normalization than in the problematization and production of the apparatus of disability (including the problematization and production of its naturalized foundation, impairment) achieved in the context of reproductive and other genetic technologies and the discourses co-constitutive with them. These technologies and the discourses co-constitutive with them have contributed to the problematization of impairment for the efficient management by the neoliberal state, a problem that demands prevention, correction, and elimination or, at least, some managed and manageable form of integration.

My discussion in this chapter of prenatal testing and screening, hESC research, and the discourses that circulate around and support these technologies is designed to illustrate how the discursive object of impairment is constituted as a disadvantageous abnormality, flaw, or defect by and through these technologies and discourses, despite the fact that they are widely claimed to be politically and normatively neutral and disinterested and to treat the subjects who engage with them as interchangeable. Prenatal testing and screening, stem cell (SC) research, and the discourses that co-constitute these technologies, I argue, bring impairment into being, that is, bring it into being as that kind of thing. My approach in this chapter has implications for both the reconstructive-conceptual dimension of my argument and its metaphilosophical dimension. The argument of the chapter demonstrates that the field of bioethics significantly contributes to the problematization of impairment and disability and thus to their naturalization and materialization; that is, as I argue, the field of bioethics, rather than merely describing impairment, actively participates in its constitution and derogation as a disadvantageous natural human attribute. Notice that insofar as I advance this argument in the chapter, I instigate a reversal of taken-for-granted assumptions about the causal relation between, on the one hand, impairment and disability and, on the other, the subfield of bioethics.

Historicizing Bioethics and Its Objects

In *The Care of the Self*, Foucault (1986, 99) drew attention to the widespread public interest in medicine during the Flavian (69 C.E.–96 C.E.)

and Antonine (138 C.E.–180 C.E) periods and to the close association between medicine and philosophy during these eras. Medicine, Foucault wrote, was regarded as a high form of culture during these periods, on the same level as rhetoric and philosophy. As he explained,

> [The American scholar of ancient Greek and Roman history] G. W. Bowersock observes that the medical model accompanied the development of the Second Sophistic and that a number of important rhetors had received medical training or manifested interests in that field. It had long been established that philosophy was closely related to medicine, even though the demarcation of boundaries posed doctrinal problems and gave rise to territorial rivalries. In the first lines of *Advice about Keeping Well*, Plutarch echoes these debates: the physician is wrong, he says, when he claims to be able to do without philosophy, and one would be quite mistaken to reproach philosophers with crossing their own boundaries when they concern themselves with health and its regimen. (99)

Plutarch, Foucault noted, concluded that medicine is not in any way inferior to the liberal arts (*eleutherai technai*) with respect to elegance, distinction, and the satisfaction that it yields. Indeed, the way in which Plutarch and other ancients perceived medicine contrasts starkly with the diagnostic style of reasoning around which modern medicine revolves insofar as, for the ancients, medicine was not conceived primarily as a technique of surveillance, examination, intervention, and remedy. Rather, for the ancients, medicine was believed "to define, in the form of a body of knowledge and rules, a way of living, a mode of reflection in relation to oneself and one's body, to food, to wakefulness and sleep, to various activities, and to the environment" (Foucault 1986, 100). As Foucault's remarks suggest, furthermore, the association that the ancients drew between philosophy and medicine was broader than the extant relation between contemporary philosophy and bioethics that is largely construed within wide swaths of the field as the application of a limited number of moral principles to medical contexts and events. As Bowersock's remarks indicate, the association between philosophy and medicine has a longer standing than many philosophers are inclined to acknowledge.

Notwithstanding the Flavians and Antonines, historians of the academic field of bioethics generally place its emergence around the early 1960s. A combination of cultural events precipitated this development, it is claimed, one of which was the Doctors' Trial that took place in Nuremberg immediately following World War II. In that twentieth-century trial, Nazi doctors who had performed grisly experiments in Nazi concentration camps on Jewish, disabled, Roma, and homosexual prisoners (among others) were tried and convicted of crimes against humanity.[1] As the evidence presented at the trial made abundantly clear, medical and scientific practices, as well as the medical and scientific personnel who perform them, can be put in the service of ghastly political ends, even in societies with so-called highly developed intellectual communities (see also Kittay 2016).

The verdict read at the Doctors' Trial included ten ethical principles—now known as the Nuremberg Code—that the jurists maintained should subsequently govern research on human subjects internationally (see Annas and Grodin 1995). In fact, the principles of the Nuremberg Code are widely regarded as precursors to the growth of the fields of research ethics, medical ethics, and bioethics, especially the first principle of the Code, which requires the informed consent of research subjects and, by association, respect for their autonomy. Historians of bioethics and bioethicists themselves acknowledge, nevertheless, that throughout the twentieth century the principles of the Nuremberg Code were repeatedly breached as scientists, doctors, and bioethicists engaged in practices that demonstrate that science, medicine, and the subfield of bioethics itself are politically interested domains and by no means value neutral. To take only one example, from the late 1800s to the 1970s (and even now), hundreds of thousands of disabled people were sterilized without their consent in institutions throughout North America and parts of Europe. Disability theorists and researchers continue to document the genealogies of these sterilization programs and the role that they played in a governmentality of eugenics (see Trent 1994, 175–77, 196–202; McWhorter 2009, 125–40; Carlson 2009, especially 21–51). That the principle of informed consent is itself the product of a certain technology of government has thus far remained unexamined.

One of the most egregious breaches of the Nuremberg Code's first principle occurred under the auspices of the Tuskegee Syphilis Study, a study that was already underway before the Doctors' Trial took place and that continued for three decades after the promulgation of the principles encompassed in the verdict of the trial. This forty-year "study" involved the withholding of treatment from 399 poor African American men with syphilis, who were deceived about the actual goals of the study, in order that various bodies of public health within the U.S. government could chart the entire course of the disease and compare its effects on black Americans with its effects on white Europeans, racist comparisons that could be made only postmortem. Susan M. Reverby (2000) has documented how, through complicity with the infamous study in the form of presentations at high-profile conferences and publications in esteemed journals over the course of the forty years during which the study took place, the scientific community, medical practitioners, and medical ethicists perpetuated racist and eugenicist scientific and medical practices that historically have been inflicted upon African Americans and facilitated the expansion of the category of race in biomedical professional discourse and public policy (see also Washington 2006; Roberts 1998, 2012).

The revelation of the extent to which medical associations, medical practitioners, and medical ethicists, as well as governmental agencies involved in the Tuskegee Study had violated the first principle of the Nuremberg Code; an exposé about horrible hepatitis experiments conducted during the late 1950s and 1960s on disabled children at Willowbrook State Hospital in Staten Island, New York; and reports of other contraventions of the Nuremberg Code led to calls (in North America and elsewhere) from the 1970s on for increased surveillance of medical and scientific practices (see Robinson and Unruh 2008). Prior to this time, ethical decision making with respect to medical practice was largely confined to the domain of sacrosanct exchanges between physicians and their patients, the latter of whom, by and large, complied with the recommendations of their doctors, who were perceived to act in their patients' best interests. With the high-profile exposure of scientific and institutional abuses and the rise of the women's health movement, among other things, the paternalistic tradition that had conditioned such interactions between doctors and their patients was to some extent undermined, augmenting the production of neoliberal forms of self-management and self-governance in medical contexts.

The narrative that historians of bioethics and bioethicists themselves tell is that their academic discipline emerged in part as a safeguard against abuses of the past and a rejection of paternalism in favor of patients' rights, framed, as I have indicated, as respect for the principle of autonomy (e.g., Ouellette 2011). By contrast, I understand the emergence of bioethics and the doctrine of informed consent as historically specific institutional responses to the demands of neoliberal subjectivity; that is, I regard the emergence of bioethics and the doctrine of informed consent as institutional responses to the relatively recent social and cultural production of a new kind of individual who is self-directed and self-legislating, endowed with the capacity to make autonomous choices that can be put in the service of certain political ends. Power is neither external to the subject's autonomy and freedom nor antithetical to these values, but rather contributes to their constitution and operates through them.

With the expansion of research into and development of new technologies in the areas of (among others) genetics and reproduction from the early to mid-twentieth century forward, an increasing number of new ethical questions and dilemmas came into being whose resolution was steadily perceived to require a novel kind of expertise and knowledge that most physicians were claimed to lack. Thus, mainstream bioethicists argue that the subdiscipline of bioethics emerged in part to train a group of philosophers in the application of accepted ethical principles to the phenomena of medical science, law, and policy for the resolution of these ethical questions and dilemmas on behalf of clinical practitioners. Although the new subdiscipline of bioethics is less than a century old, its rise and growth have been considerable. Bioethicists have substantial influence on biomedical decision making; on the generation of biomedical norms; on the design of public policy and law; on the acceptance or refusal of forms of medical and scientific research; on the identification of funding priorities; and on the inculcation of social values, expectations, and ideals. Indeed, the field of bioethics has come to occupy both a central position in the political discourse of technologically developed societies and an important (and lucrative) role in many philosophy departments. In the last several decades, the enrollment in bioethics courses has skyrocketed, in part because these courses are widely believed to be good training grounds for future practitioners in the areas of medicine, law, and public policy. Given the current financial requirements and constraints of the neoliberal university, the popularity of bioethics courses ensures that they are regularly offered in the philosophy departments of most universities.

Disability and Bioethics

Bioethicists increasingly influence the direction of research agendas, clinical protocols, and policy decisions that both directly and indirectly affect disabled people's lives; hence, disabled people pay close attention to what philosophers who work in this area of the discipline say. In fact, due to the nature of arguments about disability and disabled people that many bioethicists advance, the subfield of bioethics (and certain bioethicists especially) is held in considerable disdain within corners of the interdisciplinary field of disability studies and, more generally, within the disabled people's movement internationally. Disability theorists and disabled people are acutely aware that the field of bioethics in general and certain practitioners of it in particular provide substantial rhetorical justification for social biases and prejudices that compromise and threaten disabled people's lives. For example, Disabled People's International-Europe (DPI-Europe)—in response to both the surge of new reproductive technologies that aim to prevent and control prenatal impairment and the proliferation of bioethical arguments designed to promote the technologies—has issued a statement in which its authors assert that "congenital impairments" are not intrinsic flaws or deficits that demand to be corrected or eliminated, as many bioethicists claim, but rather are neutral characteristics integral to the species' gene pool (Disabled Peoples' International-Europe 2000).

Insofar as predictive testing strategies are directed toward progressively earlier and earlier stages of a pregnancy, along with the fact that in vitro fertilization (IVF) and preimplantation diagnosis (PGD) have become more and more widely available, disabled people and their allies are gravely concerned that the conception of impairment as a natural defect and disadvantage seems to be the chief motivation to develop the technology. The authors of the DPI-Europe statement—which relies on the BSM—argue that the use of prenatal genetic diagnosis, genetic therapies, and selective abortion to prevent lives deemed not normal (due to impairment) threatens human diversity. They argue, furthermore, that national and international governing bodies, including government bioethics task forces and think tanks, ought to declare that the selective abortion of "impaired fetuses" violates the human rights of "people with impairments." These activists and researchers also advance arguments about the expressive character of prenatal testing and selective abortion of impaired fetuses, arguments according to which the selective abortion of fetuses "with impairments" puts into public discourse a discriminatory message that disabled people's lives are not worth living, nor worthy of support. They contend that the selective abortion of impaired fetuses is on par ethically with selective abortion on the basis of "fetal sex," and therefore, de-selecting impairment ought to be recognized as a modern form of eugenics. Indeed, the authors of the DPI-Europe statement have called upon governing bodies and the bioethicists who advise them to generate policy instruments that outlaw these eugenic practices, policy instruments analogous to instruments that are already used internationally to prohibit so-called sex selection (Disabled Peoples' International-Europe 2000).

Many philosophers of disability and disabled critics of bioethics point out that most bioethicists advance arguments about disability at some distance from disabled people, that is, without the empirical and other evidence required to substantiate these arguments, including direct experience of the social, political, and economic disadvantages that accrue to disabled people, understanding of the perspectives of disabled people, and consultation with them. That is, disabled theorists and activists have for some time now argued that bioethicists must attend to the viewpoints of disabled people and involve them in the formulation of policies that affect their lives, must consult disabled people for their expertise on issues that concern them, and must respect the subjugated situated knowledges that disabled people produce.[2]

In recent years, therefore, some bioethicists, especially some feminist bioethicists, have sought collaboration with philosophers and theorists of disability. Philosophers of disability and disability theorists—some of whom identify as bioethicists—now regularly deliver papers to and participate on panels at bioethics conferences, join bioethics associations, work at bioethics institutes, and publish books on disability and bioethics. These "disability bioethicists" (as some of them refer to themselves) believe that their work, which generally assumes a (modified) sociopolitical conception of disability, will serve to educate mainstream bioethicists about the circumstances of disabled people's lives, improve the message about disability that the field of bioethics conveys to other philosophers and the public at large, broaden the range of materials that bioethicists teach their students about disability, shift the focus of research on disability that bioethicists (and other philosophers) develop and promote, and so on. The assumption that underlies the efforts of these disability bioethicists is that the field of bioethics is not itself a technology of government, that is, a mechanism of the "conduct of conduct." These philosophers of disability and disability theorists, although they are critical of the arguments about disability that some practitioners in the realm of bioethics advance, aspire to reform the field of bioethics by correcting and eliminating the biases and discriminatory assumptions that they perceive to currently condition it. For these philosophers and theorists of disability, the governmental character of bioethics with respect to disability and disabled people is an accidental feature of the enterprise rather than the impetus for the very existence of the enterprise.

Normalizing Bioethics

Force relations of normalization whose means and aims are security of the population posit conceptions of the normal from which the possibility and probability of deviations are measured and classified in order to prevent and control their actualization. The technologies of normalization that emerge to augment this security operate through calculation and management of risk and possibility, chance and probability, calculation and management that are achieved in accordance with the evidence, candidates for true and false, laws, and objects that the diagnostic style of reasoning has introduced into discourse. The philosophical renditions of these forms of calculation and management are hallmarks of contemporary bioethics. Together with the neoliberal touchstones of individual autonomy and choice, these philosophical formulations of calculation and management produce bioethics as a legitimized arena for the effective circulation of force relations that are both individualizing and totalizing, that is, force relations that contribute to the constitution of kinds of individuals (individualization) and associate these kinds with distinguishing epidemiological classifications and social categories (totalization).

In *The Birth of the Clinic*, Foucault (1973) noted that until the end of the eighteenth century—the historical moment in which biopower began to emerge—medicine was more concerned with health than with normality. Medicine before the nineteenth century, he explained, did not take as its starting point a regular functioning of the organism and proceed to discover its deviation from that functioning, the cause of this deviation, and how the organism could be returned to regular functioning. Medicine, before the end of the eighteenth century, referred to qualities of vigor, suppleness, and fluidity, which, lost in illness, it was the task of medicine to restore. Nineteenth-century medicine, on the other hand, was governed in accordance with normality. In this historical context, that is, the historical context in which biopower coalesced, a form of medicine developed that consisted primarily in the disciplinary control of the poor and working class to make them more fit for labor and less dangerous to the wealthy classes (Foucault 2003b, 336). As Foucault explained, "[In the nineteenth century, when] one spoke of the life of groups and societies, of the life of the race, or even of the 'psychological life,' one did not think first of the internal structure of *the organized being*, but of the *medical bipolarity of the normal and the pathological*" (1973, 35; emphasis in Foucault). This epistemological shift has been crucial to the proliferation of the productive strategies of biopower.

The notion of "normal species-typical functioning" that bioethicist Norman Daniels and his coauthors Daniel Brock, Allen Buchanan, and Daniel Wikler have popularized in contemporary mainstream bioethics is a mechanism of normalization through approximation to a conception of normality. The idea of species-typical functioning does not, of course, originate from within the field of bioethics itself, but rather has been imported into that discourse from the work of philosopher of science Christopher Boorse (1977). Ronald Amundson (2005) has pointed out that although the use of the word *typical* in the term *typical function* seems to suggest statistical assessment—that is, what constitutes the common or usual function—Boorse intends the notion to imply the normal function of members of a species. Boorse claims that the distinction between "normal" and "abnormal" function is an empirically grounded implication of biomedical science. Normal and abnormal function are distinct natural kinds, objective facts of the natural world. Within Boorse's theory, Amundson notes, the notion of normal function carries a double implication. First, normal function is statistically common in the species; abnormal function is rare. Second, normal function is the most successful or (in Darwinian terms) the most fit. The claim is that the more an organism diverges from its species average, the worse it will function (Amundson 2005, 105; see also Amundson 2000).

Amundson (2005) argues that Boorse's contribution to this discussion in bioethics misrepresents biomedical science. Neither functional uniformity nor the association between statistical typicality and excellence of function, Amundson states, is a scientific discovery about the biological world. As Amundson explains it, information supplied from a wide number of biological disciplines suggests that we should expect a wide range of functional variation, not a narrow match between functional typicality and functional success. He points out, furthermore, that evolutionary biology does not imply functional uniformity as an outcome of evolution; rather, functional variability is a basic assumption of Darwinian natural selection. Conformity among members of a given species is not implied by the facts of developmental biology; rather, developmental plasticity and functional adaptation, he writes, suggest that we should expect variation in the functional organization of the bodies of species members, not strict conformity. As Amundson puts it, there is so much functional variation among humans and the variation is so multidimensional that the belief in an objective correlation between typicality and functional success is scientifically untenable (2005, 106–7).

Although Boorse presented his theory as an empirical claim about biology, it has been used to support normative consequences in the bioethical writings of Daniels, Brock, Buchanan, and Wikler, among others. These normative conclusions imply that disabled people have a lower quality of life, by virtue of impairment, and that such lives should be prevented.[3] Amundson has argued, to the contrary, that these conclusions and indeed this entire discussion in biomedical ethics are biased against disabled people and the satisfaction of their civil rights because philosophers have failed to come to terms with the political conceptions of disability that the disabled people's movement has developed. Amundson has pointed out, furthermore, that these normative conclusions seem to be contradicted by a wealth of empirical data and first-person reports from disabled people who do not experience a lower quality of life than nondisabled people or experience a better quality of life than nondisabled people (Amundson 2000, 2005; see also Hall 2016; Barnes 2009, 2016; Oswald and Powdthavee 2008).

Brock, for one, has cast considerable doubt on the credibility of such first-person reports. In a presentation entitled "Genetic Testing and Selection: A Response to the Disability Movement's Critique" that Brock gave to the Tenth Genetic Technology and Public Policy in the New Millennium Symposium in November 2002, he addresses criticisms from the disabled people's movement according to which he has ignored what disabled people say about their own lives. As he explains it, "*Our* notion of how good a person's life is [isn't] fully determined by their own subjective assessment." Even with modifications to the environment, Brock claims, disabled people live with "*real* disadvantages." Thus, "severe disabilities" [among which Brock counts blindness and "mental retardation"] should be prevented with the use of amniocentesis and abortion. The prevention of "severe disabilities," Brock remarks, is not for the sake of a given child, but rather for the sake of less suffering and loss of opportunity in the world. He argues, furthermore, that "it's a mistake to think that the social and economic costs are not a legitimate concern in this context" (see Brock 2002, in Tremain 2006a, 51n3; emphasis added). In other contexts, however, Brock has expressed a very different view of one's subjective assessment of one's own quality of life. With respect to the quality of life of someone who is critically ill or dying, Brock has stated that "there is no objective standard, but only the competent patient's judgement" (2009, 166).

Notwithstanding the evidently inconsistent views that Brock seems to hold with respect to standpoint epistemologies and subjective assessments of quality of life, he and other bioethicists have invoked a certain application of the notion of "adaptive preferences" to support their conclusions. Put briefly, this construal of the notion of adaptive preferences assumes that people in disadvantaged situations adapt their personal preferences and desires to better suit the compromised or diminished circumstances in which they find themselves. When this argument from adaptive preferences is applied to the quality of disabled people's lives, the result is invariably the following: due to the diminished circumstances of their lives, disabled people lower their expectations about the amount of satisfaction and happiness they should achieve, as well as compromise their standards about which occupations, pastimes, and activities they should pursue to attain these goods. In short, this argument from adaptive preferences assumes that there is an objective and universal standard for assessing the (objective) quality of human life, below which the quality of disabled people's lives (objectively) falls. In effect, the application of the notion of adaptive preferences to disabled people's lives begins from the judgment (bias) that their circumstances are undesirable and proceeds to put a high burden of proof to show that they are not undesirable on parties who argue in some way that such generalizations cannot be made.

Many of the philosophers who advance arguments about adaptive preferences are capability theorists who assume Aristotelian and other perfectionist conceptions of the good (for instance, Nussbaum 1992, 2006; Khader 2011). Some philosophers committed to arguments about the allegedly compromised character of disabled people's preferences (and satisfactions) are utilitarians who seem to rely on John Stuart Mill's distinction between higher and lower pleasures to motivate their arguments; however, these utilitarian philosophers also seem to tendentiously set aside Mill's dictum that the best judges of the quality of preferences (and satisfactions) are individuals who have experienced "both sides of the question." Nevertheless, we can employ Mill's motto to counter claims about the allegedly diminished character of disabled people's lives by arguing that people who become disabled at some point in their lives, that is, people who "know both sides of the question," are better judges of the quality of disabled people's lives than are people who have never been disabled. Would the subjective assessments of people disabled from birth remain discredited if we employ this Millian argument? I suggest that they need not remain so if we combine the use of Mill's argument with an argument that takes seriously the insights of feminist standpoint epistemologists (among others), according to which the strategies for living and indeed the very survival of people in oppressed situations often depends on knowing and understanding well the privileged circumstances and characteristics of the people to whom they are socially subordinated, including the epistemic limits that these circumstances and characteristics entail. In short, we should recognize this application of the idea of adaptive preferences as one move among many in the theoretical repertoire of a specific situated perspective that elevates itself to the level of a universal (Tremain 2006a, 2010; see also Dotson 2012).

Given the historicist and relativist commitments that motivate my feminist philosophy of disability, I assume that there is no universal, timeless, and objective "quality of life" that can be analytically separated from the contingent concrete circumstances in which people live. This, then, is the place in which to address predictable objections to Foucault's refusal to propose normative recommendations. Since bioethics is generally conceived as a domain that developed to provide normative guidance to medical practitioners in their clinical decision making, their interactions with patients and patients' families, their use of emerging technologies, and so on, it might seem that Foucault's work is irrelevant to bioethical discourse. Nancy Fraser, for one, has argued that Foucault cannot on his own terms distinguish between acceptable and unacceptable forms of power; thus, his work is "normatively confused" (1989, 31, 33). Melinda Hall points out, however, that "this feature of Foucault's work is precisely what recommends it." As Hall explains it, Foucault's refusal to engage in normative inquiry and advance prescriptions for human actions "allows one to see what has been obfuscated—for example, power's productive functions—and thus reframe ethics by overthrowing previous normative presuppositions" (Hall 2015, 162). In a famous interview conducted in 1980, Foucault put it this way: "In a sense, I am a moralist, insofar as I believe that one of the tasks, one of the meanings of human existence—the source of human freedom—is never to accept anything as definitive, untouchable, obvious, or immobile" (1988a, 1, in Hall 2015, 162). Foucault's critical approach requires that we ask about the values, purposes, and aims of the field of bioethics itself and about the field's emergence and production through power relations that it variously obscures or purports to merely describe and adjudicate.

Government through Incremental Normalization

Despite the regularity with which medical and scientific abuses have been inflicted upon various marginalized social groups during the last century, bioethicists (predominantly nondisabled, white, and male) have tended to cast such clinical practices and research programs as anomalies and rarities, as disturbing relics of days gone by, and as disruptions in the history of an otherwise noble, emerging endeavor that strives to ensure that established practices and new developments in biomedicine and biomedical science uphold the highest ethical standards. Even the critiques of bioethical practices that feminist bioethicists and philosophers of disability and disability theorists articulate tend to implicitly assume the self-understandings and self-image that the subfield of bioethics explicitly presents; hence, the scope of these critiques has for the most part been limited to arguments against a particular biomedical practice or the position of a certain bioethicist, leaving the historical conditions of possibility for the overall enterprise of bioethics unexamined and unchallenged.

My argumentative strategy in this chapter is a distinct departure from these other critiques of bioethics. For my argument is that the subfield of bioethics (including feminist bioethics and disability bioethics)—as a concerted enterprise—is a mechanism of biopower whose increasing institutionalization and legitimation in the university, in the discipline of philosophy, and in public policy (among other contexts) consolidate and conceal the fundamental role that this field of inquiry plays in biopolitical strategies of normalization and hence the government of populations. I contend that the field of bioethics is increasingly a premier arena for racism against the abnormal; that is, I contend that the subfield of bioethics rationalizes (among other things) the proliferation and use of biotechnologies such as prenatal testing and screening and SC research and, in doing so, bioethics effectively contributes to the constitution of impairment (among other so-called anomalies) through the identification, evaluation, assessment, classification, and categorization of it, thereby expanding the purview of the apparatus of disability and extending its reach. The subfield of bioethics, I maintain, is a set of strategic discursive practices that works in the service of the mechanism of normalization and the government of conduct to eliminate impairments that medical, juridical, and administrative discourses claim to discover and manage, while simultaneously enabling these discourses to enlarge the scope of the broad outlines of the category of impairment itself.

Bioethics is generally regarded as the most suitable (if not the only) domain in philosophy for critical considerations about disability; however, bioethics actually operates as an area of philosophy whose guiding assumptions and discursive practices are significant obstacles to (1) acknowledgment that the questions—metaphysical, epistemological, political, and ethical—that the apparatus of disability raises are genuinely philosophical, and (2) recognition that disabled philosophers who investigate these questions are credible philosophers. Indeed, bioethicists serve as gatekeepers, guarding the discipline from the incursion of critical philosophical work on disability and shielding the profession from an influx of disabled philosophers. Exceptions to this exclusion are of course admissible and even serve to legitimize both the subfield of bioethics and the discipline in general, typifying the polymorphism of the (neo)liberal governmentality from which the subfield of bioethics has emerged and enabling philosophy to proceed under the guise of political neutrality, objectivity, and disinterest. The charge according to which critics of genetic technologies, physician-assisted suicide, and euthanasia employ "slippery-slope reasoning" is a striking case in point. Many bioethicists—some of whom have substantial influence on hiring practices and publishing (among other things) in philosophy, as well as on public policy and public perceptions of their field—maintain that philosophers and theorists of disability (and disabled activists) who criticize the production of these technologies and practices engage in fallacious argumentation by using "slippery-slope reasoning" to advance their claims; thus, their positions, these bioethicists argue, ought not to be taken seriously (for instance, see Schüklenk et al. 2011). That is, bioethicists who argue in favor of physician-assisted suicide, euthanasia, and genetic technologies such as prenatal testing and screening imply that although the arguments that philosophers and theorists of disability advance to oppose these practices and technologies are politically motivated, ideological, and unsound, their own arguments in favor of these practices and technologies are disinterested (yet compassionate), objective (yet caring), and rigorous (yet flexible and sensitive).

Jocelyn Downie and Susan Sherwin (1996, 316) distinguish between two kinds of slippery-slope arguments that critics of assisted suicide and euthanasia make: logical slippery-slope arguments and psychological slippery-slope arguments. Downie and Sherwin explain logical slippery-slope arguments in this way:

> If we allow assisted suicide and euthanasia, we will not be able to draw any meaningful distinction between acceptable and unacceptable killings, and, hence, we will *inevitably* slide toward the bottom of the slope (i.e., toward allowing involuntary euthanasia and thus the kill-

ing of demented patients, mentally handicapped humans, indigent humans, and any other group deemed to be "unfit" for continued existence). (emphasis in Downie and Sherwin)

Downie and Sherwin claim that there is a simple response to this sort of slippery-slope argument, namely, that if there is a morally significant difference between evaluation of life at the top of the slope and evaluation of life at the bottom of the slope, then the necessary materials to erect a barrier on the slope are available; or, if there are good reasons why practices at the top of the slope should be allowed that are not available at the bottom of the slope, then descent down the slope is not logically necessary (317).

The second type of slippery-slope argument—psychological slippery slopes—poses more difficulty, Downie and Sherwin write. Psychological slippery slopes, they explain (quoting ethicist James Rachel), take this form: "Once certain practises are accepted, people *shall in fact* go on to accept other practices as well. This is simply a claim about what people will do, and not a claim about what they are logically committed to" (Rachels 1975, 65, in Downie and Sherwin 1996, 317; emphasis in Rachels).

Downie and Sherwin state that the question of whether people will accept involuntary euthanasia if they previously accepted voluntary assisted suicide and euthanasia is an empirical one, requiring investigation that has not been conducted. They remark, furthermore, that "There are many reasons to doubt the validity of the Nazi experience as an appropriate test, since the death camps were created under a totalitarian regime with little concern for individual autonomy" (Downie and Sherwin 1996, 317). For Downie and Sherwin, the respect afforded to personal autonomy provides a safeguard against abuses of physician-assisted suicide and euthanasia, distinguishing modern uses of these practices and procedures from extermination programs of the past. To be sure, Downie and Sherwin acknowledge that there is "reason to fear that legitimization of assisted suicide and euthanasia may lead to it normalization." They point out, however, that they "do not think that this is an insurmountable obstacle" (325). Rather, they maintain that the normalization of physician-assisted suicide and euthanasia can be prevented if the appropriate regulations are put into place to ensure that people "do not feel coerced" to choose this option in response to their situation. In other words, the position that these feminist bioethicists advance on physician-assisted suicide and euthanasia relies upon a juridical conception of power and ideas about the self-originating character of the freedom and autonomy of the (neoliberal) subject that I wish to undermine.

Indeed, one of my aims in this chapter is to draw critical attention to the increasing privatization and normalization of state eugenics and the continuity between eugenic practices and policies of the past and such practices and policies in the present (see also Hall 2016).

My argument is that the critiques of physician-assisted suicide, euthanasia, and prenatal and other genetic technologies that bioethicists associate with slippery-slope reasoning astutely identify the incremental normalization of modern force relations that operates through the inculcation and utilization of a relatively recent kind of subjectivity; that is, I contend that the charge of slippery-slope reasoning that (many) bioethicists direct at critics of physician-assisted suicide, euthanasia, and genetic technologies results from the failure of these bioethicists to recognize that the critiques address the nature and operations of force relations under neoliberal governmentality, including the production of neoliberal subjects whose management and modification of biological life is taken as fundamental to self-hood and responsible citizenship (see Pitts-Taylor 2010).

Let me underscore and elaborate these assertions. I maintain that (1) these critiques cohere with a sophisticated and compelling account of the productive character of modern force relations; (2) these critiques cohere with the conception of disability as an apparatus of force relations that I have articulated throughout this investigation of disability, philosophy, and feminism; and (3) the arguments with respect to autonomy, choice, and informed consent that mainstream and feminist bioethicists advance to undermine these critiques are themselves products of and implicated in this apparatus of disability, operating in the service of neoliberal governmentality (see also Kolářová 2015; Hall 2016; Tremain 2006a, 2010). Thus, this chapter offers additional evidence of how the reconstructive-conceptual sphere of my research (from which the argument about the productive character of the apparatus of disability emerged) is inextricably intertwined with the metaphilosophical sphere of my research that aims to demonstrate the eventalization of the current state of affairs in philosophy, that is, the contingency of the discursive, disciplinary, institutional, and conceptual factors that contribute to the exclusion of disabled philosophers from the profession and the marginalization of critical philosophical work on disability in the discipline.

The argument of this chapter is certain to elicit negative and defensive responses from philosophers in general and from bioethicists especially, responses that may range from condescending amusement and dismissal to skepticism and even hostility. Since I do not wish to have my argument for a feminist philosophy of disability rejected outright, nor do

I wish to underestimate philosophers who have specialized and trained in bioethics, I should reiterate that my claims in this chapter operate at a different level of generality and differ in scope than the objections that other philosophers of disability and disability theorists have raised with respect to the positions that particular bioethicists articulate on, inter alia, prenatal testing, infanticide, physician-assisted suicide, and euthanasia. For my argumentative claims in the chapter, and indeed throughout this book, rely upon Foucault's understanding of power (force relations) as both intentional and nonsubjective. Power, Foucault (1978, 94–95) explained, is calculated and always exercised with a series of aims and objectives. In this way, power is *intentional*. Nevertheless, usually no seat of power can be located nor can a group be identified as the holders of power, that is, be identified as the decision makers who direct and coordinate the complicated network of *dispositifs* (apparatuses) that circulate in society. In this way, power is *nonsubjective*. As Foucault put it:

> [L]et us not look for the headquarters that presides over its rationality; neither the caste which governs, nor the groups which control the state apparatus, nor those who make the most important economic decisions direct the entire network of power that functions in a society (and makes *it* function); the rationality of power is characterized by tactics that are quite explicit at the restricted level where they are inscribed . . . tactics which, becoming connected to one another, but finding their base of support and their condition elsewhere, end by forming comprehensive systems: the logic is perfectly clear, the aims decipherable, and yet it is often the case that no one is there to have invented them, and few who can be said to have formulated them: an implicit characteristic of the great anonymous, almost unspoken strategies which coordinate the loquacious tactics whose "inventors" or decisionmakers are often without hypocrisy. (95)

On Foucault's understanding of power as intentional and nonsubjective, the rationality of force relations is tactical. These tactical force relations become connected with each other and attract each other, ultimately forming widespread systems of power. The logic of force relations is quite clear and its aims and objectives are discernible; nevertheless, these aims and objectives are usually not attributable to anyone who can be said to have invented them, nor are they attributable to anyone who can be said to have introduced them into practice. In other words, practices on the micro level of the subject make possible more comprehensive networks of power, though rarely can the subject be identified who performed an initial practice from which these networks of power at the macro level have derived, accumulated, and coalesced.

This account of power explains how the field of bioethics can be a fundamentally pernicious enterprise populated with many well-meaning and even critical practitioners. Notice that this account of the relation between bioethics and power does not require the attribution of bad intentions or personal responsibility to any given individual or group of individuals; on the contrary, the claim that the force relations from which the subfield of bioethics emerged and through which it persists are both intentional and nonsubjective underscores the deep and far-reaching derogation of disabled people by and through the discipline and profession of philosophy. Notice, furthermore, that insofar as this account of how the subfield of bioethics is politically motivated assumes, following Foucault, that power relations are productive and circulate between and through multiple and often conflicting sites, the account does not take recourse in foundationalist assumptions about truth and knowledge that invariably underpin appeals to "ideology" as either the font of or result of power relations. Indeed, dominant notions of ideology, insofar as they assume that power suppresses truth and authenticity, advance a juridico-discursive conception of power whereby power is fundamentally repressive, generally is held by and operates from a centralized authority such as the state or a certain social institution or group, and reigns from the top down. Foucault penned his (in)famous and evocative remark that Western political theory still has not "cut off the head of the king" in order to signal that juridical conceptions of power are outdated and do not capture the diffuse operations of contemporary force relations, that is, are inadequate to address new forms of governmentality.

Insofar as I construe force relations in nonjuridical terms, I want to argue for a new way to understand and respond to strategies of the apparatus of disability that the subfield of bioethics generates. In the following sections of this chapter, therefore, I extend my nonjuridical claims about the intentional and nonsubjective character of force relations to indicate how biopower operates through the notions of autonomy and freedom in the contexts of reproductive technologies and hESC research, as well as the bioethical and other discourses that support and reinforce these new strategies and mechanisms of government.

Reproductive Biopolitics

Genetic technologies have rapidly developed as practices that produce knowledge about the genetic bases of an expanding number of ostensibly natural human characteristics and a host of risks posed to the integrity of that biological material. The production of this new knowledge has generated new ethical and political questions with respect to (for instance) informed choice, privacy, autonomy, the moral status of the embryo, the quality of human life, and what qualifies as normal. Any given response that one offers to these questions relies upon certain epistemological and ontological assumptions about what exists, what is natural, what is a product of human invention and intervention, and what properties define a thing as a "human being" (on definitions of the human, see A. Taylor 2013). Furthermore, any given set of epistemological and ontological assumptions implies certain directives and prescriptions for human action, that is, such assumptions constitute elements of the historical a priori that defines and circumscribes the possible actions from which subjects may choose. In this section, I examine one kind of knowledge that new genetic technologies produce about impairment; that is, I indicate how knowledges about prenatal impairment and indeed prenatal impairment itself are constituted by and through reproductive genetic technologies, as well as the genetic counseling and other discourses of normalization that surround these technologies. These knowledges put in place the limits of possible conduct in the domains in which they circulate.

The prediction and presence (or absence) of prenatal impairment loom large in the information that prenatal testing and screening allegedly report, where impairment is conceived as a natural flaw or defect that can be eliminated through the termination of a given pregnancy and, ideally, will someday be correctable through use of germ-line genetic therapies, gene editing, and so on.[4] Hence, many bioethicists have attempted to articulate principled ways to determine which impairments prenatal testing should be used to predict and whether a defensible line can be drawn between the types of impairment that it is morally permissible to selectively abort and the types of impairments that it is morally impermissible to selectively abort. For example, Buchanan, Brock, Daniels, and Wikler (2000), in the book that I cite earlier in this chapter, have argued that justice demands the genetic correction and enhancement of embryos and fetuses with "defects" to enable the people that they will become to "fully participate in the cooperative framework of society," where a "fully cooperating citizen" is one whose "opportunity range" is compatible with normal species-typical functioning. As I have pointed out, Amundson, among others, has worked to destabilize the notion of normal species-typical functioning and the normative conclusions that have been derived from it.

The arguments that propel the discussion in this chapter do not advance an explicitly normative argument about prenatal genetic technologies; rather, they are designed in large part to show how the constitution of impairment by and through these technologies and discourses that surround them is a governmental technique of the apparatus of disability and the regime of biopower. Thus, these arguments extend the work already accomplished in the reconstructive-conceptual sphere of the book by demonstrating how biopower ensures that impairments are generated in utero. Although technologies to test and screen (for impairment) prenatally are claimed to enhance women's capacity to be self-determining, make informed reproductive choices, and, in effect, wrest control of their bodies from a patriarchal medical establishment, I contend that this emerging relation between pregnant women and reproductive technologies is a new strategy of biopower. Indeed, my argument is that the constitution of prenatal impairment, by and through these practices and procedures, is a widening form of modern government that increasingly limits the field of possible conduct in response to pregnancy. Hence, the government of impairment in utero is inextricably intertwined with the government of the pregnant body (Tremain 2006a).

Numerous feminists have argued that the formation of the fetus is largely the history of its visualization in medical imaging techniques such as endoscopy and ultrasound (for instance, Duden 1993, 92). Lorna Weir (1996, 374–76) has pointed out that the formation of the fetus is, in addition, the history of written statements, sampling technologies, and standardized blood tests, all of which impute a range of physiological and pathological properties upon the fetal body. From the mid-1950s, Weir explains, key experimental articles appeared in print that multiplied knowledge of the fetus: articles about sex chromatin for the diagnosis of fetal sex (1955); ultrasound imaging of fetal skulls to determine fetal age (1963); the culturing of amniotic cells for chromosome, biochemical, and later genetic analyses (1966); and so on. The exponential increase in the number of "disorders" for which prenatal diagnosis became clinically available due to the introduction of these techniques has amounted to a textual elaboration of the fetus as a discursive object.

As I have indicated, many disabled activists, philosophers of disability, and disability theorists who assume the BSM (or other sociopolitical conception of disability) argue that prenatal testing and screening for impairment violate the rights of disabled people, sending a message about the disvalue of disabled people's lives. I want to point out, however, that some of the assumptions about prenatal testing and screening for impairment that advocates of the BSM make resemble presuppositions generated from within the domains of molecular biology and biomedicine and are held by many proponents of bioethical discourses themselves. For although these opponents and proponents of prenatal testing and selective abortion do not agree about the disvalue of an impairment, they agree that impairments are intrinsic properties or attributes of individuals that exist prior to, and independent of, social norms, practices, and policies. Notwithstanding the fact that proponents of the BSM misunderstand the productive machinations of modern power, it seems politically and theoretically misguided for them to claim (with their foes) that the term *impairment* is a value-neutral—that is, "merely descriptive"—designation, for there can be no description that is not also a prescription for the formulation of the object (person, practice, or thing) to which it is claimed to innocently refer. A truth discourse (such as either the BSM or the conventional medicalized model) that is purported to (merely) describe phenomena contributes to the constitution of its objects.

The distinction between impairment and disability that proponents of the BSM draw parallels the early second-wave feminist sex-gender distinction, in whose terms *sex* denotes a universal, biological substrate and *gender* signifies the culturally variant configurations of that entity. Although (as I show in chapter 3) a great deal of feminist scholarship has demonstrated the artifactual and contingent character of the category of sex, many disability theorists have continued to use the parallel by appealing to an objective, transhistorical, and transcultural notion of sex to motivate their rhetorical strategies. To take one example, some disability theorists and activists have drawn an analogy between the ways that degrading cultural norms and values, exclusionary discursive and social practices, and biased representations produce disability and how these phenomena operate in the service of sexism (e.g., Oliver 1990). To take another example, some disability theorists and activists have used the analogy from sexism to identify inconsistencies and double standards between the treatment of sexual discrimination in public policy and law and the treatment in the same domains of disability discrimination (e.g., Silvers, Wasserman, and Mahowald 1998).

I (2006) have argued, however, that the analogical arguments that disability theorists and activists make from sex reinstitute and contribute to the naturalization and materialization of binary sex as well as facilitate and contribute to the naturalization and materialization of impairment. The analogical structure of these arguments requires that one appeal to clear distinctions between males and females and men and women, as well as assume a stable and distinct notion of impairment. In the terms of these analogical arguments, furthermore, sex and impairment are represented as separate entities, each with unique properties, and each with an identity that can be distinguished from the identity of the other.

Thus, engagement in this manner of argumentation prevents disability theorists and activists from considering the implications for work in the field of the questions that the phenomena of intersex raise; in particular, this manner of argumentation renders disability theorists and activists unable to interrogate the ways in which the biomedical-scientific arm of the matrix of heterosexual cisnormativity naturalizes and materializes intersex (a category that itself presumes binary sex) as impairment, that is, as states of affairs ("Klinefelter's syndrome," "congenital adrenal hyperplasia," and so on) to be managed, controlled, corrected, and indeed eliminated.

The previous criticisms of analogical argumentation in disability studies and activism are directed at the analogical arguments that theorists and activists make about actual living human beings; however, it seems plausible to apply these remarks to the analogical arguments that they make from selective abortion on the basis of sex to selective abortion on the basis of impairment (e.g., Saxton 2000; Wolbring 2001). It seems plausible, that is, to consider the constitutive effects of these analogical arguments from fetal sex to fetal impairment; furthermore, it seems plausible to argue that this subjectification of the embryo or fetus—this *projection* of allegedly neutral characteristics onto the embryo or fetus—contributes to both the naturalization of disability as impairment and the naturalization of gender as sex. In addition, it seems plausible to point out that this mode of argumentation subjectifies the embryo or fetus, that is, subjectifies it as an embryo or fetus with the allegedly objective, transhistorical, and transcultural human properties (attributes) of sex and impairment. Indeed, because "the fetus" has been turned into a subject in this way, it has become a site of contestation between activists, antiabortionists, and feminists (among others), as well as an object of government, even though in most jurisdictions "the fetus" does not exist as a legal entity (Weir 1996). When disability theorists and activists argue that selective abortion on the basis of impairment is on par ethically with selective abortion of the basis of sex, their claims apply only to the abortion of female fetuses. They do not interrogate, indeed, do not acknowledge, the selective abortion of fetuses predicted to be ambiguously sexed humans, except if these fetuses are deemed to be impaired. This, then, is another way in which the analogical arguments that disability theorists and activists make from sex to impairment implicitly reinforce a naturalized dichotomy of sex and simultaneously prop up the way that intersex remains pathologized in current medical and juridical practices. Interestingly, many feminist arguments against selective abortion on the basis of sex continue to make reference to the expressive character of sex selection as it pertains to the social standing of women and girls only, with the proviso that sex selection is permissible if it prevents the birth of infants with so-called sex-linked disorders. Notice that these feminist arguments elide the tired distinction between sex and gender by appealing to a form of sex determinism and, in doing so, they, too, serve to naturalize binary sex and pathologize intersex.

The Government of Risk

The inventors of prenatal testing and screening did not intend them as universal procedures to be applied in all pregnancies; yet they have been steadily institutionalized within standard protocols for prenatal care and maternal "risk management" (Browner and Press 1995; Rapp 1999; Lippman 1991). For example, although sonar screening was initially developed to benefit women deemed to be at "increased risk" in pregnancy, it is a screening technique that is now advocated for use in every pregnancy. This incremental normalization of prenatal diagnostics contributes to the objectification of impairment insofar as it cultivates the notion that pregnancies can be classified and that the classifications generated imply risks of an entity called "impairment" whose existence is logically and temporally prior to the identification of these risks.

The state-administered program of maternal serum alpha-fetoprotein (AFP) screening that was instituted in California in the mid-1980s to provide universal screening for Down syndrome, spina bifida, and other neural tube "defects" offers an early example of the incremental normalization of prenatal diagnosis. In 1986, California became the first state in the United States to mandate that all providers of prenatal care must offer the AFP screen to every pregnant client who enters care prior to the twentieth completed week of pregnancy; in addition, the state mandated that all prenatal care providers must maintain records that demonstrate that they have offered the AFP screen to each of these eligible clients. By 1990, more than 60 percent of eligible Californians were screened with the AFP test, in comparison to 40 percent in 1986 (State of California 1990, 28, in Browner and Press 1995, 310–14).

The neural tube formations that the AFP screen was designed to predict occur in the United States in approximately one to two live births per thousand. For every one thousand women who undergo the AFP test, however, between fifty and one hundred of them receive positive—or "abnormal"—readings. Since the AFP test is only a screen, each of the women in the latter group requires additional testing before she can receive a definitive diagnosis: repeat AFP screening, one or more sonograms, amniocentesis, or some combination of these screens and tests. In one of several articles based on their study of the California state-mandated program of prenatal screening, Carol Browner and Nancy Press point out that although the AFP screen cannot provide definitive diagnoses and that few of the women whose intake interviews they observed were given sufficient information about the test, most of the women accepted the offer of it. That the test has been offered universally and is state administered lends legitimacy to the notion that prenatal testing is an inherently good and, therefore, necessary intervention of which pregnant women can avail themselves (Browner and Press 1995, 314–17).

Kathryn Morgan (1998) has pointed out that although some pregnant women are reluctant to undergo prenatal testing and screening, many women derive a sense of satisfaction and personal fulfillment from the fact that their pregnancies are technologically managed. When the elements of a medical matrix are incorporated into the self-understandings and self-knowledge of individuals like this, Morgan writes, the subjects constituted through the process experience themselves as people who are autonomous and active in their medical encounters. As Morgan explains it, a medical gaze and surveillance are most effectively produced when individual subjects actively support, use, and demand to use medicalizing concepts, vocabularies, and practices by claiming them as their own and by seeking an active involvement in the medical technologies in which they become subjected. As this kind of medicalized self-management ensues, she notes, the discourse generated frequently appeals to certain conceptions of responsibility, self-control, self-interest, and self-determination; moreover, many people who become ensconced in this self-management characterize the lived reality that they experience in terms of a genuine increase in their personal power and decision making (Morgan 1998, 96–97).

The claim that the practices and mechanisms of a medical regime operate most effectively when they position subjects as autonomous and free implicates those practices in neoliberal governmentality. Foucault (2003c) coined the term *governmentalities* to refer to rationalities of government, that is, systems of thinking about the practice of government that have the capacity to rationalize some form of that activity to the subjects who practice it and to the subjects upon whom it is practiced. As I have indicated, neoliberal governmentality operates at a distance from individuals by guiding, influencing, and limiting their actions in ways that accord with the exercise of their freedom. In other words, power operates most effectively when subjects are enabled to act. Although power appears to be only repressive, its most effective exercise consists in guiding the possibilities of conduct—"the conduct of conduct"—and putting in order the possible outcomes. The production of these practices, these *limits* of possible conduct, allows the discursive formation in which they circulate to be naturalized and legitimized.

Disability theorist Anne Waldschmidt (1992, 2015) has assumed this conception of power to argue that genetic testing and prenatal diagnoses are elements of a new form of eugenics that is practiced with the active participation of the individuals concerned, once they have been informed of the supposed facts and have given their consent. Neo-eugenics, Waldschmidt writes, has shed its past authoritarian roots and has developed an apparently democratic approach. Neo-eugenics does not need to operate through direct forms of coercion, pressure, open repression, or control. The state and society no longer need to intervene to urge people to do their eugenic duty, Waldschmidt remarks, because now people "voluntarily" adhere to eugenic lines of reasoning individually, without having been expressly told to do so. Waldschmidt contends that neo-eugenics functions so well precisely because it is supported and practiced "from below," that is, by the average person on the street. It does not need to be enforced from above by the police and the authorities, she notes. Not even the human geneticists and genetic counselors appear to be acting on their own authority. Rather, they seem merely to accord with the wishes of their own women clients (Waldschmidt 1992, 165).

In a comprehensive, ethnographic study of genetic counseling discourse, Rayna Rapp (1999) writes that the genetic counselors whom she observed described their goals as to give their clients "reassurance." In the discourse of genetic counseling, "to give reassurance" means to return one's clients to the general population of pregnant subjects, each of whose "background risk" of giving birth to an infant "with an impairment" is 2 to 3 percent. If "older" clients (that is, clients over age thirty-five) decide to forgo testing—in particular, amniocentesis—their genetic counselors tell them that they will undertake a *larger* risk because their "age-related risk" must be added to that "background risk" (Rapp 1999, 70). The demarcation of "age-related risk"—a statistical marker that fluctuates in accordance with modifications in the technology itself—is intended to outweigh the percentage of procedure-induced miscarriages, which, by current estimates, occur about 1 percent of the time (Rapp 1999; see also Rapp 1995).

The constitution and circulation of age-related risk produces what Abby Lippman has referred to as "iatrogenic anxiety" (1991, 3). Although it has long been known that older women are more likely than younger women to give birth to babies who present with what gets called "Down syndrome," only the recent generations of statistically graded pregnant women have been given specific risk figures and led to identify generic pregnancy anxieties with their respective ages and the statistical category to which they have been assigned. It is no coincidence that the prenatal procedures offered to pregnant women to assess and alleviate risk in pregnancy fostered this iatrogenic anxiety in the first place (Lippman 1991, 3). For although the medical and scientific communities represent genetic counseling as a value-neutral means through which to elaborate the options for action available to pregnant women that would enable them to make decisions regarding testing and its possible outcomes, the reification of age-related risk (that the practice of genetic counseling facilitates) is a technique of government that enlists women to become self-regulating and self-disciplining (Weir 1996; Lippman 1991; Rapp 1999).

Recall Foucault's (2003d) claim that the practice of government in Western societies has tended toward a form of political sovereignty that is government "of all and of each," the effects of which are to totalize and to individualize. My argument is that the conception of risk that conditions genetic counseling and prenatal diagnosis is an individualizing and totalizing strategy of government. This conception, with its language of "age-related risk," "added risk," "background risk," and "reassurance," individualizes insofar as it attaches risk to the bodies of discrete subjects; in addition, this conception of risk in pregnancy totalizes insofar as it generates statistical subpopulations, that is, "risk groups." In terms of this conception of risk in pregnancy, an increasing number of allegedly prediscursive variations between humans are attributed to allegedly prediscursive genetic structures. Lippman has referred to the epistemological trajectory of this assumption as "geneticization," which she defines as the ongoing process by which differences among individuals are reduced to their DNA codes and assumed to be genetic in origin (1991, 18). Both a rationality and a practice, geneticization attaches risk to genes and, in doing so, creates putative populations whose members are linked only by the fact that they share the same statistical probability with respect to that genetic risk. As Rapp has repeatedly shown, this conception of risk in pregnancy relies upon rather culturally specific assumptions that in many cases muffle or conflict with other epistemic strategies by which pregnant women from diverse cultural backgrounds understand risks that are posed to them and to their children (1995, 176; 1999, 70). In short, the government of risk in pregnancy is a culturally contested domain.

Since the end of the nineteenth century, the technology of risk, in all its various epistemological, economic, moral, juridical, and political modalities, has become a central organizing principle of governmentality in the West. The political and conceptual power that risk has gained is concomitant with the rise of statistical and probabilistic thinking from the eighteenth century onward. As I have pointed out, Foucault attributed the cascade of statistical assessments and interventions that has prevailed to the strategies of biopower, which from the late eighteenth century has worked toward increasingly comprehensive management of the "life" of individuals and populations (Foucault 2003g, 243). In fact, the collection of statistics about populations and deviancy is an integral and constitutive component of the modern state. Hacking has noted that the bureaucracy of statistics and probabilities does not merely create administrative rulings; rather, statistics and probabilities also determine classifications within which people must think of themselves and the options that are open to them (1991a, 182, 194). Many of the categories used to think about people and their activities were put in place by attempts to collect numerical data. Thanks to these efforts on the part of a host of administrative, juridical, medical, industrial, and economic bureaucracies, new kinds of people have come to be counted and new statistical metaconcepts—of which the most notable is "normalcy"—have been engendered (182–83). Hence, the emergence of risk as a technology of modern government.

One of the foundational premises of prenatal diagnosis and genetic counseling is that risks in pregnancy exist in reality—that is, they have an objective, prediscursive existence. Without the tests that make prenatal risk calculable, however, there would be no risk in pregnancy per se. Risk does not exist apart from the rationalities, practices, and techniques that make risk calculable and attach it to certain objects, which the technologies effectively bring into being as certain kinds of things. As François Ewald remarks, "Nothing is a risk in itself, but anything *can* be a risk; it all depends on how one analyses the danger, considers the event" (1991, 199; emphasis in Ewald). Risk is a means by which to order reality. The category of risk enables previously incalculable events to be represented in a form that makes them governable in certain ways, with certain techniques, for the satisfaction of certain goals. Risk is one element of the diverse forms of calculative rationality that are deployed "to [govern] the conduct of individuals, collectivities, and populations" (Dean 1999, 177). As calculative rationalities, forms of risk assessment incite compliance with techniques and practices that regulate, manage, and shape human conduct in certain ways, in the service of specific ends. For to describe the possibility of a certain future event as a risk is to ascribe negative value to the actual occurrence of such an event and to imply that certain measures ought to be taken to avoid it. Since the possible courses of action from which people may choose are not independent of the descriptions available to them under which they may act, and since the available descriptions are embedded in a cultural matrix of (among other things) institutions, practices, and power relations, analyses of risk must consider the kinds of objects to which risk gets attached, the kinds of knowledge that risk makes possible, the techniques employed to identify and discover risk, the technologies mobilized to govern it, and the political rationalities and programs that deploy it (175–97).

When the constitutive efficacy of risk is appreciated, the eugenic impetus behind prenatal testing and screening becomes evident. If analyses of prenatal testing and screening were to shift their emphasis to governmentality, that is, if theoretical analyses of these practices were redirected from their current location in the realm of bioethics and situated within the domain of biopolitics, the starting point of inquiry could shift from argumentative claims that take the impaired fetus as a natural kind to a thick description of the administrative, medical, prenatal, scientific, and discursive constitution of impairment by and through these technologies of normalization. The (neo)liberal governmentality that facilitates the birth of the practices of biopower also spawns reactions to that apparatus, some of which have been articulated in the language of reproductive freedom. A governmental approach to prenatal testing and screening enables one to recognize that the feminist achievement of "reproductive choice" and the genetic counseling claimed to enhance that ostensible autonomy operate as effects of the polymorphous character of liberalism, which is its capacity to both foster and engage criticism of itself, as well as to subsequently recuperate that critique in the service of certain political ends (Foucault 1991; see also Weir 1996).

The importance of the government of prenatal impairment for normalization cannot be overstated. Over the past two centuries, a vast apparatus, erected to secure the well-being of the general population, has caused both the disabled subject and the idea that disability has a biological foundation—impairment—to emerge into discourse and social existence. An understanding of biopower's normalizing strategies allows one to analyze the constitution of prenatal impairment in ways that avoid the reductive arguments about misogynistic science and patriarchal medical practices that tended to condition earlier feminist analyses of reproductive technologies and control of the maternal body (see Sawicki 1991, 67–94). The argument from governmentality does not assume that pregnant subjects who undergo prenatal testing and screening or who insert themselves in genetic counseling contexts have been duped by the ideological forces of some distant and overarching external power, nor does the argument from governmentality imply that these subjects make morally bad personal decisions. Instead, the argument from governmentality indicates how practices of neoliberal governmental power produce people with certain kinds of subjectivities, that is, these practices have constituted subjects whose actions are governed through the exercise of their own capacity to choose in accordance with the norm(al).

The Metaphysics of SC Research

In the introductory chapter, I point out that mainstream philosophical inquiries into disability take for granted the metaphysical and epistemological status of disability, casting it as self-evident and thus philosophically uninteresting. Recall that on the terms of the cluster of motivational assumptions that underlie these inquiries, disability is a prediscursive, transcultural, and transhistorical disadvantage, an objective human defect or characteristic that ought to be prevented, corrected, eliminated, and cured. That disability is a historically and culturally specific and contingent social phenomenon, a complex apparatus of power rather than a natural attribute or property that certain people possess, is not considered, let alone seriously investigated. Over the course of the book, I have argued that many feminist philosophers, too, hold these assumptions about the ontological and epistemological character of disability. Nowhere are these assumptions more evident than in mainstream and feminist bioethical discussions about disability and genetic technologies, including prenatal testing and screening and SC research.

Until recently, philosophical debate about hESC research has largely been limited to its ethical dimensions and implications. Although the importance and urgency of these ethical debates should not be underestimated, the almost undivided attention that mainstream and feminist philosophers have paid to the ethical dimensions of hESC research suggests that the only philosophically interesting questions and concerns about the technology are by and large ethical in nature. In this section of my inquiry into the biopolitics of bioethics, I challenge the assumption that ethical considerations alone must be foregrounded in philosophical discussions about hESC research by introducing a critical stance on the epistemological and ontological assumptions that underlie and condition the research and discussions that surround it. I also argue that heretofore these debates have been formulated in ways that obscure their own governmental production, that is, ways that obscure their imbrication in the problematization of disability and the government of disabled people.

The question of whether the U.S. federal government should fund hESC research became a pivotal issue of debate in the weeks and months leading up to the 2008 U.S. presidential election. Every American voter, it seemed, held strong convictions on a matter that, not all that long ago, had been the specialized province of embryologists, geneticists, some bioethicists, and a handful of politicians: fundamentalist Christians and other members of the "pro-life" movement decried the destruction of the human embryo that hESC requires; left-leaning intelligentsia argued that the current prohibitions on hESC research were a legacy of Bush-era anti-intellectualism; leaders of the American scientific community circulated the terrible truth that the United States was losing its ground at the forefront of genetic research internationally; so-called average Americans, under the influence of a media consistently producing hype about the successes of SC technology, expressed frustration about the fact that potentially lifesaving medical treatments were being withheld from them; and some pro-choice feminists, convinced that Bush's restrictions on the growth of hESC lines encroached on women's reproductive rights, implied that opposition to hESC research threatened gains made in the realm of gender equality. For example, in an op-ed piece appearing in the *Los Angeles Times* on September 4, 2008, the feminist icon Gloria Steinem asserts that one of the three most troubling and antifeminist aspects of Republican vice presidential candidate Sarah Palin's policy stances was her refusal to support federal funding for hESC research. As Steinem explains it, Palin's pledge to oppose funding for hESC research was as troubling and antifeminist as her opposition to *Roe v. Wade* and her support for the introduction of creationism and intelligent design in public school instruction. For Steinem, it seems, reproductive freedom and other civil liberties are themselves at stake in the SC debates and thus support for hESC research should be taken up as a feminist issue.

In their introduction to a special issue of *Metaphilosophy* devoted to the ethics of SC research, Laura Grabel and Lori Gruen provide one account of the ethical reflection and debate about hESC research in which a growing number of philosophers are engaged. Due to the development of the atomic bomb, they write, there have been legitimate worries that ethical debate about scientific and technological developments occurs too late. They note, with some relief, that ethical discussion with respect to hESC research is, however, taking place at the same time as the research proceeds. In the United States, they explain, discussions continue about how to maintain the highest ethical standards with respect to regulation and oversight, which embryos can be used, what forms of consent must be provided, how privacy can be maintained, whether payment should be made to embryo and gamete donors, and so on. At the international level, they point out, philosophers increasingly enter conversations with scientists, policy makers, religious leaders, and others about how to move hESC research forward in the most ethically defensible ways (Grabel and Gruen 2007, 137).

The almost exclusive attention that philosophers have paid to the ethical dimensions of hESC research has seriously limited the sorts of questions about the research that philosophers have formulated and are prepared to consider. Certain epistemological and ontological assumptions about disability (e.g., about its origins, effects, and so on) that underlie and condition the research and the motivation to develop it have been taken for granted as self-evidently true, remaining unexamined in mainstream and almost all feminist bioethical discussions about it. Hence, the argument in this section adds another dimension to feminist bioethical and other philosophical discussion about hESC research by challenging the self-evidence and alleged objectivity of these epistemological and ontological commitments. That neither mainstream nor feminist bioethical approaches to hESC research consider the potentially detrimental effects for disabled people of these epistemological and ontological assumptions underscores the historically situated character of bioethical discourses and their conceptual objects (Tremain 2006b, 2008, 2010). The argument of this section is thus designed to show how these epistemological and ontological assumptions about hESC research, as well as the research itself, play a role in the efficient and economical operation of a relatively recent regime of knowledge-power, namely, biopower. Indeed, the discussion in this section shows how bioethical discourses about hESC research have been a local center through which the constitution of impairment has traversed.

SCs can be functionally defined in terms of their ability to self-renew and their multipotency. In mammalian development, embryonic stem cells (ESCs), which are undifferentiated (i.e., unspecialized), are considered the most multipotent cells because they contribute to all three germ layers of the developing embryo and have the ability to form any differentiated (specialized) cell type. Adult stem cells (ASCs), which are differentiated (specialized) and located in many adult tissues, maintain the ability to generate all the cell types required to build the tissue, or organ, of origin (Van der Kooy and Weiss 2000). For example, a neural SC derived from the adult brain can generate all the cell types required to build a brain (astrocytes, neurons, and ogliodendrocytes). Scientists believe, therefore, that SCs can provide ideal models for understanding the bases and developments of specific diseases and are potential sources of transplantable tissue to be used to treat, for instance, Parkinson's disease and spinal cord injury (Gruen 2007, 285). Most scientists who work on SC technology argue, however, that although ASCs and SCs derived from cadaveric fetal tissue have been shown to serve some of these purposes, ESCs can do so more effectively. Hence, the trend is to focus SC research on ESCs. Gruen has written that to realize its full promise hESC research would ideally entail the creation of hESC lines with specific genotypes that could (1) model certain diseases (such as Alzheimer's or Parkinson's) and (2) provide histocompatible transplantation therapies able to resist rejection and minimize the need for immunosuppressive drugs. These developments, Gruen (2007, 286) notes, will require oocytes—some researchers estimate a lot of oocytes—in both the research and therapeutic phases of the work. That these diseases have a prediscursive existence and should be eliminated with the use of ESC technology is taken for granted in the research and in the bioethical literature about it.

hESCs are typically derived from the inner cell mass of embryos that remain after IVF treatments. They can also be derived from embryos deemed "unsuitable" following PGD or with the use of other nongenetic evaluative criteria, such as "morphology." Insofar as the derivation of SCs from the inner cell mass of an embryo requires the embryo's destruction, the moral status of the embryo has been the crux of public debate and controversy about hESC research. Until relatively recently, mainstream bioethical discussion about issues in hESC research has also focused almost exclusively on the question of the embryo's moral status, suggesting that this is the only relevant question to ask about the technology. (The judgment that some embryos are "unsuitable" for implantation and the criteria on which such a judgment is predicated have gone unquestioned by both mainstream and feminist critics and proponents of hESC research—though these judgments are increasingly issues of concern to disabled people.) Thus, mainstream bioethical opposition to hESC research has generally been grounded in one of two assumptions: the embryo is a human being or the embryo is a potential human being. Although most embryologists and geneticists maintain that early hESCs are too unspecialized to constitute a unique identity, bioethicists who hold that the embryo has the same moral status as persons argue that human life begins at conception, that all human life is sacred, and that the destruction of the embryo during hESC research is tantamount to the sacrifice of a person to scientific knowledge.

In an article with the evocative title "The Point of a Ban; or, How to Think about Stem Cell Research," Gilbert Meilander (2001) demonstrates that at one time the question of the embryo's moral status was indeed the only question that mainstream bioethicists regarded as important to ask about the research. As Donna Dickenson explains it, although Meilander attempts to provide a more nuanced consideration of the assertion that it is wrong to destroy an existing or potential human being than other opponents of the technology do, he nevertheless remains preoccupied with the harms that the research poses to the embryo. Meilander claims that to take the notion of respect for the embryo seriously, we may need to regard the relief from suffering through scientific progress that SC research promises as a "real but not supreme imperative" (Meilander 2001, 15, in Dickenson 2007, 62). Dickenson remarks that although Meilander set out to widen the debate beyond "a seemingly endless argument about the embryo's moral status," he did not widen it much at all. To the contrary, Dickenson writes, respect for the embryo remained the sole ethical issue in relation to hESC research, with the only difference being that the important question to ask became this: is respect for the embryo an absolute imperative when consequentialist arguments about the relief of human suffering are weighed against it, or is it not? (2007, 63).

Whereas Meilander suggests that the counterweight of relief from human "suffering" might render scientific progress in the area of SC research a prima facie rather than an absolute, imperative, some bioethicists who believe that embryos deserve special respect, though not the full respect afforded to persons, have argued that the future of hESC research is worth the sacrifice of embryos that remain after IVF treatments. For example, Patricia Roche and Michael Grodin (2000, 139) have argued that from the perspective of justice it would be unethical to rank respect for embryos over the good that might accrue to actual living human beings because of the knowledge that scientists hope to gain from hESC research: the good of actual living human beings always outweighs the good of potential human beings. Note that although these authors seem to have shifted discussion of the ethics of hESC research away from consideration of harms to the embryo by moving the goalposts of argumentation in a more consequentialist direction than Meilander did, their argument nevertheless presumes that such a move must be made in terms of the embryo's moral status.

Roche and Grodin notwithstanding, one might have expected mainstream proponents of hESC research to bypass or even avoid claims about the moral status of the embryo; however, they have not really done so. In 1994, the Human Embryo Research Panel (HERP) in the United States recommended that federal funds should be forthcoming for both research on embryos remaining after IVF treatment and embryos created solely for research purposes. In an article that appeared in the *New England Journal of Medicine* in 1996, American bioethicists George Annas, Arthur Caplan, and Sherman Elias—who wished to secure congressional funding for embryo research yet avoid hurdles that the American antiabortion movement erected—critique the HERP recommendations by drawing a distinction between embryos created for IVF procreative attempts and embryos created for research only. They distinguish between embryos in this way by arguing that "the embryo research conflict" cannot be resolved solely based on moral properties inherent to the embryo because the circumstances under which conception occurs are also morally relevant considerations. As these bioethicists explain it, "The embryo's moral status derives not only from a cluster of properties it possesses, but also from the interests that potential parents and society bring to procreation and reproduction" (Annas, Caplan, and Elias 1996). The rhetorical strategy of these bioethicists is noteworthy for the following reason: although they argued that the "embryo research conflict" cannot be resolved on the basis of a set of moral properties inherent to the embryo because the moral status of the embryo is socially constituted, they nevertheless assumed that the product of such constitution— namely, the embryo's moral status—is the single most important factor that needs to be addressed in response to the question of whether or not hESC research should be publicly funded.

Insofar as Annas and colleagues argue that the moral status of the embryo is socially constituted, deriving at least in part from personal and societal interests, they acknowledge the value-laden character of the public and bioethical debates about hESC research that revolve around and contribute to the constitution of that status. I will eventually show that through a process of social and political constitution certain properties are projected onto certain embryos, in addition to the properties that combine to constitute the embryo's moral status. In this context, however, I am concerned to underscore that although Annas and colleagues point to the interested and value-laden character of the embryo's moral status, they do not seem to think that embryo research itself should be regarded as a product and an effect of certain interests and values, let alone that embryo research should be regarded as a technique of government, that is, the direction of conduct. Rather, these authors point to the social constitution of the embryo's moral status and its value-laden character to argue that these contingencies should not hamper the putatively value-neutral and objective domain within which embryo research is undertaken. In other words, one of the assumptions that underpins their critique of the HERP recommendations is this: although the moral status of the embryo is a site of social and political contestation, embryo research itself is a morally and politically neutral endeavor and should be allowed to stand apart from the noise of these public debates. Contra Annas and his colleagues, however, many feminist bioethicists have compellingly argued that embryo research, like a host of other scientific and medical research endeavors, is a value-laden enterprise. Let us consider these arguments in feminist bioethics.

Feminist Critiques of hESC Research

As I note at various places throughout the previous chapters, one of the guiding assumptions of a great deal of feminist scholarship and practice is that questions and claims are always situated and interested. Feminist scholars have sought to demonstrate that much of what in recent Anglo-European societies has been accepted as value-neutral and objective knowledge and truth reflects androcentric and masculinist biases. Feminist critiques of abstraction and of the theoretical gesture that elevates a specific historical experience to the level of an absolute universal have conditioned feminist approaches to bioethics. Feminist bioethics has, from its inception, been suspicious of how this logic of abstraction operates in medicine, as well as in ethical and bioethical inquiry. Thus, feminist bioethicists have sought to dethrone the abstract principles assumed

in mainstream ethics and bioethics by scrutinizing the concrete consequences for women (and other marginalized groups) of certain scientific and medical practices, as well as the bioethical discussions about them
(e.g., Sherwin 1992, 2008). As Mary Rawlinson (2008, 2) explains, feminist approaches to bioethics have challenged mainstream bioethics for
its reliance on abstract principles disconnected from the material conditions of action and the specificities of the relationships in which ethical
urgencies arise. From the beginning, she continues, feminist bioethics
also insisted on turning to women's experience and women's bodies as
points of departure in science, politics, and philosophy and as resources
or sites for the production of concepts that might function generically,
informing us about human (not just women's) experience.

Given that feminist bioethicists have precipitated a conceptual and
theoretical shift away from abstraction and false universalism to consider the bioethical questions and concerns that arise when women's
lives are fully accounted for, it is not surprising that some of them have
challenged the almost exclusive attention that mainstream bioethical
approaches to hESC research had at one time paid to the moral status
of the embryo. Dickenson, for instance, has argued that this "obsession"
with the embryo's moral status has obscured regulatory and other issues
that pertain to women whose ova make the research possible. She notes,
for example, that it has been widely assumed that if techniques in hESC
research could be developed that did not require embryos, the technologies would be ethically unobjectionable (Dickenson 2007, 59–60).

Only in the aftermath of the scandal involving Dr. Hwang Woo Suk
did mainstream bioethicists begin to consider the sorts of measures that
should be enacted to protect the women from whom the ova required
for embryo research would be taken. Hwang, who at one time was
revered as a pioneer in hESC research, used over twenty-two hundred
eggs from 129 women, some of whom were his junior researchers, in
what was eventually exposed as fraudulent research. Heather Widdows
(2009) has reported that over half the women who supposedly gave their
eggs to Hwang had sold them to him, many of these transactions taking place through a profit-making international agency, the DNA bank,
that recruited Malaysian, Chinese, and other Asian women in addition
to Korean women (Paik 2006, in Widdows 2009, 12). More than half of
these women, Widdows notes, were paid an average of $1,400 U.S. for
their eggs (Joung 2006, in Widdows 2009, 12). With these inducements
in view, some of the women underwent the "donation" process (which
may result in ovarian hyperstimulation[5] and other sequelae) as many as

three times, with one woman providing forty-three eggs (Widdows 2009, 12). Although the case of Hwang is the best-known example of (among other things) the unethical use of female members of an embryo research team for their ova, many recent reports have documented a flourishing trade in human ova for IVF, in which eggs are contracted for extraction from Eastern European women and sold to infertile couples in wealthier countries such as Britain, Germany, and Israel (Dickenson 2007, 58–60). Angela Ballantyne and Sheryl de Lacey (2008, 155) have pointed out that reports have also been made in the European Parliament that in the Ukraine eggs have been removed postmortem from babies without parental consent.

Due to the very public furor over egg donation that has ensued due to the Hwang scandal and because of the international nature of most SC research teams, there has been growing pressure to produce harmonized standards on egg procurement. Although some specific guidance for research-oriented human egg procurement has been produced, disagreements with respect to the ethics of egg donation and ongoing controversies about payment for ova nevertheless persist and have prevented the construction of binding international governance on the matter among interested countries (Dickenson and Idiakez 2008, 129; Witherspoon Council on Ethics and the Integrity of Science 2012). Dickenson remarks that insofar as the women from whom eggs are extracted derive no therapeutic benefit themselves from the pharmaceutical and surgical interventions that egg extraction involves, it should be asked whether doctors who perform the interventions contravene their duty to "do no harm." Indeed, Dickenson responds in the affirmative to the question she rhetorically poses by arguing that women who undergo egg extraction are used solely as means to another's ends, in contravention of the Kantian categorical imperative and the medical duty of nonmaleficence, regardless of whether informed consent has been obtained from them (Dickenson 2007, 65–67; see also Ballantyne and de Lacey 2008, 149). To be sure, some feminist bioethicists have argued that a regulated market in oocytes would provide recognition and validation of women's autonomy, promote their options, and be a partial remedy for the racial discrimination that permeates "egg donation" (Grabel and Gruen 2007, 148; see also Gruen 2007). Dickenson and Itziar Alkorta Idiakez (2008, 134) have argued, however, that many of the arguments that appeal to informed consent and payment in order to justify claims according to which the procedures have been freely chosen conceal the deception and exploitation that surround them. As with prenatal testing and screening, so, too, with embryo research and the egg donation that it requires: the historically and culturally specific ideals of autonomy and informed consent facilitate the depoliticization and normalization of neoliberal governmental practices.

SC Research and the Apparatus of Disability

Whereas mainstream (or nonfeminist) bioethical considerations of hESC research had at one time focused almost exclusively on the moral status of the embryo, feminist bioethical inquiries into the research have concentrated almost solely on ethical questions and issues about "sourcing" and "harvesting" ova from women, especially with respect to autonomy and consent, as well as on the fact that these questions and issues had been largely overlooked in mainstream bioethical accounts of the research. Although mainstream bioethics is now more apt to acknowledge the potential and actual harms of hESC research and technology for women than it was in the past, it has yet to acknowledge the potentially harmful effects of the research and technology for disabled people; that is, mainstream bioethics has not critically examined the epistemological and ontological understandings about disability that underlie the research. Rather, mainstream proponents of hESC research, and even some of its opponents, take for granted (and indeed have contributed to) the (paradoxical) conviction that the development of SC research is both inherently good—insofar as it promises to minimize or eliminate certain forms of disease, impairment, and disability—and value neutral—insofar as it is an outcome of disinterested and objective scientific knowledge. With few exceptions, feminist bioethicists, too, have both implicitly or explicitly endorsed the taken-for-granted conviction that SC technology itself is inherently good and value neutral and that disabled people universally regard its development as a desirable and unequivocally momentous outcome of scientific progress. This conviction—that SC technology is inherently good and value neutral—is propped up by news agencies and other media that widely and frequently report the poignant testimonies of disabled people who urgently argue that they have a human right to benefit from SC research and that opponents to it in effect condemn them to a diminished life, if not a death sentence. By contrast, disabled people who articulate concerns about and objections to the technology are largely ignored by or discounted in the press and other media, which foster the public perception that their views are eccentric, if not unintelligible (see Tremain 2006b; Goggin and Newell 2004).

These ideas about the diminished lives of disabled people—and the cluster of assumptions about restoration, repair, health, and cure on which they rely—simultaneously provide the impetus to develop the research and contribute to the naturalization and materialization of both impairment and the apparatus of disability more generally. Given my claims thus far, it should now be evident that these assumptions and their constitutive effects are generated in accordance with the requirements of the diagnostic style of reasoning, which emerged through and in tandem with the apparatus of disability. hESC technology and the discourses that surround and interact with it significantly contribute to the constitution of impairment, that is, to its materialization and naturalization. Medical, scientific, and virtually all bioethical discourses on hESC research presuppose that impairment is a universal, stable, and distinct human attribute or characteristic, with transhistorical and transcultural properties, from which a recognizable and scientifically indisputable notion of "normal" can be distinguished. In the terms of these discourses on hESC technology, these allegedly transhistorical and transcultural properties and the human characteristic (attribute) that they constitute (impairment) must be eliminated from the actual living subjects who currently embody them and must be "de"-selected to prevent future embodiment of them.

Within the context of hESC research, that is, the process of normalization that is constitutive of impairment begins in the lab with the allegedly value-neutral clinical perception of an objectively detrimental human characteristic (a "defect") and its projection onto the embryo, followed by the determination that any given embryo that manifests such a characteristic is unsuitable for implantation and hence should be donated for research purposes. Often this perception and impending decision are based on criteria—"morphology"—that are no more objective than a judgment that the embryo "doesn't look nice" (J. Nisker, personal communication, 2005; see also Ballantyne and de Lacey 2008, 149). The evaluation of unsuitability may also be based on PGD, itself an interpretive procedure. Although several feminist bioethicists have drawn attention to the value-laden character of these judgments, they have overlooked their constitutive effects. Ballantyne and de Lacey have asserted, for instance, that embryo-grading practices are "contentious" and that the process of evaluating and grading gametes and embryos is arguably grounded in "subjective opinions." However, these authors have been concerned to show only that the practices of grading and evaluating ova heighten the vulnerability of women who undergo IVF by increasing the pressure on them to donate their "low-quality" ova for research; that is, these authors have neglected to consider the extent to which such grading and evaluating practices contribute to the constitution of the very prenatal defects, abnormalities, and other discursive objects that they are claimed to innocently identify and assess (see Ballantyne and de Lacey 2008, 149).

Biopower—as both a governmental rationality that aims to harness the vagaries of life and the dispersed network of force relations through which this governmentality circulates—normalizes people in order to make them governable. Within the constraints of this normalizing governmentality, certain characteristics among populations have been materialized and made perceptible as pathology, while the subjects who come to bear these ostensibly natural and objective characteristics are rendered as "abnormal" and "defective," are regarded as naturally disadvantaged, and are signified as either less than fully human, or as fully human, but in need of repair. Through the apparatus of disability, biopower produces these subjects as the embodiment of a "problem" that must be resolved or eliminated. Technologies of normalization that emerge from the apparatus of disability are designed to identify and isolate such anomalous subjects who can in turn be normalized through the regulatory strategies of other technologies that biopower generates. Such technologies of normalization are thus both individualizing and totalizing. That is, technologies of normalization are neither merely benign nor merely benevolent responses to the identification of anomalies in the social body; rather, these technologies are vital to the systematic creation, classification, and control of such anomalies. Grading and evaluating practices of hESC research, for example, both mobilize technologies designed to eliminate embryos unsuitable for implantation in virtue of impairment and systematically contribute to the constitution of the perception of impairment in the first place.

Feminist discussions of hESC research and a growing number of mainstream discussions of the technology, insofar as they focus on autonomy and informed consent, assume a juridical notion of power whereby power stands in opposition to freedom, is possessed, and can be exchanged; thus, these discussions preclude analysis of the incremental normalization and problematization of impairment and disability that the technology facilitates and extends. Yet, the problematization of disability (and its naturalized antecedent, impairment) that emerged from biopower has been increasingly integral to the framework of liberal governmentality from the eighteenth century on, that is, integral to the governmental rationality based on a conception of autonomous legal subjects endowed with rights and individual freedoms (see also Hall 2016). As noted throughout this book, the management and administration of people's actions in ways that accord with the exercise of their freedom is most effectively and efficiently achieved indirectly through the distribution and prescription of norms and standards that people more or less freely endeavor to approximate. Under such a regime, a strategy of eugenics is most effective when it enlists individuals to become self-governing, that is, to take responsibility for the management and maximization of the prospects of their own lives and the lives of future generations. The development of embryo research, the refinement of prenatal testing and screening, and the institutionalization of an academic discipline that (among other things) adjudicates their value, as well as the incremental normalization of these technologies and practices—normalization that contributes to the stabilization of previously unrecognized laws, the emergence of new types of evidence, and the constitution of new types of objects—are elements of this eugenic strategy.

This chapter was designed to show that the subfield of bioethics is a technology of modern government. I have argued that prenatal testing and screening, hESC research, and physician-assisted suicide and euthanasia, as well as the bioethical (and other) discourses that surround and are mutually constitutive with these technologies and practices, contribute to the problematization of disability and its allegedly natural foundation, impairment. A particular coalescence and movement of force relations—biopower—has produced these technologies, practices, and discourses and facilitated their incremental normalization in order to secure the life of a distinctive population.

Afterword

A Call for More Dialogue about Disability*

⎯⎯⎯ ⁘ ⎯⎯⎯

Reprising the Book

Foucault and Feminist Philosophy of Disability has drawn upon Foucault and feminist philosophers (among others) to consider how the problematization of disability that emerged from a relatively recent form of power (biopower) has been produced in philosophy. The arguments of the book were developed in two distinct, but interrelated and mutually constitutive, spheres: a reconstructive-conceptual sphere and a metaphilosophical sphere. In the reconstructive-conceptual sphere, I argued that philosophers take for granted that disability is a natural—that is, prediscursive—and disadvantageous attribute or characteristic of certain individuals that, therefore, is philosophically uninteresting. In this sphere, I elaborated and advanced an alternative historicist and relativist conception of disability as an apparatus (in Foucault's sense) of power.

---

*Some philosophers of disability have cautioned that calls for increased "dialogue" and other communicative practices operate as individualizing and totalizing strategies in the service of neoliberal capitalism by fostering subjectivities that are more productive, compliant, predictable, and interchangeable (among other things). I hope that my call for more dialogue about the apparatus of disability will be understood as a strategic call to action of a different kind, namely, a strategic call that, in the service of counterhegemonic resistance, makes available previously unavailable discursive space in which subjugated knowledges about apparatuses of force relations can circulate and practices to subvert these force relations can be created.

In the metaphilosophical sphere, I offered theoretical arguments and empirical evidence to show that the understanding of disability that (most) philosophers continue to hold contributes significantly to the exclusion of disabled philosophers from the profession through, among other things, the production of an environment that is hostile to them. Let me highlight the course that the arguments took over the five chapters of the book.

The introductory chapter identified the problematization of disability and advanced the thesis that disability should be understood as an apparatus of productive force relations rather than as a personal characteristic, an identity, a difference, or a form of social oppression. This discussion of the apparatus of disability enabled me to distinguish my historicist and relativist approach to disability from the medicalized and individualized understanding of disability that mainstream philosophers hold; from a dominant model in disability studies; and, in addition, from the understandings of disability that other feminist philosophers of disability hold.

The second chapter identified and explained aspects of Foucault's work that are central to an understanding of disability as an apparatus, including his claims about the practice of genealogy, the subject, the mechanisms and strategies of biopower, governmentality, and the disciplinary and regulatory power of the norm and normalization. In the second chapter, I also drew upon Hacking's claims about styles of reasoning to introduce the diagnostic style of reasoning through which the apparatus of disability has brought impairment—the naturalized foundation of disability—into being.

In the third and fourth chapters, by responding to charges that disability theorists and feminist philosophers have directed at Foucault, I elaborated the conception of disability as a productive apparatus. In the third chapter, I used Foucault's ideas about genealogy, the subject, and the individualizing and totalizing character of modern government, as well as Butler's claims about the performativity of gender, to respond to charges from disability theorists that Foucault ignores materiality and subjectivity. In the fourth chapter, I relied upon Foucault's nominalism and examination of his Collège de France lectures to respond to feminist charges that his work is masculinist and reflects sexist and androcentric biases.

In the fifth and final chapter, Foucault's claim that modern force relations are intentional and nonsubjective enabled me to advance the argument that the subfield of bioethics is a technology of government that emerged by and through the apparatus of disability to facilitate normalization. I illustrated this argument by considering a charge directed at critics of physician-assisted suicide and euthanasia and more closely examining prenatal testing and screening and hESC research, as well as the discourses constituted by, around, and through these technologies. I pointed out that insofar as bioethics has emerged to facilitate normalization, this subfield of philosophy operates to homogenize the population and thus, ultimately, cannot be reconciled with efforts within the discipline and profession to increase the heterogeneity of philosophy and the university and society more broadly.

Dialogues on Disability

The work to improve the professional situation of disabled philosophers and garner support in the discipline for philosophy of disability extends beyond the pages of this book and any other. Disabled philosophers constitute one of the most underrepresented groups in the profession. In concrete, experiential, and material terms, many disabled philosophers—like disabled people in general—remain isolated, are underemployed or unemployed, and are marginalized and oppressed. As I indicated in the introductory chapter, the data available, to date, indicates that disabled philosophers account for roughly 1–2 percent of faculty employed in North American philosophy departments, although disabled people make up an estimated 22 percent of the general North American population. Many disabled philosophers in academic positions have no job security and no health or dental insurance and are forced to endure inaccessible and even dangerous working conditions because of the precarious nature of their employment. Hence, there has been a pressing need for disabled philosophers to publicize the discrimination and disadvantages that they encounter throughout the profession. Some disabled philosophers have experienced significant professional repercussions due to their attempts to resist and subvert the marginalization and discrimination that they have confronted in philosophy.

Since April 2015, I have conducted monthly interviews with disabled philosophers and have posted them to the *Discrimination and Disadvantage* blog, the philosophy blog that I coordinate with Kevin Timpe, initiated by Kevin and Thomas Nadelhoffer. The interview series, called Dialogues on Disability, provides a public venue for discussion with disabled philosophers about a range of topics, including their philosophical work on disability; the place of philosophy of disability vis-à-vis the discipline and profession; their experiences of institutional discrimination and personal prejudice in philosophy and in academia more generally; resistance to ableism; accessibility; and anti-oppressive pedagogy. Dialogues on Disability represents a collective effort to counter the isolation and disenfranchisement that accrue to disabled philosophers. The interviews in the series have, each in its own way, enabled disabled philosophers to draw attention to professional, institutional, and personal issues pertinent to them that are not adequately or appropriately addressed in venues such as philosophy journal articles or philosophy conferences (conferences that are financially, discursively, and structurally inaccessible to many of them), providing role models and mentorship to disabled students and faculty. Among other things, the interview series provides a forum through which disabled philosophers can articulate their circumstances and experiences of oppression and exclusion without fear that they will be shut down, disparaged, or attacked, all strategies that have been employed against disabled philosophers to maintain ableist power asymmetries in philosophy.

The Dialogues on Disability series is important, furthermore, because it also shines a spotlight on critical philosophical approaches to disability that have been dismissed or obscured in recognized areas of philosophy. This book has attempted to show that the claims that philosophers make about disability in the areas of mainstream bioethics, political philosophy and ethics, cognitive science, and even feminist philosophy have been conditioned by and circumscribed within the terms of medicalized, individualizing, pathologizing, and paternalistic ideas and assumptions about disability that the apparatus of disability generates. My interviewees in the Dialogues on Disability series repeatedly demonstrate how uncritical acceptance of these medicalizing assumptions and condescending beliefs about disability reproduces biases within philosophy, across the university, and beyond academia.

Thus, Dialogues on Disability is shifting relations of knowledge-power in philosophy with respect to disability. Indeed, the Dialogues on Disability series is a hub for production of new forms of knowledge about disability and should therefore be recognized as a critical and vital contribution to social epistemology. In particular, Dialogues on Disability enables disabled philosophers to demonstrate—in very specific and concrete ways—to their nondisabled colleagues that the disadvantages they confront are not medical in nature and are not natural, nor are they isolated occurrences to be rectified through individualized means; on the contrary, as my interviewees continue to show, these disadvantages are political and socially constituted products of the apparatus of disability whose elimination requires that the wider philosophical community develop broad structural and institutional strategies and solutions for that distinct purpose. The Dialogues on Disability series is a guide to that end.

Notes

———— ෴ ————

Preface

1. The framework of the PhilPapers database has been transported to other databases external to the PhilPapers organization, such as the database "Diversity Reading List in Philosophy." These databases, too, marginalize philosophical work on disability because of their infrastructure and design. See Folk, n.d.

2. In "Introducing Feminist Philosophy of Disability," my introduction to the special issue of *Disability Studies Quarterly*, I advance arguments designed to show how the phrases "women and underrepresented groups in philosophy" and "women and minorities in philosophy" operate to obscure power relations in philosophy that advantage nondisabled white women. See Tremain 2013b.

Chapter 1

1. Increasing attention is paid to the relations between disability and the domination of nonhuman animals. See, for instance, S. Taylor (2017) and Donaldson and Kymlicka (2011).

2. An interlocutor might object that my use of terms such as *metaphysical, ontological,* and *ontology* flies in the face of the historicist and antifoundationalist approach to disability that I aim to advance in this book. Such an interlocutor might argue that insofar as the approach that I advance draws on Foucault and antiessentialist feminist philosophers, I should emphasize *practices* rather than metaphysics. Although I understand the twentieth-century criticisms of metaphysics from which this sort of objection derives, my use of these terms serves a different purpose than is the target of these criticisms. My use of these terms should be understood as similar to the way that Ian Hacking has used the term *ontology*. As Hacking explains it: "suppose we want to talk in a quite general way about all types of objects, and what makes it possible for them to come into being. It is convenient to group them together by talking about

'what there is,' or ontology" (2002, 1). I want to point out, furthermore, that Foucault himself used the term *ontology* in this way when he referred to (for instance) "critical ontology" and "historical ontologies."

3. Selection bias can be defined as the phenomenon whereby individuals, groups, or data are selected for analysis in a way that is not representative of the population or field of inquiry analyzed.

4. Confirmation bias can be defined as the phenomenon whereby information that is sought, favored, interpreted, or recalled confirms one's preexisting beliefs or hypotheses.

5. Sander L. Gilman and James M. Thomas have pointed out that a strict distinction between an "old" approach and a "new" approach to the scientific study of humans and social categories is historically unfounded and theoretically misguided. Gilman and Thomas caution against adoption of the idea that there has been a linear progression from a consensus with respect to biological determinism about humans and social categories to a consensus with respect to social constructionism about humans and social categories. I want to point out that Roberts avoids this mistake, as I indicate later in the chapter. See Gilman and Thomas 2016.

6. Twomey's article notes that Gage's skull and mask are currently housed at the Warren Anatomical Museum on the Harvard Medical School campus, where they are quite popular items in the collection. I cannot help but see an obvious and troubling likeness between this state of affairs and the case of Saartjie (Sarah) Baartman ("the Hottentot Venus"), whose body was used to advance the apparatus of (scientific) racism and whose remains were, until recently, displayed at the Muséum d'Histoire Naturelle in Angiers. Thanks to Kevin Tobia and Joshua Knobe for an engaging discussion about how Phineas Gage has been used in cognitive science, philosophy of mind, and other areas of academic research. For writing about the phenomenology and ontology of brain injuries, narratives about the lives of people who have experienced brain injuries, and legal and ethical arguments that take account of the marginalized social position and status of such people, see Sherry 2006; Fins 2015; Wright 2016.

7. In *Dark Ghettos: Injustice, Dissent, and Reform*, Tommie Shelby (2016) uses the term *medical model* to refer to a broad understanding of the "problem of the ghetto" that assumes it to be a "pathology" of given black individuals who thus ought to be fixed or helped in some way. Although many philosophers will regard Shelby's book as squarely positioned within analytic philosophy, I think that his identification of the individualizing and pathologizing emphasis of this approach to the "problem" of the ghetto aligns with both Foucault's claims about "racism against the abnormal," which I discuss in chapters 2 and 5, and with the historicist conception of disability as an apparatus that I advance in this book. See Shelby 2016, 2–4, 21.

8. For a very interesting discussion of the cultural and historical specificity of the notion of "brain death," see Lock 2002.

9. Despite Foucault's explicit denial that his claims rely upon skepticism, Colin Koopman has argued that Foucault's ideas about power derive from a skeptical stance. See Koopman 2017b.

10. See Nichols 2012 for an account of queerness as an apparatus. See Repo 2015 for an account of gender as an apparatus. At the outset of the chapter, I identified both sexuality and gender as apparatuses.

11. My understanding of disability as an apparatus resembles Sally Haslanger's now familiar conception of race, though in the next chapter I advance an argument

that converges the seemingly separate and distinct notions of race and disability and, in doing so, I reconfigure them. See Haslanger 2000, 2006, 2012.

12. At the outset of her book *The Minority Body* (2016), Elizabeth Barnes stipulates that the book is about physical disability which she distinguishes from cognitive and psychological disability. One of the main reasons that Barnes focuses on physical disability concerns the emphasis that, as she explains it, she gives to first-person testimony. As Barnes puts it, "psychological and cognitive disabilities raise complicated issues for the reliability of testimony that simply aren't present in the case of physical disability." Physical disability, she writes, is "the easiest and most straightforward case" (3). This rationale should not be unquestioningly accepted and seems to be an example of epistemic injustice. Indeed, as Barnes might have expected, her assertions in this context have met with considerable disapproval in some corners of disability studies, not least because they could reinstate a hierarchy of recognition that many disability theorists have worked hard to eliminate. I want to point, furthermore, that first-person testimony plays a relatively minor role in Barnes's book. In short, the justification for the distinction seems unsubstantiated. The assertion that the book is about physical disability seems to be undermined by the fact that many of the arguments and examples that Barnes uses to support and illustrate her claims throughout the book concern blindness and deafness which are commonly regarded as *sensory* disabilities rather than *physical* disabilities. As my argument in this context makes clear, I eschew these descriptions of disability as a personal characteristic or attribute of given individuals.

13. In an interview published in February 2016, Dr. Marc Edwards, whose studies revealed high rates of lead in the Flint, Michigan, water supply, asserted that "the perverse incentive structures" of academia prevented scientists from exposing the problem with the water in Flint sooner. As Edwards put it, "In Flint the agencies paid to protect these people weren't solving the problem. They *were* the problem. What faculty person out there is going to take on their state, the Michigan Department of Environmental Quality, and the U.S. Environmental Protection Agency?" As Edwards explained it, the incentive structures that early-career academics face directed them away from the kind of work that he, in collaboration with community organizers and other Flint residents, did in Flint and toward more lucrative work that had questionable social value. See Kolowich 2016; emphasis in Kolowich. Thanks to Olúfẹ́mi O. Táíwò, who directed me to this interview.

14. Other examples of ableist exceptionism in philosophy arise from and reproduce the virtual exclusion of disabled philosophers from the profession: first, the common failure of nondisabled philosophers to include the knowledge and perspectives of disabled people in work that impacts upon their own lives, even though these philosophers advocate such inclusion with respect to the insights and perspectives of members of other marginalized social groups (in chapter 5, I discuss this issue with respect to the claims and research endeavors of bioethicists); and, second, the lack of concern that many nondisabled feminist philosophers who publish and teach about disability and disabled people demonstrate for the low number of disabled philosophers employed in the profession, though they are outspoken about gender inequality in philosophy.

15. For example, none of the feminist and other philosophers who (now) argues that analyses of power should concentrate (at least in part) on the institutional and structural mechanisms of power has thus far broached the institutional and structural constraints and exclusions with respect to disability (such as the composition of the

PhilPapers and PhilJobs databases) that I described in my 2013 article "Introducing Feminist Philosophy of Disability." See Tremain 2013b.

16. My discussion in this context should suggest some of the ways in which Fricker fails to capture Foucault's ideas about power (among others). For example, Fricker's (2007, 10, 12–13) remark that Foucault does not understand power as a capacity that can operate when no one is present to ensure its operation fails to account for his ideas of government as "the conduct of conduct," normalization, discipline and disciplinary constraints, and panopticism. Most of these ideas in Foucault's work are explained and discussed in the following chapter. In another context, I show that Fricker misunderstands how the apparatus of disability is racialized. See Tremain 2017. For another critique of Fricker's approach to epistemic injustice, see Dotson 2012.

17. I would like to thank Alison Reiheld, Chandra Kumar, Sally Haslanger, Zara Bain, Lydia Nunez, Axel Arturo Barceló, Kristie Dotson, and Daniel J. Brunson, who engaged me in a Facebook discussion about arguments that I make in this paragraph. These arguments improved because of the discussion. I would also like to thank Evan Thompson, who shared with me both an unpublished paper that he delivered to the International Symposium for Contemplative Studies held in San Diego in November 2016 and his chapter "Looping Effects and the Cognitive Science of Mindfulness Meditation" (2017).

Chapter 2

1. I realize that this division is an artifact of discourse and that my use of it in the book may lend credence to the criticisms that some cultural theorists and feminist theorists have made according to which Foucault's work (and hence use of it) is anthropocentric. As some authors in disability studies and critical animal studies have noted, however, Foucault (2007) himself demonstrated that his ideas could be used in nonanthropocentric ways and in nonanthropocentric contexts. For instance, see Fritsch 2015.

2. In *Are Racists Crazy? How Prejudice, Racism, and Antisemitism Became Markers of Insanity*, Gilman and Thomas claim that the term *biopower* was coined in 1905 when Rudolph Kjellén introduced it in *Stormaterna* (1920), one of the first sociological works on "geopolitics." Gilman and Thomas point out that the term was reworked in the critical literature of the 1930s, such as Morley Roberts's *Bio-politics: An Essay in the Physiology, Pathology, and Politics of the Social and Somatic Organism* (1938). See Gilman and Thomas 2016, 13.

3. Although Foucault himself gave considerable attention to dividing practices, normalization, classification of anomalies, racism against the abnormal, and other discursive objects that concern the apparatus of disability, Foucault scholars who are not philosophers and theorists of disability have largely neglected to analyze the apparatus of disability or use the work of philosophers and theorists of disability who draw upon his claims to analyze disability themselves.

4. Self-advocates in the United Kingdom, where these authors were located when this article was published, prefer the term *learning difficulties* to terms such as *cognitive disabilities* or *cognitive impairments*.

5. For an account of Foucault's critique of, and critical appropriation of, rights discourse, see Golder 2015.

6. In chapter 1, I cited work by the medical anthropologist Margaret Lock on the cultural and historical specificity of the notion of brain death. In that work, Lock

draws upon Hacking's and Arnold Davidson's (2001) discussions of styles of reasoning to explain how, in a relatively short span of time, systematization of the methods and reasoning used to determine brain death have changed radically, and thus the significance of brain death has likewise been radically transformed. See Lock 2002.

Chapter 3

1. The term *disability rights movement* is used by activists in the U.S., while the term *disabled people's movement* is used in the U.K. The use of these different terms reflects the fact that activists (and theorists) in the U.S. and U.K. disagree about what disability is.

2. As I recall, the disabled philosopher of biology Ronald Amundson, who was the first disability studies scholar to correct this error, did so initially on the Disability Studies in the Humanities (DS-HUM) listserv. See Amundson, n.d.

3. I should point out, as I have done elsewhere (see Tremain 2015, 30), that Kittay's remarks in this context conflate the categories of impairment and disability, as well as naturalize and (re)medicalize impairment. Although my argument in this book and elsewhere effectively collapses the distinction between impairment and disability, it does so in a way that politicizes both impairment and disability rather than (re)medicalizes them.

Chapter 4

1. See my discussion of the sex-gender distinction in chapter 3.

Chapter 5

1. Kittay (among others) has shown resemblances between the eugenic reasoning of the Nazi doctors and some arguments advanced in contemporary moral philosophy about the moral status of disabled people. See Kittay 2016.

2. The research endeavor described in an article entitled "Professors Lead Call for Ethical Framework for New 'Mind Control' Technologies," seems to be an example of the failure to take account of disabled people's perspectives and subjugated knowledges on issues that directly affect them, as well as an example of the failure to draw upon the arguments and insights of (disabled) philosophers of disability on such matters. Indeed, I would argue that this research project incorporates an epistemology of domination with respect to (the apparatus of) disability. See University of Pennsylvania 2017.

3. In feminist bioethics and feminist philosophy more generally, assumptions about the allegedly diminished character of disabled people's quality of life have motivated arguments according to which certain people (i.e., people who are "at risk" of reproducing disabled infants) have a moral imperative not to reproduce. For instance, Purdy 1995, 2009; Cassidy 2006.

4. Discussions about the development and unregulated implementation of gene editing technologies (also referred to as "germline genetic technologies") intensified in 2017, with some of these discussions entering the public domain and everyday discourse to an extent that they had not before (see Cobb 2017). While my arguments with respect to genetic technologies are foremost directed at the productive and political dimensions of these technologies, I want to note the contested character of

scientific claims according to which attempts at gene editing have already been "successful." In an article published in *Nature* on August 2, 2017, Heidi Ledford reported that an international team of researchers, led by reproductive biologist Shoukhrat Mitalipov at the Oregon Health and Science University, had used CRISPR-Cas9 gene editing to "correct" a dominant "mutation" in a gene called *MYBPC3*, that is, to "correct" a "mutation" in the density of heart muscle. In an article posted to the bioRxiv preprint server on August 28, 2017, however, a team led by Dieter Egli, a stem-cell scientist at Columbia University, and Maria Jasin, a developmental biologist at Memorial Sloan Kettering Cancer Center, questioned whether the "mutation" was actually "fixed." See Heidi Ledford (2017) and Egli et al. (2017).

5. Angela Ballantyne and Sheryl de Lacey (2008) have pointed out that specialists in reproductive medicine acknowledge that there is insufficient data about the long-term effects of the drugs used to hyperstimulate ovaries, that practitioners in the field do not adequately understand the possible consequences of rounds of ovulation stimulation subsequent to the initial round, and that women who sell their eggs (in the commercial U.S. environment in particular) are not sufficiently informed about the possible consequences of ovarian hyperstimulation procedures and the extent of uncertainty that surrounds them.

References

Abberley, Paul. 1996. "Work, Utopia and Impairment." In *Disability and Society: Emerging Issues and Insights*, edited by Len Barton, 61–79. Harlow, UK: Longman.

Alcoff, Linda Martín. 1996. "Dangerous Pleasures: Foucault and the Politics of Pedophilia." In *Feminist Interpretations of Foucault*, edited by Susan J. Hekman, 99–135. University Park: Pennsylvania State University Press.

Alcoff, Linda Martín. 2000. "Who's Afraid of Identity Politics?" In *Reclaiming Identity: Realist Theory and the Predicament of Postmodernism*, edited by Paula M. L. Moya and Michael R. Hames-Garcia, 213–44. Berkeley: University of California Press.

Alcoff, Linda Martín. 2006. *Visible Identities: Race, Gender, and the Self.* New York: Oxford University Press.

Allen, Barry. 2015. "Foucault's Nominalism." In *Foucault and the Government of Disability*, rev. ed., edited by Shelley Tremain, 93–107. Ann Arbor: University of Michigan Press.

American Philosophical Association. 2016. Demographic Survey 2016. Available at http://www.apaonline.org/

Amundson, Ron. 2000. "Against Normal Function." *Studies in the History and Philosophy of Biological and Biomedical Sciences* 31C: 33–53.

Amundson, Ron. 2005. "Disability, Ideology, and Quality of Life: A Bias in Biomedical Ethics." In *Quality of Life and Human Difference*, edited by David Wasserman, Robert Wachbroit, and Jerome Bickenbach, 101–24. Cambridge: Cambridge University Press.

Amundson, Ron. N.d. "About the Meaning of Handicap." https://hilo.hawaii.edu/~ronald/HandicapDefinition.htm

Annas, George, Arthur Caplan, and Sherman Elias. 1996. "The Politics of Human-Embryo Research—Avoiding Ethical Gridlock." *New England Journal of Medicine* 334:1329–32.

Annas, George J., and Michael A. Grodin. 1995. *The Nazi Doctors and the Nuremberg Code: Human Rights in Human Experimentation.* Oxford: Oxford University Press.

Appiah, Kwame Anthony. 2016. "Mistaken Identities: Culture." The Reith Lectures. Produced by BBC Radio 4. http://www.bbc.co.uk/programmes/b00729d9/epi sodes/player

Bailey, Moya. 2011. "'The Illest': Disability as Metaphor in Hip Hop Music." In *Blackness and Disability*, edited by Chris Bell, 141–48. East Lansing: Michigan State University Press.

Bailey, Pearce. 1922. "A Contribution to the Mental Pathology of Races in the United States." *Archives of Neurology and Psychiatry* 7:183–201.

Ballantyne, Angela, and Sheryl de Lacey. 2008. "Wanted—Egg Donors for Research: A Research Ethics Approach to Donor Recruitment and Compensation." *International Journal of Feminist Approaches to Bioethics* 1 (2): 145–64.

Banaji, Mahzarin, and Anthony Greenwald. N.d. "Implicit Association Test." Project Implicit. https://implicit.harvard.edu/implicit/

Barad, Karen. 2007. *Meeting the Universe Halfway: Quantum Physics and the Entanglement of Matter and Meaning.* Durham: Duke University Press.

Barad, Karen. 2008. "Posthumanist Performativity." In *Material Feminisms*, edited by Stacy Alaimo and Susan Hekman, 120–54. Bloomington: Indiana University Press.

Barnes, Elizabeth. 2009. "Disability and Adaptive Preference." *Philosophical Perspectives* 23 (1): 1–22.

Barnes, Elizabeth. 2016. *The Minority Body: A Theory of Disability.* Oxford: Oxford University Press.

Bartlett, Tom. 2017. "Can We Really Measure Implicit Bias? Maybe Not." *Chronicle of Higher Education.* January 5. http://www.chronicle.com/article/Can-We-Really-Measure-Implicit/238807

Baylis, Françoise, and Carolyn McLeod. 2007. "The Stem Cell Debate Continues: The Buying and Selling of Eggs for Research." *Journal of Medical Ethics* 33:726–31.

Beauchamp, Tom, and James F. Childress. 2012. *Principles of Biomedical Ethics.* Oxford: Oxford University Press.

Benhabib, Seyla. 1987. "The Generalized and the Concrete Other: The Kohlberg-Gilligan Controversy and Feminist Theory." In *Feminism as Critique: Essays on the Politics of Gender in Late-Capitalist Societies*, edited by Seyla Benhabib and Drucilla Cornell. Minneapolis: University of Minneapolis Press.

Bonnet, H., and J. Bulard. 1868. *Rapport medico-légal sur l'état mental de Charles-Joseph Jouy, inculpé d'attendats aux moeurs.* Nancy.

Boorse, Christopher. 1977. "Health as a Theoretical Concept." *Philosophy of Science* 44:542–73.

Brock, Dan. 2002. "Genetic Testing and Selection: A Response to the Disability Movement's Critique." Paper presented at the Tenth Genetic Technology and Public Policy in the New Millennium Symposium, November.

Brock, Dan. 2009. "Voluntary Active Euthanasia." In *Biomedical Ethics: A Canadian Focus*, edited by Johnna Fisher, 164–76. Don Mills, ON: Oxford University Press. Reprinted from *Hastings Center Report* 22 (2) (2002).

Brown, Wendy. 2015. *Undoing the Demos: Neoliberalism's Stealth Revolution.* New York: Zone Books.

Browner, Carole H., and Nancy Ann Press. 1995. "The Normalization of Prenatal Diagnostic Screening." In *Conceiving the New World Order: The Global Politics of Reproduction*, edited by Ruth Ginsberg and Rayna Rapp, 307–22. Berkeley: University of California Press.

Brownmiller, Susan. 1990. *In Our Time: Memoir of a Revolution.* New York: Dial Press.

Brownstein, Michael, and Jennifer Saul, eds. 2016. *Implicit Bias and Philosophy.* Vols. 1 and 2. Oxford: Oxford University Press.

Buchanan, Allen, Dan W. Brock, Norman Daniels, and Daniel I. Wikler. 2000. *From Chance to Choice: Genetics and Justice.* Cambridge: Cambridge University Press.

Butler, Judith. 1993. *Bodies That Matter: On the Discursive Limits of "Sex."* New York: Routledge.

Butler, Judith. 1999. *Gender Trouble.* 2nd ed. New York: Routledge. First published in 1990.

Cahill, Ann J. 2000. "Foucault, Rape, and the Construction of the Feminine Body." *Hypatia: A Journal of Feminist Philosophy* 15 (1): 43–63.

Carlson, Licia. 2009. *The Faces of Intellectual Disability: Philosophical Reflections.* Indianapolis: Indiana University Press.

Carlson, Licia. 2015. "Docile Bodies, Docile Minds: Foucauldian Reflections on Mental Retardation." In *Foucault and the Government of Disability*, rev. ed., edited by Shelley Tremain, 133–52. Ann Arbor: University of Michigan Press.

Carlson, Licia. 2016. "Feminist Approaches to Cognitive Disability." *Philosophy Compass* 11/10 (2016): 541–53. http://dx.doi.org/10.1111/phc3.12350

Cassidy, Lisa. 2006. That Many of Us Should Not Parent. *Hypatia: A Journal of Feminist Philosophy* 21 (4): 40–57.

Centers for Disease Control and Prevention. 2015. "Disability Impacts All of Us: A Snapshot of Disability in the United States." https://www.cdc.gov/ncbddd/dis abilityandhealth/infographic-disability-impacts-all.html

Clark, Andy. 1998. "Where Brain, Body, and World Collide." *Daedalus* 127 (2): 257–80.

Cobb, Matthew. 2017. "The Brave New World of Gene Editing." *New York Review of Books*, July 13. http://www.nybooks.com/articles/2017/07/13/brave-new-world-of-gene-editing/

Cooper, Rachel. 2004. "Why Hacking Is Wrong About Human Kinds." *British Journal of Philosophy of Science* 55 (1): 73–85.

Corker, Mairian, and Tom Shakespeare, eds. 2002. *Disability/Postmodernism: Embodying Disability Theory.* London: Continuum.

Crow, Liz. 1996. "Including All of Our Lives: Renewing the Social Model of Disability." In *Encounters with Strangers: Feminism and Disability*, edited by Jenny Morris, 206–22. London: Women's Press.

Davidson, Arnold. 2001. *The Emergence of Sexuality: Historical Epistemology and the Formation of Concepts.* Cambridge, MA: Harvard University Press.

Davidson, Arnold. 2003. Introduction to *Abnormal: Lectures at the Collège de France, 1974–75*, by Michel Foucault, xvii–xxvi. New York: Picador.

Dean, Mitchell. 1999. *Governmentality: Power and Rule in Modern Society.* London: Sage.

De Lauretis, Teresa. 1984. *Alice Doesn't: Feminism, Semiotics, Cinema.* Bloomington: Indiana University Press.

De Lauretis, Teresa. 1987. *Technologies of Gender: Essays on Theory, Film, and Fiction.* Bloomington: Indiana University Press.

Desjardins, Michel. 2012. "The Sexualized Child: Parents and the Politics of 'Voluntary' Sterilization of People Labeled Intellectually Disabled." In *Sex and Disability*, edited by Robert McRuer and Anna Hollow, 69–85. Durham: Duke University Press.

Dickenson, Donna. 2002. "Commodification of Human Tissue: Implications for Feminist and Development Ethics." *Developing World Bioethics* 2 (1): 55–63.

Dickenson, Donna. 2007. *Property in the Body: Feminist Perspectives*. Cambridge: Cambridge University Press.

Dickenson, Donna, and Itziar Alkorta Idiakez. 2008. "Ova Donation for Stem Cell Research: An International Perspective." *International Journal of Feminist Approaches to Bioethics* 1 (2): 125–44.

Disabled Peoples' International Europe. 2000. "Disabled People Speak on the New Genetics." DPI Europe Position Statement on Bioethics and Human Rights. http://www.dpi-europe.org/bioethics_issues/bioethics_issues/

Dolmage, Jay. 2005. "Between the Valley and the Field." *Prose Studies* 27 (1/2): 108–19.

Dolmage, Jay. 2017. *Academic Ableism*. Ann Arbor: University of Michigan Press.

Donald, Merlin. 1991. *The Origins of the Modern Mind: Three Stages in the Evolution of Cognition and Culture*. Cambridge, MA: Harvard University Press.

Donald, Merlin. 2001. *A Mind So Rare: The Evolution of Human Consciousness*. New York: W. W. Norton.

Donaldson, Sue, and Will Kymlicka. *Zoopolis: A Political Theory of Animal Rights*. Oxford: Oxford University Press.

Dotson, Kristie. 2011. "Tracking Epistemic Violence, Tracking Practices of Silencing." *Hypatia: A Journal of Feminist Philosophy* 26 (2): 236–57.

Dotson, Kristie. 2012. "A Cautionary Tale: On Limiting Epistemic Oppression." *Frontiers* 33 (1): 24–47.

Downie, Jocelyn, and Susan Sherwin. 1996. "A Feminist Exploration of Issues Around Assisted Death." *St. Louis University Public Law Review* 15 (2): 303–30.

Drinkwater, Chris. 2015. "Supported Living and the Production of Individuals." In *Foucault and the Government of Disability*, rev. ed., edited by Shelley Tremain, 229–44. Ann Arbor: University of Michigan Press.

Duden, Barbara. 1993. *Disembodying Women: Perspectives on Pregnancy and the Unborn*. Cambridge, MA: Harvard University Press.

Egli, Dieter, Michael Zuccaro, Michal Kosicki, George Church, Allan Bradley, and Maria Jasin. 2017. "Inter-Homologue Repair in Fertilized Human Eggs?" bioRxiv, https://doi.org/10.1101/181255

Erevelles, Nirmala. 2015. "Signs of Reason: Rivière, Facilitated Communication, and the Crisis of the Subject." In *Foucault and the Government of Disability*, rev. ed., edited by Shelley Tremain, 45–64. Ann Arbor: University of Michigan Press. Reprinted from *Studies in Philosophy and Education* 21 (1) (2002): 17–35.

Ewald, François. 1991. "Norms, Discipline, and the Law." In *Law and the Order of Culture*, edited by Robert Post, 138–61. Berkeley: University of California Press.

Ewald, François, and Alessandro Fontana. 2003. Foreword to *Abnormal: Lectures at the Collège de France, 1974–75*, by Michel Foucault, xi–xv. New York: Picador.

Fausto-Sterling, Anne. 2000. *Sexing the Body: Gender Politics and the Construction of Sexuality*. New York: Basic Books.

Fineman, Martha. 2005. *The Autonomy Myth: A Theory of Dependency*. New York: The New Press.

Fins, Joseph J. 2015. *Rights Come to Mind: Brain Injury, Ethics, and the Struggle for Consciousness*. Cambridge: Cambridge University Press.

Florence, Maurice [Foucault]. 1994. "Foucault." In *The Essential Foucault: Selections from Essential Works of Foucault, 1954–1984*, edited by Paul Rabinow and Nikolas Rose, 1–5. New York: The New Press.

Folk, Simon. N.d. "Diversity Reading List in Philosophy." http://www.diversityreadinglist.org/

Foucault, Michel. 1970. *The Order of Things: An Archaeology of the Human Sciences*. Translated by Alan Sheridan. New York: Vintage Books.

Foucault, Michel. 1972. *The Archaeology of Knowledge and the Discourse of Language*. Translated by Alan Sheridan. London: Tavistock.

Foucault, Michel. 1973. *The Birth of the Clinic: An Archaeology of Medical Perception*. Translated by A. M. Sheridan Smith. New York: Vintage Books.

Foucault, Michel. 1977a. *Discipline and Punish: The Birth of the Prison*. Translated by Alan Sheridan. New York: Vintage Books.

Foucault, Michel. 1977b. "Nietzsche, Genealogy, History." In *Language, Counter-memory, Practice: Selected Essays and Interviews by Michel Foucault*, edited by Donald F. Bouchard, 139–64. Ithaca: Cornell University Press.

Foucault, Michel. 1977c. "Power and Sex." In *Michel Foucault: Politics, Philosophy, Culture: Interviews and Other Writings, 1977–1984*, edited by Lawrence D. Kritzman, 110–24. New York: Routledge.

Foucault, Michel. 1978. *The History of Sexuality*. Vol. 1, *An Introduction*. Translated by Robert Hurley. New York: Vintage Books.

Foucault, Michel. 1980a. "The Confession of the Flesh." In *Power/Knowledge: Selected Interviews and Other Writings, 1972–1977*, edited by Colin Gordon, 194–228. New York: Pantheon Books.

Foucault, Michel. 1980b. "Two Lectures." In *Power/Knowledge: Selected Interviews and Other Writings, 1972–1977*, edited by Colin Gordon, 78–108. New York: Pantheon Books.

Foucault, Michel. 1982. "The Subject and Power." Appended to *Michel Foucault: Beyond Structuralism and Hermeneutics*, edited by Hubert L. Dreyfus and Paul Rabinow, 208–26. 2nd ed. Chicago: University of Chicago Press.

Foucault, Michel. 1985. *The Use of Pleasure*. Translated by Robert Hurley. New York: Vintage Books.

Foucault, Michel. 1986. *The Care of the Self*. Translated by Robert Hurley. New York: Vintage Books.

Foucault, Michel. 1988a. "Power, Moral Values, and the Intellectual." *History of the Present* 4.

Foucault, Michel. 1988b. "Sexual Choice, Sexual Act: Foucault and Homosexuality." In *Michel Foucault: Politics, Philosophy, Culture: Interviews and Other Writings, 1977–1984*, edited by Lawrence D. Kritzman, 286–303. New York: Routledge.

Foucault, Michel. 1988c. *Technologies of the Self: A Seminar with Michel Foucault*. Edited by Luther H. Martin, Huck Gutman, and Patrick H. Hutton. Amherst: University of Massachusetts Press.

Foucault, Michel. 1990. "Confinement, Psychiatry, Prison." In *Politics, Philosophy, Culture: Interviews and Other Writings, 1977–1984*, edited with an Introduction by Lawrence D. Kritzman, 178-210. New York: Routledge.

Foucault, Michel. 1991. *Remarks on Marx: Conversations with Duccio Trombadori*. Translated by R. J. Goldstein and J. Cascaito. Brooklyn, NY: Semiotext(e).

Foucault, Michel. 1994. *Dits et écrits*. Vol. 4.

Foucault, Michel. 1997a. "The Birth of Biopolitics." In *The Essential Work of Michel Foucault, 1954–1984: Ethics: Subjectivity and Truth*, edited by Paul Rabinow, 73–79. New York: The New Press.

Foucault, Michel. 1997b. "What Is Enlightenment?" In *The Essential Works of Michel Foucault, 1954–1984, Ethics: Subjectivity, and Truth*, edited by Paul Rabinow, 303–19. New York: The New Press.

Foucault, Michel. 2003a. *Abnormal: Lectures at the Collège de France, 1974–75*. New York: Picador.

Foucault, Michel. 2003b. "The Birth of Social Medicine." In *The Essential Foucault: Selections from Essential Works of Foucault, 1954–1984*, edited by Paul Rabinow and Nikolas Rose, 319–37. New York: The New Press.

Foucault, Michel. 2003c. "Governmentality." In *The Essential Foucault: Selections from Essential Works of Foucault, 1954–1984*, edited by Paul Rabinow and Nikolas Rose, 229–45. New York: The New Press.

Foucault, Michel. 2003d. "Omnes et Singulatim: Toward a Criticism of Political Reason." In *The Essential Foucault: Selections from Essential Works of Foucault, 1954–1984*, edited by Paul Rabinow and Nikolas Rose, 180–201. New York: The New Press.

Foucault, Michel. 2003e. "Polemics and Problematizations: An Interview with Michel Foucault." In *The Essential Foucault: Selections from Essential Works of Foucault, 1954–1984*, edited by Paul Rabinow and Nikolas Rose, 10–24. New York: The New Press.

Foucault, Michel. 2003f. "Questions of Method." In *The Essential Foucault: Selections from Essential Works of Foucault, 1954–1984*, edited by Paul Rabinow and Nikolas Rose, 246–58. New York: The New Press.

Foucault, Michel. 2003g. *"Society Must Be Defended": Lectures at the Collège de France, 1975–1976*. Edited by Mauro Bertani and Alessandro Fontana. Translated by David Macey, 1–21. New York: Picador.

Foucault, Michel. 2006. *Psychiatric Power: Lectures at the Collège de France, 1973–74*. New York: Picador.

Foucault, Michel. 2007. *Security, Territory, Population: Lectures at the Collège de France, 1977–1978*. Edited by Michel Senellart. Translated by Graham Burchell. New York: Palgrave Macmillan.

Foucault, Michel. 2008. *The Birth of Biopolitics: Lectures at the Collège de France, 1978–1979*. Edited by Michael Senellart. Translated by Graham Burchell. New York: Palgrave Macmillan.

Foucault, Michel. 2014. "Interview with Jean François and John de Wit (May 22, 1981)." In *Wrong-Doing Truth-Telling: The Function of Disavowal in Justice*, edited by Fabienne Brion and Bernard E. Harcourt, translated by Stephen W. Sawyer, 253–69. Chicago: University of Chicago Press.

Fraser, Nancy. 1989. *Unruly Practices: Power, Discourse, and Gender in Contemporary Social Theory*. Cambridge: Polity Press.

French, Sally. 1993. "Disability, Impairment, or Something in Between?" In *Disabling Barriers, Enabling Environments*, edited by John Swain, Vic Finkelstein, Sally French, and Michael Oliver, 17–25. London: Sage.

Fricker, Miranda. 2007. *Epistemic Injustice: Power and the Ethics of Knowing*. Oxford: Oxford University Press.

Fritsch, Kelly. 2015. "Desiring Disability Differently: Neoliberalism, Heterotopic Imagination, and Intra-corporeal Configurations." *Foucault Studies* 19:43–66.

Garland-Thomson, Rosemarie. 2011. "Misfits: A Feminist Materialist Disability Concept." *Hypatia: A Journal of Feminist Philosophy* 26 (3): 591–609.

Gendler, Tamar. 2011. "On the Epistemic Costs of Implicit Bias." *Philosophical Studies* 156:33–63.

Gill, Michael. 2012. "Sex Can Wait, Masturbate: The Politics of Masturbation Training." *Sexualities* 15 (3/4): 472–93.

Gilman, Sander L., and James M. Thomas. 2016. *Are Racists Crazy? How Prejudice, Racism, and Antisemitism Became Markers of Insanity*. New York: New York University Press.

Goggin, Gerard, and Christopher Newell. 2004. "Uniting the Nation? Disability, Stem Cells, and the Australian Media." *Disability & Society* 19 (1): 47–60.

Golder, Ben. 2015. *Foucault and the Politics of Rights.* Redwood City: Stanford University Press.

Gordon, Colin. 1991. "Governmental Rationality: An Introduction." In *The Foucault Effect: Studies in Governmentality,* edited by Graham Burchell, Colin Gordon, and Peter Miller, 1–51. Chicago: University of Chicago Press.

Gould, Stephen J. 1996. *The Mismeasure of Man.* New York: W.W. Norton.

Grabel, Laura, and Lori Gruen. 2007. "Introduction: Ethics and Stem Cell Research." *Metaphilosophy* 38 (2–3): 137–52.

Grigely, Joseph. 2017. "The Neglected Demographic: Faculty Members With Disabilities." *Chronicle of Higher Education,* June 27. Available at http://www.chronicle.com

Gruen, Lori. 2007. Oocytes for Sale? *Metaphilosophy* 38 (2–3): 285–308.

Gutting, Gary. (2003) 2008. "Foucault." In *The Stanford Encyclopedia of Philosophy,* edited by Edward N. Zalta. http://plato.stanford.edu/entries/foucault/

Hacking, Ian. 1990. *The Taming of Chance.* Cambridge: University of Cambridge Press.

Hacking, Ian. 1991a. "How Should We Do the History of Statistics?" In *The Foucault Effect: Studies in Governmentality,* edited by Graham Burchell, Colin Gordon, and Peter Miller, 181–95. Chicago: University of Chicago Press.

Hacking, Ian. 1991b. "The Making and Molding of Child Abuse." *Critical Inquiry* 17 (2): 253–88.

Hacking, Ian. 1992a. "Making Up People." In *Forms of Desire: Sexual Orientation and the Social Constructionist Controversy,* edited by Edward Stein, 69–88. New York: Routledge.

Hacking, Ian. 1992b. "'Style' for Historians and Philosophers." *Studies in History and Philosophy of Science* 23 (1): 1–20.

Hacking, Ian. 1995. "The Looping Effects of Human Kinds." In *Causal Cognition: A Multidisciplinary Debate,* edited by Dan Sperber, David Premack, and Anne James Premack, 351–94. New York: Oxford University Press.

Hacking, Ian. 2000. *The Social Construction of What?* Cambridge, MA: Harvard University Press.

Hacking, Ian. 2002. *Historical Ontology.* Cambridge, MA: Harvard University Press.

Hacking, Ian. 2007. "Natural Kinds: Rosy Dawn, Scholastic Twilight." *Royal Institute of Philosophy Supplements* 61:203–39.

Hahn, Harlan. 1985. "Toward a Politics of Disability: Definitions, Disciplines, and Policies. *Social Science Journal* 22 (4): 87–105.

Hall, Melinda. 2015." Continental Approaches in Bioethics." *Philosophy Compass* 10 (3): 161–72. http://dx.doi.org/10.1111/phc3.12202

Hall, Melinda. 2016. *The Bioethics of Enhancement: Transhumanism, Disability, Bioethics.* Lanham, MD: Rowman and Littlefield.

Hamilton, Jon. 2017. "Why Brain Scientists Are Still Obsessed With the Curious Case of Phineas Gage." *Shots: Health News From NPR* (blog). NPR. May 21. http://www.npr.org/sections/health-shots/2017/05/21/528966102/why-brain-scientists-are-still-obsessed-with-the-curious-case-of-phineas-gage

Haraway, Donna J. 1990. *Primate Visions: Gender, Race, and Nature in the World of Modern Science.* New York: Routledge.

Haraway, Donna J. 1991. *Simians, Cyborgs, and Women: The Reinvention of Nature.* New York: Routledge.

Harding, Sandra. 1986. *The Science Question in Feminism.* Ithaca: Cornell University Press.

Harding, Sandra. 1991. *Whose Science? Whose Knowledge? Thinking from Women's Lives.* Ithaca: Cornell University Press.

Harding, Sandra. 2015. *Objectivity and Diversity: Another Logic of Scientific Research.* Ithaca: Cornell University Press.

Hartsock, Nancy C. M. 1983. "The Feminist Standpoint: Developing the Ground for a Specifically Feminist Historical Materialism." In *Discovering Reality*, edited by Sandra Harding and Merrill B. Hintikka, 283–310. Dordrecht: D. Reidel.

Haslanger, Sally. 2000. "Gender and Race: (What) Are They? (What) Do We Want Them To Be?" *Noûs* 34 (1): 31-55.

Haslanger, Sally. 2006. "Philosophical Analysis and Social Kinds: What Good Are Our Intuitions?" *Aristotelian Society Supplementary* 80 (1): 89–118.

Haslanger, Sally. 2012. *Resisting Reality: Social Construction and Social Critique.* New York: Oxford University Press.

Henderson, Holly. 2007. "Feminism, Foucault, and Rape: A Theory and Politics of Rape Prevention." *Berkeley Journal of Gender, Law & Justice* 22 (1): 225-53. http://scholarship.law.berkeley.edu/bglj

Hengehold, Laura. 1994. "An Immodest Proposal: Foucault, Hysterization, and the 'Second Rape.'" *Hypatia: A Journal of Feminist Philosophy* 9 (3): 88–107.

Hughes, Bill. 2015. "What Can a Foucauldian Analysis Contribute to Disability Theory?" In *Foucault and the Government of Disability*, rev. ed., edited by Shelley Tremain, 78–92. Ann Arbor: University of Michigan Press.

Hughes, Bill, and Kevin Patterson. 1997. "The Social Model of Disability and the Disappearing Body: Towards a Sociology of Impairment." *Disability & Society* 12: 325–40.

Institute on Disability. 2016. *Annual Disability Statistics Compendium.* Durham: University of New Hampshire. http://www.disabilitycompendium.org/statistics/poverty

Joung, Phillan. 2006. "Breaking the Silence: The Aftermath of the Egg and Cloning Scandal in South Korea." Paper presented at the Connecting Civil Society-Implementing Basic Values Workshop, Berlin, March 17–19.

Khader, Serene J. 2011. *Adaptive Preferences and Women's Empowerment.* Oxford: Oxford University Press.

King, Barbara J. 2016. "'Disabled': Just #SayTheWord." *13.7: Cosmos & Culture* (blog). NPR. February 25. http://www.npr.org/sections/13.7/2016/02/25/468073722/disabled-just-saytheword

Kittay, Eva Feder. 1999. *Love's Labor: Essays on Women, Equality, and Dependency.* New York: Routledge.

Kittay, Eva Feder. 2016. "Deadly Medicine: Project T4, Mental Disability, and Racism." *Res Philosophica* 93 (4): 715–41. http://dx.doi.org/10.11612/resphil.1568

Kjellén, Rudolf. 1920. *Grundriß zu einem System der Politik.* Leipzig: S. Hirzel Verlag.

Knobe, Joshua. 2016. "Personal Identity and the True Self." *Flickers of Freedom* (blog). http://philosophycommons.typepad.com/flickers_of_freedom/2016/07/personal-identity-and-the-true-self.html#more

Knobe, Joshua. 2017. "Cognitive Science Suggests Trump Makes Us More Accepting of the Morally Outrageous." *Vox.* January 10. http://www.vox.com/the-big-idea/2017/1/10/14220790/normalization-trump-psychology-cognitive-science

Kolářová, Kateřina. 2015. "Death by Choice, Life by Privilege: Biopolitical Circuits of Vitality and Debility in the Time of Empire." In *Foucault and the Government of Disability*, rev. ed., edited by Shelley Tremain, 396–423. Ann Arbor: University of Michigan Press.

Kolowich, Steve. 2016. "The Water Next Time: Professor Who Helped Expose the Crisis in Flint Says Public Science Is Broken." *Chronicle of Higher Education,* February 2. http://www.chronicle.com/article/The-Water-Next-Time-Profes sor/235136

Koopman, Colin. 2017a. Review of *Foucault's Futures: A Critique of Reproductive Reason* by Penelope Deutscher (New York: Columbia University Press, 2017). *Notre Dame Philosophical Reviews,* June 27. http://ndpr.nd.edu/news/foucaults-futures-a-cri tique-of-reproductive-reason/

Koopman, Colin. 2017b. "The Power Thinker." *Aeon.* March 15. https://aeon.co/ essays/why-foucaults-work-on-power-is-more-important-than-ever

Krafft-Ebing, Richard von. (1886) 2011. *Psychopathia Sexualis: The Classic Study of Deviant Sex.* New York: Arcade Books.

Krafft-Ebing, Richard von. 1965. *Psychopathia Sexualis.* Translated by Henry E. Wedeck. New York: G. P. Putnam's Sons.

Laqueur, Thomas. 2003. *Solitary Sex: A Cultural History of Masturbation.* New York: Zone Books.

Ledford, Heidi. 2017. "CRISPR Fixes Disease Gene in Viable Human Embryos." *Nature* 548, no. 7665 (August 2). http://dx.doi.org/10.1038/nature.2017.22382

Le François, Brenda A., Robert Menzies, and Geoffrey Reaume. 2013. *Mad Matters: A Critical Reader in Canadian Mad Studies.* Toronto: Canadian Scholars' Press.

Lippman, Abby. 1991. "Prenatal Testing and Screening: Constructing Needs and Reinforcing Inequities." *American Journal of Law and Medicine* 17 (1 & 2): 15–50.

Lloyd, Genevieve. 1993. *The Man of Reason: "Male and "Female" in Western Philosophy.* New York: Routledge.

Lloyd, Moya. 1996. "A Feminist Mapping of Foucauldian Politics." In *Feminist Interpretations of Foucault,* edited by Susan J. Hekman, 241–64. University Park: Pennsylvania State University Press.

Lock, Margaret. 2002. *Twice Dead: Organ Transplants and the Reinvention of Death.* Berkeley: University of California Press.

Machery, Edouard. 2016. "What Is an Attitude?" *The Brains* (blog). http://philoso phyofbrains.com/2016/04/14/what-is-an-attitude.aspx

Macmillan, Malcolm. 2002. *An Odd Kind of Fame: Stories of Phineas Gage.* Cambridge, MA: A. Bradford/MIT Press.

Madva, Alex. 2016. "A Plea for Anti-Anti-Individualism: How Oversimple Psychology Misleads Social Policy." *Ergo: An Open Access Journal of Philosophy* 3 (27). http:// dx.doi.org/10.3998/ergo.12405314.0003.027

May, Vivian M., and Beth A. Ferri. 2005. "Fixated on Ability: Questioning Ableist Metaphors in Feminist Theories of Resistance." *Prose Studies* 27 (1–2): 120–40.

McCallum, E. L. 1996. "Technologies of Truth and the Function of Gender in Foucault." In *Feminist Interpretations of Foucault,* edited by Susan J. Hekman, 77–97. University Park: Pennsylvania State University Press.

McLaren, Margaret. 2002. *Feminism, Foucault, and Embodied Subjectivity.* Albany: SUNY Press.

McQuillan, Colin. 2010. "Philosophical Archaeology in Kant, Foucault, and Agamben." *Parrhesia* 10: 39–49.

McWhorter, Ladelle. 1999. *Bodies & Pleasures: Foucault and the Politics of Sexual Normalization.* Bloomington: Indiana University Press.

McWhorter, Ladelle. 2007. "In Perpetual Disintegration." Paper presented at Vanderbilt University Divinity School, September 25.

McWhorter, Ladelle. 2009. *Racism and Sexual Oppression: A Genealogy.* Bloomington: Indiana University Press.

McWhorter, Ladelle (with Shelley Tremain). 2010. "Normalization and Its Discontents: An Interview with Ladelle McWhorter." *Upping the Anti: A Journal of Theory and Practice* 11. http://uppingtheanti.org/journal/article/11-normalization-and-its-discontents-an-interview-with-ladelle-mcwhorter/

Meilander, Gilbert. 2001. "The Point of a Ban; or, How to Think about Stem Cell Research." *Hastings Center Report* 31:9–15.

Mills, Catherine. 2011. *The Future of Reproduction: Bioethics and Biopolitics.* Sydney: Springer.

Mills, Charles W. 1997. *The Racial Contract.* Ithaca: Cornell University Press.

Mills, Charles W. 2005. "'Ideal Theory' as Ideology." *Hypatia: A Journal of Feminist Philosophy* 20 (3): 166–84.

Mills, China. 2014. *Decolonizing Global Mental Health: The Psychiatrization of the Majority World.* London: Routledge.

Minow, Martha. 1991. *Making All the Difference: Inclusion, Exclusion, and American Law.* Ithaca: Cornell University Press.

Money, John, and Anke Ehrhardt. 1972. *Man and Woman, Boy and Girl: The Differentiation and Dimorphism of Gender Identity from Conception to Maturity.* Baltimore: Johns Hopkins University Press.

Morgan, Kathryn. 1998. "Contested Bodies, Contested Knowledges: Women, Health, and the Politics of Medicalization." In *The Politics of Women's Health: Exploring Agency and Autonomy*, edited by Susan Sherwin, 83–121. Philadelphia: Temple University Press.

Morris, Jenny, ed. 1996. Introduction to *Encounters with Strangers: Feminism and Disability*, 1–15. London: Women's Press.

Nichols, Robert. 2012. "Empire and the *Dispositif* of Queerness." *Foucault Studies* 14:41–60.

Novas, Carlos, and Nikolas Rose. 2000. "Genetic Risk and the Birth of the Somatic Individual." *Economy and Society* 29 (4): 485–513.

Nussbaum, Martha. 1988. "Nature, Functioning and Capability: Aristotle on Political Distribution." *Oxford Studies in Ancient Philosophy* (Supplementary Vol.) 6:145–84.

Nussbaum, Martha. 1992. "Human Functioning and Social Justice: In Defense of Aristotelian Essentialism." *Political Theory* 20 (2): 202–46.

Office of Disability Employment Policy. U.S. Department of Labor. "Disability Employment Policy Resources by Topic." https://www.dol.gov/odep/topics/Disability EmploymentStatistics.htm

Oksala, Johanna. 2005. *Foucault on Freedom.* Cambridge: Cambridge University Press.

Oksala, Johanna. 2011. "Sexual Experience: Foucault, Phenomenology, and Feminist Theory." *Hypatia: A Journal of Feminist Philosophy* 26 (1): 207–23.

Oksala, Johanna. 2016. *Feminist Experiences: Foucauldian and Phenomenological Investigations.* Evanston: Northwestern University Press.

Oliver, Michael. 1990. *The Politics of Disablement.* London: Macmillan Education.

Oliver, Michael. 1996. *Understanding Disability: From Theory to Practice.* London: Macmillan.

Oswald, Andrew J., and Nattavudh Powdthavee. 2008. "Does Happiness Adapt? A Longitudinal Study of Disability with Implications for Economists and Judges." *Journal of Public Economics* 92 (5–6): 1061–77.

Oudshoorn, Nellie. 1994. *Beyond the Natural Body: An Archaeology of Sex Hormones.* London: Routledge.

Ouellette, Alicia. 2011. *Bioethics and Disability: Toward a Disability-Conscious Bioethics.* Cambridge: Cambridge University Press.

Overall, Christine. 2006. "Old Age and Ageism, Impairment and Ableism: Exploring the Conceptual and Material Connections." *National Women's Studies Association Journal* 18 (1): 126–37.

Overall, Christine (with Shelley Tremain). 2016. "Dialogues on Disability: Shelley Tremain Interviews Christine Overall." *Discrimination and Disadvantage* (blog). http://philosophycommons.typepad.com/disability_and_disadvanta/2016/03/dialogues-on-disability-shelley-tremain-interviews-christine-overall.html

Oyěwùmí, Oyèrónkẹ́. 1998. "De-confounding Gender: Feminist Theorizing and Western Culture: A Comment on Hawkesworth's 'Confounding Gender.'" *Sign: Journal of Women in Culture and Society* 23:1049–62.

Paik, Young-Gyung. 2006. "Beyond Bioethics: The Globalized Reality of Ova Trafficking and the Possibility of Feminist Intervention." Paper presented at the International Forum on the Human Rights of Women and Biotechnology, Seoul, September 21.

PhilJobs: Jobs for Philosophers. N.d. https://philjobs.org/

PhilPapers: Online Research in Philosophy. N.d. https://philpapers.org/

Picciuto, Elizabeth. 2015. "They Don't Want an Autism Cure." *Daily Beast*, Feb. 25. http://www.thedailybeast.com/articles/2015/02/25/they-don-t-want-an-autism-cure.html

Pitts-Taylor, Victoria. 2010. "The Plastic Brain: Neoliberalism and the Neuronal Self." *Health* 14 (6): 635–52.

Plaza, Monique. 1981. "Our Damages and Their Compensation. Rape: The Will Not to Know of Michel Foucault." *Feminist Issues* 1:25–35.

Priestley, Mark. 1998. "Constructions and Creations: Idealism, Materialism, and Disability Theory." *Disability & Society* 13:75–94.

Prinz, Jesse J. 2007. *The Emotional Construction of Morals.* Oxford: Oxford University Press.

Prinz, Jesse J. 2011. "Culture and Cognitive Science." In *The Stanford Encyclopedia of Philosophy*, edited by Edward N. Zalta. Winter 2011 edition. http://plato.stanford.edu/archives/win2011/entries/culture-cogsci/

Prinz, Jesse J. 2012. *Beyond Human Nature: How Culture and Experience Shape the Human Mind.* New York: W. W. Norton.

Prinz, Jesse (with Shelley Tremain). 2016. "Dialogues on Disability: Shelley Tremain Interviews Jesse Prinz." *Discrimination and Disadvantage* (blog). http://philosophycommons.typepad.com/disability_and_disadvanta/2016/02/dialogues-on-disability-shelley-tremain-interviews-jesse-prinz.html

Prinz, Jesse (with Joe Gelonesi). 2016. "The Truth, Beauty, and Power of Punk." Audio recording at *The Philosopher's Zone* (blog). September 4. http://www.abc.net.au/radionational/programs/philosopherszone/the-truth,-beauty,-and-power-of-punk/7798108

Puar, Jasbir K. 2009. "Prognosis Time: Towards a Geopolitics of Affect, Debility and Capacity." *Women & Performance: A Journal of Feminist Theory* 19 (2): 161–72.

Purdy, Laura. 1995. "Loving Future People." In *Reproduction, Ethics, and the Law*, edited by Joan C. Callahan, 300–330. Bloomington: Indiana University Press.

Purdy, Laura. 2009. "Genetics and Reproductive Risk: Can Having Children Be Immoral?" In *Biomedical Ethics: A Canadian Focus*, edited by Johnna Fisher, 341–47. Don Mills, ON: Oxford University Press. Reprinted from *Reproducing Persons: Issues in Feminist Bioethics*, edited by Laura M. Purdy. Ithaca: Cornell University Press, 1996.

Rabinow, Paul. 1997. "Introduction: The History of Systems of Thought." In *The Essential Works of Michel Foucault, 1954–1984, Ethics: Subjectivity and Truth*, edited by Paul Rabinow, xi–xlii. New York: The New Press.

Rabinow, Paul, and Nikolas Rose. 2003. "Introduction: Foucault Today." In *The Essential Foucault, Selections from 1954–1984*, edited by Paul Rabinow, vii–xxxv. New York: The New Press.

Rachels, James. 1975. "Medical Ethics and the Rule Against Killing: Comments on Professor Hare's Paper." In *Philosophical Medical Ethics: Its Nature and Significance*, edited by F. Spricker and H. Tristram Englehardt, 63–72. Jr. Proceedings of the Third Trans-Disciplinary Symposium on Philosophy and Medicine, Farmington, Connecticut. Dordrecht: D. Reidel.

Rajchman, John. 1991. *Truth and Eros: Foucault, Lacan, and the Question of Ethics*. New York: Routledge.

Rapp, Rayna. 1995. "Risky Business: Genetic Counseling in a Shifting World." In *Articulating Hidden Histories: Exploring the Influence of Eric R. Wolf*, edited by Jane Schneider and Rayna Rapp, 175–89. Berkeley: University of California Press.

Rapp, Rayna. 1999. *Testing Women, Testing the Fetus: The Social Impact of Amniocentesis in America*. New York: Routledge.

Rawlinson, Mary. 2008. "Introduction." *International Journal of Feminist Approaches to Bioethics* 1(1): 1–6.

Rawls, John. 1971. *A Theory of Justice*. Cambridge, MA: Belknap Press of Harvard University Press.

Reverby, Susan M. 2000. "More Than a Metaphor: An Overview of the Scholarship of the Study." In *Tuskegee's Truths: Rethinking the Tuskegee Syphilis Study*, edited by Susan M. Reverby, 1–11. Chapel Hill: University of North Carolina Press.

Roberts, Dorothy. 1998. *Killing the Black Body: Race, Reproduction, and the Meaning of Liberty*. New York: Vintage Books.

Roberts, Dorothy E. 2012. *Fatal Invention: How Science, Politics, and Big Business Re-create Race in the Twenty-First Century*. New York: The New Press.

Roberts, Dorothy E. 2016. "The Ethics of the Biosocial: The Old Biosocial and the Legacy of Unethical Science." Tanner Lectures on Human Values, Mahindra Humanities Center, Harvard University. November 2.

Roberts, Morley. 1938. *Bio-politics: An Essay in the Physiology, Pathology and Politics of the Social and Somatic Organism*. London: Dent.

Robinson, Walter M, and Brandon T. Unruh. 2008. *The Oxford Textbook of Clinical Research Ethics*, edited by Ezekel J. Emmanuel, Chrstine Grady, Raboert A. Couch, Reider K Lie, Franklin G. Miller, and David Wendler, 80–85. Oxford: Oxford University Press.

Roche, Patricia, and Michael Grodin. 2000. "The Ethical Challenge of Stem Cell Research." *Women's Health Issues* 10 (3): 136–49.

Rose, Nikolas. 1996. "Governing 'Advanced' Liberal Democracies." In *Foucault and Political Reason: Liberalism, Neo-liberalism, and Rationalities of Government*, edited by Andrew Barry, Thomas Osborne, and Nikolas Rose, 37–64. Chicago: University of Chicago Press.

Rubin, Gayle. 1975. "The Traffic in Women: Notes on the 'Political Economy' of Sex." In *Toward an Anthropology of Women*, edited by Rayna R. Reiter, 157–210. New York: Basic Books.

Sawicki, Jana. 1991. *Disciplining Foucault: Feminism, Power, and the Body*. New York: Routledge.

Sawicki, Jana. 2005. Review of *Abnormal: Lectures at the Collège de France, 1974–75*, by Michel Foucault. *Notre Dame Philosophical Reviews: An Electronic Journal.* http://ndpr.nd.edu/news/23977-abnormal-lectures-at-the-college-de-france-1974–1975/

Saxton, Marsha. 2000. "Why Members of the Disability Community Oppose Prenatal Diagnosis and Selective Abortion." In *Prenatal Testing and Disability Rights*, edited by Erik Parens and Adrienne Asch, 147–64. Washington, DC: Georgetown University Press.

Schalk, Sami. 2013. "Metaphorically Speaking: Ableist Metaphors in Feminist Writing." *Disability Studies Quarterly* 33 (4). http://dx.doi.org/10.18061/dsq.v33i4.3874

Scheiber, Noam. 2015. "Study Says Disabled Face Clear Job Bias." *New York Times.* November 2.

Schüklenk, Udo, Johannes J. M. van Delden, Jocelyn Downie, Sheila McLean, Ross Upshur, and Daniel Weinstock. 2011. "End-of-Life Decision-Making in Canada: The Report by the Royal Society of Canada Expert Panel on End-of-Life Decision-Making." *Bioethics* 25 (1): 1–4. http://dx.doi.org/10.1111/j.1467-8519.2011.01939.x

Schwitzgebel, Eric, and Carolyn Dicey Jennings. 2016. "Women in Philosophy: Quantitative Analyses of Specialization, Prevalence, Visibility, and Generational Change." Unpublished manuscript.

Scott, Joan W. 1991. "The Evidence of Experience." *Critical Inquiry* 17 (4): 773–97.

Scully, Jackie Leach. 2008. *Disability Bioethics: Moral Bodies, Moral Differences*. Latham, MD: Rowman & Littlefield.

Shelby, Tommie. 2007. *We Who Are Dark: The Philosophical Foundations of Black Solidarity*. Cambridge, MA: Harvard University Press.

Shelby, Tommie. 2016. *Dark Ghettos: Injustice, Dissent, and Reform*. Cambridge, MA: Harvard University Press.

Sherry, Mark. 2006. *If Only I Had A Brain: Deconstructing Brain Injury*. New York: Routledge.

Sherwin, Susan. 1992. *No Longer Patient: Feminist Ethics and Health Care*. Philadelphia: Temple University Press.

Sherwin, Susan. 2008. "Whither Bioethics? How Feminism Can Help Reorient Bioethics." *International Journal of Feminist Approaches to Bioethics* 1 (1): 7–27.

Shildrick, Margrit. 2001. *Embodying the Monster: Encounters with the Vulnerable Self*. London: SAGE Publications.

Shildrick, Margrit, and Janet Price. 1996. "Breaking the Boundaries of the Broken Body." *Body & Society* 2:93–113.

Siebers, Tobin. 2008a. "Disability Experience on Trial." In *Material Feminisms*, edited by Stacy Alaimo and Susan Hekman, 291–305. Bloomington: Indiana University Press.

Siebers, Tobin. 2008b. *Disability Theory*. Ann Arbor: University of Michigan Press.

Silvers, Anita. 1995. "Reconciling Equality to Difference: Caring (F)or Justice for People with Disabilities." *Hypatia: A Journal of Feminist Philosophy* 10 (1): 30–55.

Silvers, Anita, David Wasserman, and Mary B. Mahowald. 1998. *Disability, Difference, Discrimination: Perspectives on Justice in Bioethics and Public Policy*. Lanham, MD: Rowman & Littlefield.

Simons, Maarten, and Jan Masschelein. 2015. "Inclusive Education for Exclusive Pupils: A Critical Analysis of the Government of the Exceptional." In *Foucault and the Government of Disability*, rev. ed., edited by Shelley Tremain, 208–28. Ann Arbor: University of Michigan Press.

Simplican, Stacy Clifford. 2015. *The Capacity Contract: Intellectual Disability and the Question of Citizenship*. Minneapolis: University of Minnesota Press.

Spencer, Quayshawn (with Shelley Tremain). 2017. "Dialogues on Disability: Shelley Tremain Interviews Quayshawn Spencer." *Discrimination and Disadvantage* (blog).

Stoler, Ann Laura. 1995. *Race and the Education of Desire: Foucault's "History of Sexuality" and the Colonial Order of Things*. Durham, NC: Duke University Press.

Stramondo, Joseph. 2015. "The Medicalization of Reasonable Accommodation." *Discrimination and Disadvantage* (blog). http://philosophycommons.typepad.com/disability_and_disadvanta/2015/01/the-medicalization-of-reasonable-accommodation-in-higher-education.html

Stramondo, Joseph. 2016. "Why Bioethics Needs a Disability Moral Psychology." *Hastings Center Report*. http://dx.doi.org/10.1002/hast.585

Strohminger, Nina. 2014. "The Self Is Moral." *Aeon*. November 17.

Stuckey, Zosha. 2017. "Race, Apology, and Public Memory at Maryland's Hospital for the 'Negro' Insane." *Disability Studies Quarterly* 37 (1). http://dsq-sds.org/article/view/5392

Sullivan, Shannon, and Nancy Tuana, eds. 2007. *Race and Epistemologies of Ignorance*. Albany: SUNY Press.

Taylor, Ashley. 2013. "'Lives Worth Living.' Theorizing Moral Status and Expressions of Human Life." *Disability Studies Quarterly* 33 (4). http://dx.doi.org/10.18061/dsq.v33i4.3875

Taylor, Chloë. 2009. "Foucault, Feminism, and Sex Crimes." *Hypatia: A Journal of Feminist Philosophy* 24 (4): 1–25.

Taylor, Sunaura. 2017. *Beasts of Burden: Animal and Disability Liberation*. New York: The New Press.

Terzi, Lorella. 2004. "The Social Model of Disability: A Philosophical Critique." *Journal of Applied Philosophy* 21 (2): 141–57.

Thomas, Carol. 1999. *Female Forms: Experiencing and Understanding Disability*. Buckingham, UK: Open University Press.

Thompson, Evan. 2016. "What Is Mindfulness? An Embodied Cognitive Science Perspective." Paper presented at the International Symposium for Contemplative Studies, San Diego, November 13.

Thompson, Evan. 2017. "Looping Effects and the Cognitive Science of Mindfulness Meditation." In *Meditation, Buddhism, and Science*, edited by David McMahan and Erik Braun, 47–61. Oxford: Oxford University Press.

Titchkosky, Tanya. 2001. "Disability—A Rose by Any Other Name? People-First Language in Canadian Society." *Canadian Review of Sociology and Anthropology* 38 (2): 125–40.

Tobia, Kevin. 2016. "The Phineas Gage Effect." *Aeon*. https://aeon.co/essays/how-a-change-for-the-worse-makes-for-a-different-person

Tremain, Shelley. 2001. "On the Government of Disability." *Social Theory and Practice* 27 (4): 617–36.

Tremain, Shelley. 2006a. "Reproductive Freedom, Self-Regulation, and the Government of Impairment In Utero." *Hypatia: A Journal of Feminist Philosophy* 21 (1): 35–53.

Tremain, Shelley. 2006b. "Stemming the Tide of Normalization: An Expanded Feminist Analysis of the Ethics and Social Impact of Embryonic Stem Cell Research." *Journal of Bioethical Inquiry* 3 (1&2): 33–42.

Tremain, Shelley. 2008. "The Biopolitics of Bioethics and Disability." *Journal of Bioethical Inquiry* 5 (2&3): 101–6.

Tremain, Shelley. 2010. "Biopower, Styles of Reasoning, and What's Still Missing from the Stem Cell Debates." *Hypatia: A Journal of Feminist Philosophy* 25 (3): 577–609.

Tremain, Shelley. 2011. "Ableist Language and Philosophical Associations." *New APPS: Arts, Politics, Philosophy, Science* (blog). http://newappsblog.com/2011/07/ableist-language-and-philosophical-associations.html

Tremain, Shelley. 2012. Review of *The Faces of Intellectual Disability: Philosophical Reflections*, by Licia Carlson, and *Racism and Sexual Oppression in Anglo-America: A Genealogy*, by Ladelle McWhorter. *Hypatia: A Journal of Feminist Philosophy* 27 (2): 440–45.

Tremain, Shelley. 2013a. "Educating Jouy." *Hypatia: A Journal of Feminist Philosophy* 28 (4): 801–81.

Tremain, Shelley. 2013b. "Introducing Feminist Philosophy of Disability." *Disability Studies Quarterly* 33 (4). http://dsq-sds.org/article/view/3877/3402

Tremain, Shelley. 2014. "Disabling Philosophy." *Philosopher's Magazine* 65 (2): 15–17.

Tremain, Shelley. 2015. "This Is What a Historicist and Relativist Feminist Philosophy of Disability Looks Like." *Foucault Studies* 19:7–42. http://rauli.cbs.dk/index.php/foucault-studies/article/view/4822/5268

Tremain, Shelley. 2016. Review of *Civil Disabilities: Citizenship, Membership, and Belonging*, edited by Nancy J. Hirschmann and Beth Linker. *APA Newsletter on Feminism and Philosophy* 15:7–10. http://c.ymcdn.com/sites/www.apaonline.org/resource/collection/D03EBDAB-82D7-4B28-B897-C050FDC1ACB4/FeminismV15n2.pdf

Trent, James, Jr. 1994. *Inventing the Feeble Mind: A History of Mental Retardation in the United States.* Berkeley: University of California Press.

Twomey, Steve. 2010. "Phineas Gage: Neuroscience's Most Famous Patient." *Smithsonian*, January. http://www.smithsonianmag.com/history/phineas-gage-neuroscience-most-famous-patient-11390067/

University of Pennsylvania. 2017. "Professors Lead Call for New Ethical Framework for 'Mind Control' Technologies." *Medical Press* (blog). https://medicalxpress.com/news/2017-07-professors-ethical-framework-mind-technologies.html

UPIAS. 1976. *The Fundamental Principles of Disability.* London: Union of the Physically Impaired Against Segregation.

Van der Kooy, D., and S. Weiss. 2000. "Why Stem Cells?" *Science* 287:1439–41.

Verstraete, Pieter. 2005. "The Taming of Disability: Phrenology and Bio-power on the Road to the Destruction of Otherness in France (1800–1860)." *History of Education* 34 (2): 119–34.

Waldschmidt, Anne. 1992. "Against Selection of Human Life: People with Disabilities Oppose Genetic Counseling." *Issues in Reproductive and Genetic Engineering* 5 (2): 155–67.

Waldschmidt, Anne. 2015. "Who Is Normal? Who Is Deviant? 'Normality' and 'Risk' in Genetic Diagnostics and Counseling." In *Foucault and the Government of Disability*, rev. ed., edited by Shelley Tremain, 191–207. Ann Arbor: University of Michigan Press.

Washington, Harriet A. 2006. *Medical Apartheid: The Dark History of Medical Experimentation on Black Americans from Colonial Times to the Present.* New York: Harlem Moon.

Weir, Lorna. 1996. "Recent Developments in the Government of Pregnancy." *Economy and Society* 25 (3): 372–92.

Wendell, Susan. 1996. *The Rejected Body: Feminist Reflections on Disability.* New York: Routledge.

Widdows, Heather. 2009. "Border Disputes across Bodies: Exploitation in Trafficking for Prostitution and Egg Sale for Stem Cell Research." *International Journal of Feminist Approaches to Bioethics* 2 (1): 5–24.

Williams, Lindsay, and Melanie Nind. 1999. "Insiders or Outsiders: Normalisation and Women with Learning Difficulties." *Disability & Society* 14 (5): 659–72.

Witherspoon Council on Ethics and the Integrity of Science. 2012. "Overview of International Human Embryonic Stem Cell Laws. Appendix E." *The New Atlantis: A Journal of Technology and Society* Winter (34). http://www.thenewatlantis.com/publications/appendix-e-overview-of-international-human-embryonic-stem-cell-laws

Wolbring, Gregor. 2001. "Where Do We Draw the Line? Surviving Eugenics in a Technological World." In *Disability and the Life-Course: Global Perspectives,* edited by Mark Priestley, 38–50. Cambridge: Cambridge University Press.

Wong, David. 2006. *Natural Moralities: A Defense of Pluralistic Relativism.* Oxford: Oxford University Press.

Wright, Megan, and Joseph J. Fins. 2016. "Rehabilitation, Education, and the Integration of Individuals with Severe Brain Injury into Civil Society: Towards an Expanded Rights Agenda in Response to New Insights from Translational Neuroethics and Neuroscience." *Yale Journal of Health, Policy, Law, and Ethics* 16 (2): 233.

Wylie, Alison. 2003. "Why Standpoint Matters." In *Science and Other Cultures: Issues in Philosophies of Science and Technology,* edited by Robert Figueroa and Sandra Harding, 26–46. New York: Routledge.

Yates, Scott. 2015. "Truth, Power, and Ethics in Care Services for People with Learning Difficulties." In *Foucault and the Government of Disability,* rev. ed., edited by Shelley Tremain, 65–77. Ann Arbor: University of Michigan Press.

Index